Plymouth's Railways in the 1930's

including the GWR's Poor Relation

By
Russell Leitch

RCTS

The Railway Correspondence and Travel Society

ISBN 0901115 91 6
www.rcts.org.uk

Published by Railway Correspondence and Travel Society
7 Cherryfields, Peterborough, PE2 5XD, England

Typesetting by Highlight Type Bureau Limited, Bradford
Printed by The Amadeus Press, Cleckheaton

Cover: Four 1930s posters promoting the Plymouth area. The White Star line sailed from Plymouth, and the air service map shows how Railway Air Services developed from the initial Plymouth – Cardiff route.
Author's collection

CONTENTS

APPENDICES

Aerial view of Millbay Docks with Drake's Island behind in Early 1927. Tender at nearest pier is believed to be the "Sir Walter Raleigh". Two other tenders are just visible above the buildings on nearest pier. Passengers were landed on pier just behind and to the right of the locomotive. The three chocolate and cream coaches nearest camera are "Dreadnought" ocean mail vans.

M J Dart collection

1. INTRODUCTION

The story related in this book is railway history with a difference. There are no references to Acts of Parliament, opening ceremonies, and only a few to historical events from down the years. Rather, it is a chronicle of memories of the railway in Plymouth covering the decade up to the outbreak of World War II in 1939. Those memories have been authenticated, where possible, by reference back to old diaries and other surviving documentation, local newspapers, timetables, magazines, and visits to the Public Record Office at Kew. Where possible, an attempt has been made to relate activity back to the very different lifestyles that appertained at the time. Some readers, no doubt, will have difficulty in relating to the seemingly ridiculous low price for railway tickets which, in fact, equated with the normal cost of living. A short chapter attempts to deal with that problem.

How did it all begin? Where do the memories come from? It started with a group of schoolboys who met in The Lane overlooking North Road Station. The Lane, known to several generations of young enthusiasts, was at the rear of Glen Park Avenue with convenient hoardings upon which to lean whilst we watched the comings and goings on the railway. The lane was unmade, and at the station end ankle deep in mud during the winter, unlit, and unprotected from a ten feet drop on to the railway below.

It was important that at least one member of the group visited the Laira engine shed each day to obtain a complete picture of what was going on. With one exception, we were able to walk around the shed without challenge, wearing short trousers and our schoolboy caps which were de rigueur in those days. The head foreman was Dave Warren who was always on duty on Sunday afternoons. The other three were Shepherd (who died c1930), Urell, and Crook. Memory is a bit dim, but I believe it was Luscombe who replaced Shepherd. All except Crook were amenable, although they never spoke to us. The three all worked on the then standard weekly rotating eight hour shift system, so we always knew when Crook was on duty. We never went around the shed when he was on duty so as to avoid "being chucked out when doing a bunk". A most unpleasant experience.

We lived in an era when money was very tight for everybody, and as young teenage enthusiasts we were no exception. The monthly *Railway Magazine* was far too expensive at one shilling (5p), but the *Great Western Railway Magazine*, available from the station bookstall for one penny each month, at least told us which engines were withdrawn and which new ones had been constructed. (There was also an insurance edition of the Magazine at twice the price i.e. two pence (1p)).

Two Plymouth schoolboys, complete with school caps during one of their regular visits to Laira Shed in August 1936. Aberdare 2648 was a Laira resident.
Authors collection

There was little interest in the technical side of the railway, or the rolling stock, for there was little available information at a price we could afford. The RCTS was in its infancy, and dare it be said, viewed with suspicion. However, it can now be said that the RCTS was a forerunner in the field to cater solely for the enthusiast and the forerunner of the avalanche of pocket guides, magazines, and books historical, technical, biographical and pictorial which grace to-day's bookstalls and bookshops.

I am grateful to my friend and fellow RCTS member Peter Orton for permission to use some of his contemporary photographs taken with a contemporary inexpensive folding camera of the day.

There was also H.W. Adams, the Station Master's clerk at North Road, also an enthusiast, who provided a daily "paper" listing the main line trains, the engines which worked them, and the drivers who drove them, information culled from guards' journals. Additionally, from time to time, there were important bits of inside information. Therefore, it should be apparent that there was not much that escaped the attention of that group of schoolboys who met in the Lane. Unfortunately, Harry Adams died in June 2000 at the ripe old age of 90. Therefore, I am grateful to his son, John, for permission to reproduce some of his period photographs.

The massive damage sustained by Plymouth during the blitz of the 1939-45 conflict resulted in the loss of many photographic collections. This has had the effect of limiting the choice of illustrations in this book.

Train times in the narrative are generally taken from the May 1934 edition of the Bradshaw timetable, unless otherwise stated.

Individual engine allocations are taken from the Swindon engine registers to be found at the Public Record Office under reference RAIL 254.

Working Timetables (WTTs) can also be found at the Public Record Office under reference RAIL 937. Working Timetables are published by the railway for internal use only.

Closed station dates are as per Clinker's Register of Closed Stations.

To be consistent, all times are shown in the am or pm notation: the 24 hour clock is one of the dictates of the computer age. Again, to be consistent, they were steam engines and they dwelt in engine sheds. Even on Ordnance Survey maps they were shown as engine sheds.

Plymouth St Andrews Cross/Batemans Corner in late 1930s. All the buildings in this photograph were destroyed by fire in the blitz except for the Guildhall on the extreme left which although gutted was rebuilt. *Authors collection*

2. AN INTRODUCTION TO PLYMOUTH

A sketch map of the present day City of Plymouth is reproduced on page 10 and superimposed thereon is the City of the 1930s. It becomes immediately obvious how compact the City was before the war. That compactness hides the fact that much of the housing was sub-standard and in multiple occupation. Inner City areas surrounding Friary, Millbay and both Devonport stations were characterised by densely populated housing, some of which could be classified as slums.

Reproduced on page 12 is a schematic diagram of the railway map during the 1930s. At one time there were no less than twenty stations, halts or platforms within the city boundary. Leaving North Road Station and travelling 3½ miles to St Budeaux, both the GWR and LSWR (later SR) originally had six stopping points apiece on roughly parallel tracks no more than a mile or so apart. Two of the Halts closed very early on: Wingfield Villas (GWR) and Weston Mill (LSWR) both in June 1921. Mount Gould and Tothill Halt, which was served by the Yealmpton branch also closed early, in February 1918. During the 1930s, Laira Halt closed in July 1930 following discontinuance of the Plympton Motors. At the other end of the decade Mutley Station closed on 3rd July 1939 in anticipation of the continued redevelopment of North Road station, but much delayed by the outbreak of war.

All that is left to-day is 1.The main line through Laira, onwards to North Road and out over the Royal Albert Bridge at Saltash and onwards into Cornwall. 2. The almost defunct Cattewater branch into Friary. 3. The rump of the Southern main line from St. Budeaux to Bere Alston and the Callington branch as far as Gunnislake. Almost miraculously, still in the timetable are the Halts at Devonport, Dockyard and Keyham. Devonport and Keyham were once stations in their own right.

Not included elsewhere is reference to the 4'6" gauge Lee Moor Tramway. A familiar sight were the trains of four somewhat primitive trucks, double headed by two horses en route from Lee Moor to the Cattewater, conveying china clay destined for export. Famous was the on the level crossing of the Great Western main line under the eagle eye of the Laira Junction signalman. The horse drivers usually sat on the edge of the trucks with their legs dangling over the side. The Tramway had two 0-4-0T steam engines, Peckett 783/4 of 1899. They only worked at the Lee Moor end of the system. However, there is the memory of one, dead, adjacent to Laira yard waiting for transportation to Pecketts at Bristol for overhaul. No. 1 is preserved at the China Clay Museum at St Austell and No. 2 has recently moved to the South Devon Railway at Buckfastleigh.

Laira crossing with LeeMoor tramway china clay empties heading back to the moor. First wagon is loaded with coal so one hopes it was cleaned before reloading with china clay. Motive power is two horse power. Circa 1920's Storage sidings for Rail Motor coaches for the Saltash service on right and Laira shed top left of centre. *M J Dart collection*

SKETCH MAP OF THE PLYMOUTH CITY LIMITS DURING THE 1930'S COMPARED WITH THE EXPANDED CITY OF THE 21ST CENTURY

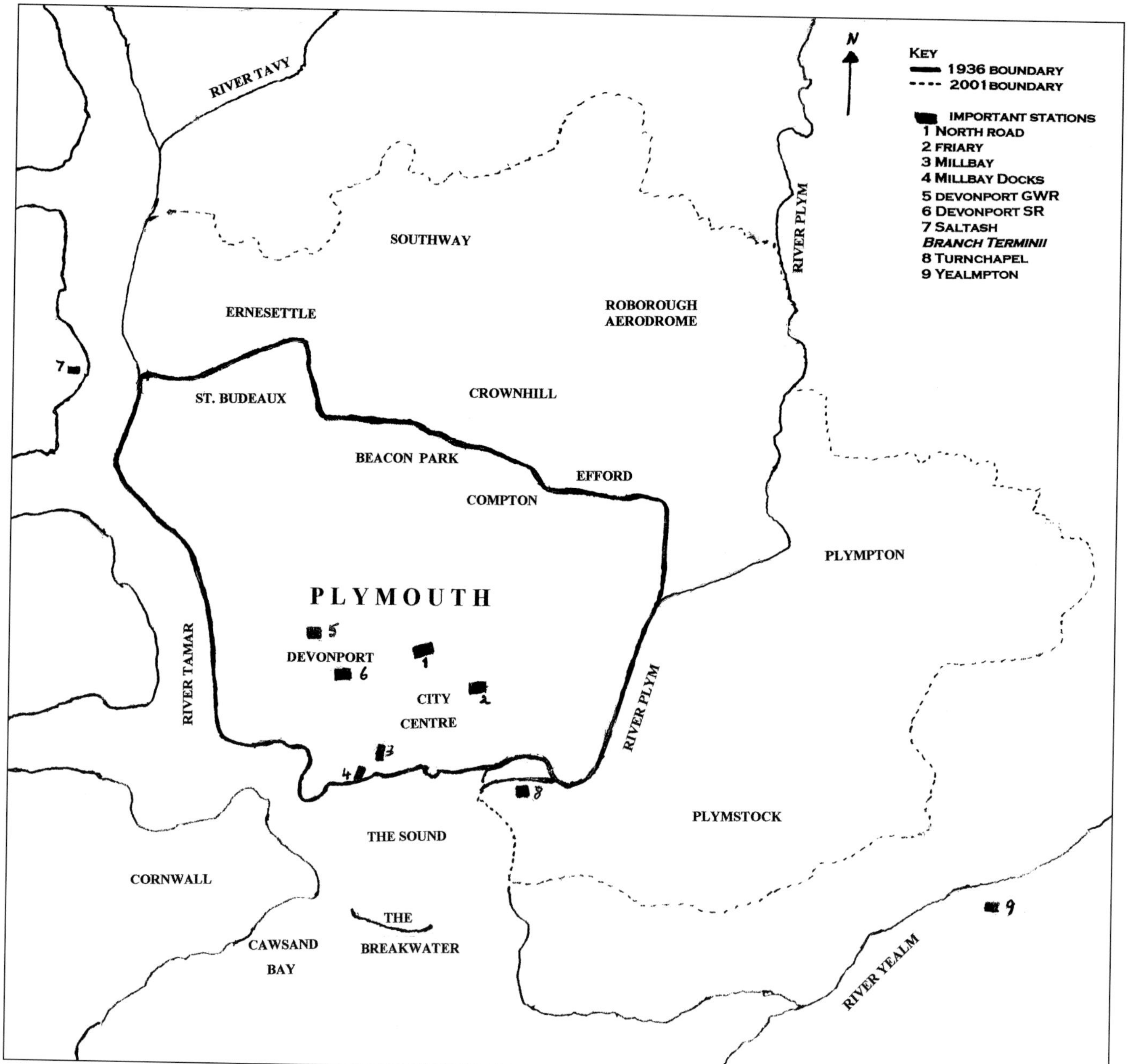

Sketch map of the Plymouth City limits during the 1930s compared with the expanded city of the 21st century.

The Great Western had an interest in modes of transport other than the railway. Perhaps, the most important was the ownership of Millbay Docks. Here were based four sea going vessels, known as tenders, whose principal employment was to meet the prestigious trans-Atlantic liners which dropped anchor in Cawsand Bay, just beyond the breakwater. From those liners there disembarked the glitterati of the day, brought in to land at the Great Western's Ocean Terminal by Great Western tenders and conveyed to London in Great Western trains.

Outside Millbay Station, and latterly North Road Station, could be found Great Western omnibuses in chocolate and cream livery whose pedigree can be traced back to the Railway's pioneer bus services in Cornwall in 1903.

Chocolate and cream livery was used on the plane which pioneered the first railway operated air service in Great Britain in 1933. The internal upholstery was the same as that in a Great Western first class compartment.

The pre-war railway was a basic railway, it ran with basic technology and it worked. That trains ran to time was the norm. It only fell apart at peak holiday times when the system became overloaded, particularly summer Saturdays. Many of the troubles that bedevil the railway to-day were unknown. Signal failures, points failures, power failures, train failures were unheard of, although there were occasional engine failures, occasional being the operative word. A significant proportion of to-day's failures can be put down to the complexity of modern technology. Cancellations? The pre-war railwayman would stand aghast at the very thought.

The Government was the major Plymouth employer by virtue of the Dockyard and, although all got one week's holiday, wages were low. That, together with two million unemployed during the great depression, there was not much by way of affluence. Thus one arrives at the prevalent day trip mentality with the sea, the country and the moorland close at hand.

As the national economy improved during the decade there emerged the infant holiday trade with the gradually increasing number of Saturday Only trains arriving from London and the North and proceeding onwards into Cornwall. Plymouth did not benefit a great deal as it did not have the attractions provided by the expanding resorts. A comparison between pages 44 to 46 illustrates how the Saturday holiday traffic grew between 1932 and 1938.

A rare picture of Lee Moor No 2 one of the 0-4-0T's actually at work in typical Dartmoor weather conditions on 27 December 1933.No five day Christmas breaks in those days. *Authors collection*

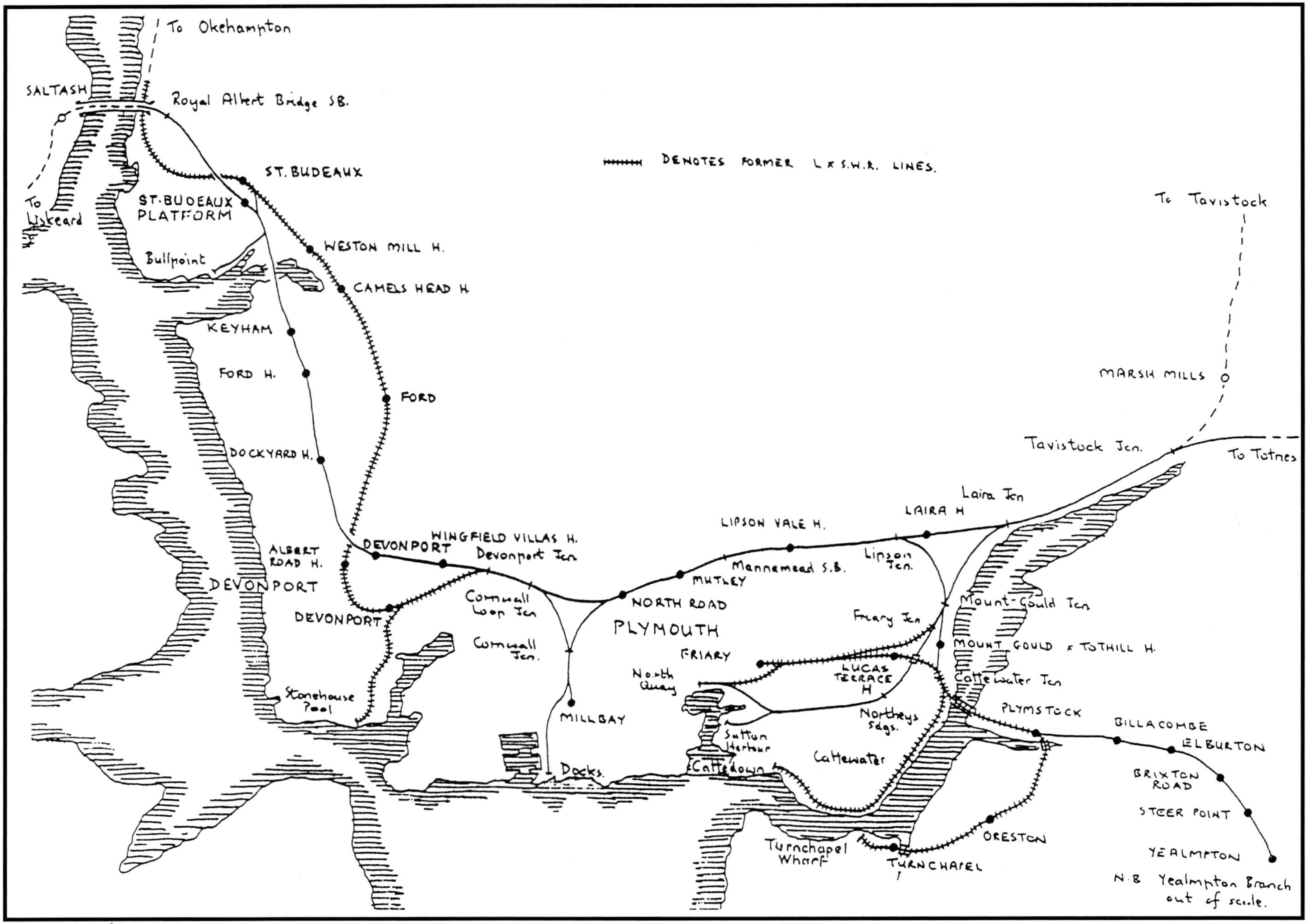

Based on an original by R. A. Cooke

3. THE KINGS

The Kings were the pride and joy of the Great Western Railway, but in pre war days they were very temperamental machines. The last visits of the City Class 4-4-0s to Plymouth were the Reading pilots, 3707 *Malta* and 3716 *City of London*, both in 1928, and as replacements for Kings which had to be removed from their trains.

The class had a very restricted route availability until the war days, being confined to the following routes:

1. Paddington to Plymouth Millbay via Badminton, Bath or Westbury.
2. Paddington to Wolverhampton Low Level via Bicester
3. Newton Abbot to Kingswear.

The Kings were, in fact, permitted beyond Plymouth North Road to Keyham. That permission was rarely exercised except when some parts of the summer Saturday Cornish Riviera Express omitted their North Road stops but called at Devonport to change engines. Kings could also be seen, from time to time, between Banbury and Didcot en route to or from Swindon Works.

The first of the class emerged from Swindon in June 1927 as 6000 *King George V* and by July 1928 6019 *King Henry V* was on the road. As might have been expected, the premier engine was allocated to the premier shed, then known as Paddington, although, as now, located at Old Oak Common. Following on from 6000, the odd numbers were allocated to Paddington and the even numbers to Plymouth Laira, except for the final three. Thus by July 1928 the allocation of the class was:

Paddington	6000/1/3/5/7/9/11/3/5	(9)
Laira	6002/4/6/8/10/2/4/6	(8)
Newton Abbot	6018	(1)
Wolverhampton	6017/9	(2)

The appearance of a further ten engines in 1930 caused four of the originals to be transferred to Wolverhampton Stafford Road. Paddington surrendered 6005, whilst Laira's 6006/8/14 were replaced by three of the new engines 6020/2/4. Newton Abbot got one extra with 6023 and the remaining six went to Paddington. The allocation then became:

Paddington	6000/1/3/7/9/11/3/5/21/5-9	(14)
Laira	6002/4/10/2/6/20/2/4	(8)
Newton Abbot	6018/23	(2)
Wolverhampton	6005/6/8/14/7/9	(6)

Until the end of 1939, when the onset of war caused further changes, there were only four shed changes, viz 6026 of Paddington was exchanged for 6014 from Wolverhampton when the latter was streamlined in 1935. During the same year Laira received 6019 from Wolverhampton to replace 6024 which had earlier been transferred to Newton Abbot.

One of the features of the Kings in Plymouth was the very rare appearance of the Wolverhampton allocation, there being only six recorded occasions up to the end of 1939. A summary is set out below:

6005 To Wolverhampton in 1930. There were three visits to Plymouth in 1931 (probably consecutive over a week or so) but no more until December 1939.

6006 To Wolverhampton in 1930, but not recorded in Plymouth again until 1943.

6008 To Wolverhampton in 1930. Turned up once in June 1934, but not recorded again until the end of 1943.

6014 At Wolverhampton from 1930 until 1935 but never visited Plymouth during that period.

6017 At Wolverhampton as new in 1928. One trip to Plymouth during July 1928 shortly after release from Swindon Works, but not again until February 1940, by which time it had been transferred to Bristol.

6019 To Wolverhampton as new in 1928 but there was no appearance in Plymouth until transferred to Laira in 1935.

6026 To Wolverhampton in 1935 but never came to Plymouth again until January 1940, by which time it had been transferred to Bristol.

The reason for that state of affairs can be attributed to the non-appearance of the Wolverhampton Kings at Old Oak Common. They were employed on the Birmingham two hour expresses with their overlying periods in London spent at the Ranelagh Bridge stabling point to await the time for setting out on their rostered journey to Birmingham and Wolverhampton.

The Kings provided a sort of basic workload for Swindon Works. A visit on 13th January 1935 found no less than nine of the thirty present. During the five years 1935 to 1939 there were 252 recorded visits of the class to the Works. Three visits during a twelvemonth were by no means uncommon and there were a few which even managed four visits during that same timescale. The worst offender was 6010 from Laira with twelve visits over the five year period. 6004 from Laira and 6015 from Paddington were runners up with eleven visits. At the other end of the scale 6009 from Paddington with four visits and the only engine to consistently go more than twelve months between visits.

Over the same five year period an analysis by engine allocation gives:

Wolverhampton	6.80 visits per engine
Newton Abbot	8.00 visits per engine
Paddington	8.32 visits per engine
Laira	9.62 visits per engine

Two reasons can be suggested for the better performance of the Wolverhampton engines (1) They did not have to contend with the South Devon banks and (2) they were home to Wolverhampton each night and therefore received a higher standard of maintenance than those who spent alternative nights in "foreign" sheds.

The Laira Kings reached their nadir on August Bank Holiday week-end 1938 with only one of the eight on the road. A worse week-end to cope with heavy traffic demands could not be imagined. The diary for 30th July summarised the position thus: 6002 was the sole engine in service; 6004/10/22 were in works, 6012 had been missing but reappeared at Laira that day, 6016 had also been missing but returned home next day, 6019 had been stopped at Laira but now disappeared and 6020 failed to return home the previous Thursday.

Quite fortuitously, a report appeared in the *Railway Observer* of a visit to Swindon Works on 15th August which listed nine Kings inside, five of which belonged to Laira. The two missing ones, 6019 and 6020 were there, 6004/22 were still there and, additionally 6012. Thus, Laira was struggling in mid August with only three of their eight Kings on the road i.e. 6002/16 plus 6010 back from works. Significantly, there was apparently no attempt to borrow from Wolverhampton.

The position can be summarised thus:

	30th July 1939	15th August 1938
6002	In service	In service
6004	In works	In works
6010	In works	In service
6012	Reappeared that day. How not known	In works
6016	Reappeared next day. Missing for 10 days	In service
6019	Stopped at Laira. Now disappeared	In works
6020	Failed to return previous Thursday	In works
6022	In works	In works

Nine months later on 8th May 1939 the *Railway Observer* reported that Laira only had three Kings on the road, three in works and 6002/20 unaccounted for.

A record which maintained throughout the 1930s was a points system which awarded one point for each journey between Plymouth and Paddington and vice versa. That covered virtually the whole of the work performed by the Laira Kings, for it was only between Laira Kings that any viable comparison could be made. The average performance worked out around 225 single journeys per annum, more or less coincidental with 225 day's work. There were three occasions during the decade when individual engines excelled and topped the 300 mark during one twelvemonth period, but there were twelve occasions when individual engines could not reach the 200 mark, bearing in mind that 182 points indicated less than 50% employment during the year. The worst performer was 6002 which could not achieve 200 points on four occasions during the decade, yet managed 301 in 1937.

To keep the matter in perspective the paucity of the

6016 *King Edward V* climbing Hemerdon Bank. with the last Paddington service of the day, the 4.10pm from North Road (1.15 from Penzance). The front van and syphons conveyed milk in churns. 4 May 1934. *P D Orton*

During one period in the 1930s the winter roster for Kings is remembered as:

1. Laira and Paddington engines on alternate days

	Plymouth to Paddington			Paddington to Plymouth	
up	8.35am	from Millbay	down	10.30am	Paddington to Penzance (Cornish Riviera)
	11.15am	(8.50am from Penzance)		1.30pm	Paddington to Penzance
	12.30pm	(10am from Penzance) (Cornish Riviera)		3.30pm	Paddington to Truro
	4.10pm	(1.15pm from Penzance)		4.30pm	Paddington to Millbay

2. Paddington engines every day

2pm	(11am from Penzance)	6.30pm	Paddington to Millbay (previous day)
4.33pm	Paddington Perishables (taken on from Tavistock Junc.)	12.50am	Newspaper train (returning home same day)

winter Sunday service has to be remembered, so that most of the Kings only worked a six day week. Bradshaw for May 1934 only shows four Sunday trains through from Plymouth to London, but three of them were endurance tests. (See Chapter 8).

The best and the worst of the Laira Kings can be identified by recourse to the points system and the total number of points earned in the decade 1930 to 1939.

6002	2174
6004	2339
6010	2274
6012	2342
6016	2286
6020	2087
6022	2287
Total	15789

Annual average 1579

Divided by 7 = 225 days worked per engine per year

Note 6020/22 did not come into service until the second half of 1930.

A normal day's work for a King was to work one trip to or from Paddington which meant that the engine was only earning revenue from four to six hours per day when actually hauling a train. That goes a long way to explain why the modern railway needs so little diesel or electric motive power as compared with steam days.

These were all lodging turns for the footplate men and their rosters followed the same pattern as their engines.

Castles would deputise for Kings on occasion, usually indicating a lack of availability. It was unusual for a Laira engine to work a Paddington duty, or vice versa, or for an engine not to take up its balancing return duty. That was vividly illustrated on one occasion when Paddington turned out Star class 4038 *Queen Berengaria* for the 1.30pm Paddington which Laira rostered in the normal way for the next day's up Cornish Riviera Express. That was the only occasion that a Star was known to have hauled that prestige train during the whole of the 1930s.

It may not be generally known that Laira and Paddington top link men had their own allocated engines. If his engine was available there was an even chance that he would get it when rostered for a King duty. There is a widely published photograph of Driver Parsons beside *6015 King Richard III,* his own engine, at Paddington prior to making the inaugural run of the 12.50am West of England newspaper train on 12th March 1934.

The Laira top link is remembered as:

6002	Salter
6004	Lakey
6010	Coleman
6012	Emery
6016	Tipton
6020	Osborn
6022	Luscombe
6024	Mitchelmore

The link was not rostered in that sequence.

The Paddington link is much more imprecise, the detail having been lost.

Those remembered are:

6000	Sparrow
6007	Elkins
6011	James or Dale
6013	Wilmhurst
6015	Parsons

There were 15 men in the link, but only 14 engines, therefore it was either James or Dale who did not have his own engine.

A monthly record of Kings, Castles and Stars which visited Plymouth was maintained from August 1927 through to the war years and an extract for the Kings is shown on page 16. That which has gone before in this chapter is now displayed pictorially, covering the period from August 1927 through to the end of 1934. A few words of interpretation may be appropriate.

6000 did not appear on the record until December 1927, that is after its return from America.

MONTHLY RECORD OF KINGS VISITING PLYMOUTH

		1927 (AUG–DEC)	1928 (JAN–DEC)	1929 (JAN–DEC)	1930 (JAN–DEC)	1931 (JAN–DEC)	1932 (JAN–DEC)	1933 (JAN–DEC)	1934 (JAN–DEC)
6000	PDN	-- -- 12	123456789 10 11 12	12--5678 9 10 11 12	12345678 9 10 --	23456789 10 11 12	123-56789 10 11 12	12-456789 10 11 12	1234-
6001	PDN	89 10 11 12	1234-6789 10 11 12	1-3456789 10 11 12	123--6789 10 11 12	12345-789 10 11 12	1-3456789 10 11 12	1-3456789 10 11 12	1-3456789 10 11 12
6002	LA	89 10 11 12	123456789 10 11 12	1234-6789 10 11 12	123456789 10 11 12	123-56789 10 11 12	123456789 10-12	123456789 10 11 12	12-456789 10 11 12
6003	PDN	89 10 11 12	12345678-10 11 12	-2345-789 10 11 12	12--567-9 10 11 12	123456789 10---	-23456789 10 11 12	1--456789 10 11 12	1-3456789 10 11-
6004	LA	89 10 11 12	123456789 10 11-	1234-6789 10 11 12	123456789 10 11 12	1234-6789 10 11 12	-23456789 10 11 12	12345-789 10 11 12	12345-789 10 11 12
6005	PDN/WSR	89 10 11 12	123-56789 10 11 12	--3456789 10 --	1234 12	1	2		1
6006	LA/WSR		3456789 10 11 12	1234-6789 10 11 12	1234--7				
6007	PDN		456789 10 11 12	12-456789 10 11 12	-2345678-10--	----567-----	-2345678-10 11 12	123456789 10--	12345-789 10 11 12
6008	LA/WSR		456789 10 11 12	1234-6789 10 11 12	12				4
6009	PDN		456789 10-12	12--56789 10--	-23456789 10 11 12	1234--789 10 11 12	1-34567-9 10 11 12	1--456789 10 11 12	1234-56789 10 11 12
6010	LA		456789 10 11 12	-23456789 10-12	1234-6789 10 11 12	12345-789 10 11 12	123456789 10-12	123456789 10 11 12	23456789 10 11 12
6011	PDN		56789 10 11 12	1-3456789 10 11 12	1---56789 10--	1-34--78--11 12	123456789--12	123456789 10--	123456789-11 12
6012	LA		56789 10 11 12	12-456789 10 11 12	--3456789 10 11 12	123456-89 10 11 12	123--6789 10 11 12	123456789 10-12	123456789 10 11-
6013	PDN		56789 10 11 12	12-456789 10 11 12	---456789 10 11-	-23456789 10 11 12	1-34--789 10 11 12	123-56789 10 11 12	1234-6789 10 11 12
6014	LA/WSR		789 10 11 12	-23--6789 10 11 12	123456-8				
6015	PDN		789 10 11 12	1--456789 10 11 12	1-3456789 10 11 12	12--56789 10 11 12	123456789-11 12	123456789-11 12	12345678-10 11 12
6016	LA		6789 10 11 12	123456789--12	12345-789 10 11 12	1234--789 10 11 12	-23456789 10 11-	123456789 10 11 12	1-3456789 10 11 12
6017	WSR		7						
6018	NA		789 10 11 12	123--6--9 10--	-23---789 ---	--345-789 10 11 12	1234--789-11-	12-456~~78~~-10--	123456789 10 11 12
6019	WSR								
6020	LA				78-10 11 12	1234-6789 10 11 12	123456789-11 12	1234--789 10 12	123-56789 10 11 12
6021	PDN				9 10 11 12	123456789 10 11 12	1--456789 10 11 12	123456789 10-12	123 456789 10--
6022	NA				789 10 11 12	123456789 10 11 12	123456789 10 11 12	123456789 10 11 12	1-3 456789 10 11 12
6023	NA				78---12	-2----789 10 11 12	1--456789 10 11 12	1--456789 10 11-	1234-6789 10 11 12
6024	LA				789 10 11 12	123456789 10 11 12	1-3456789 10 11 12	12345-789 10 11 12	1234-6789 10--
6025	PDN				789 10-12	123456789---	123456789--12	1234---89 10 11-	123456--9 10 11 12
6026	PDN				789 10 11 12	1-3456-89 10 11 12	--3456789 10 11 12	-234--789 10--	123456789 10 11 12
6027	PDN				89 10 11 12	123456789 10 11 12	-23--6789 10 11 12	12---6789 10 11 12	12345--89 10 11 12
6028	PDN				10 12	123456789 10 11 12	1--456789 10 11 12	1--456-89-11 12	1234567--10 11 12
6029	PDN				10 11 12	123456789 10 11 12	1---56789 10 11 12	123456789--12	123-456789 10--

6005/6/8/14 all departed for Wolverhampton during the months of April-June 1930, slightly in advance of the final tranch of new construction 6020-9. Following their transfer their very spasmodic reappearance in Plymouth is most noticeable.

6006 to 6019 depicts their arrival as new construction from Swindon from March to July 1928. As already explained 6017 made one appearance only in July 1928 and 6019 made none until 1935.

The erratic appearance of 6018 *King Henry VI* in Plymouth was because it was allocated to Newton Abbot for working the Torbay Express. Some of the Laira and all the Paddington engines had extended visits to Swindon Works over the years and this is shown up where certain engines did not appear in Plymouth for two or more consecutive months.

Mystery surrounded the activities of 6007 *King William III* during 1930/31. Until July 1930 all appears normal, although, in fact, it only did 47 return journeys to Plymouth for the whole year. It entered works in August 1930 and reappeared in the October. There then followed a six month gap until entering Swindon Works again in March 1931. During May, June and July it did 14 return trips to Plymouth, followed by another six months gap, not recorded as entering Swindon Works until December of that year. It resumed normal service in February 1932.

There were also problems with 6011 *King James I* spread over from February 1930 until November 1931. Was there any significance in the two cases running concurrently?

Most of the final batch 6020-9 had problems. 6020 *King Henry IV* on arrival new from Swindon, was initially run in on the 1pm from Millbay to the North West as far as Bristol – that is if it ever got that far. There were at least two such occasions when it failed to return home to Laira. It was well over a month before it ventured on to a London train. 6021 *King Richard II* seemingly had similar problems for it was two months late with an appearance in Plymouth. 6022 *King Edward III* was best of the batch, although not missing a month between July 1930 and February 1934 only means that there were no extended visits to Swindon Works. 6023 *King Edward II* was a Newton Abbot engine and, therefore, it is not appropriate to comment. The years 1932 to 1934 appear to have been disastrous for 6025 to 6029, all Paddington engines. 6025 *King Henry III,* 6026 *King John and* 6027 *King Richard I* all had long periods of absence from Plymouth during the early months of 1933 and all three were absent during the month of May. Finally, 6028, then *King Henry II,* had three individual extended breaks in 1933.

Retirement farewell in 1930's. On arrival at North Road Station with the down Cornish Riviera Express Driver Salter's hand is shaken by Laira's head foreman, Dave Warren with his badge of office – a bowler hat. Such was the standing of top link drivers that despite it being a dirty job such an event would often merit a photograph in local newspapers.

Authors collection

4. OTHER PASSENGER CLASSES

THE CASTLES

At the end of 1927 Laira had twelve Castles on the books. They were:

4032	*Queen Alexandra* (Castle Class)
4080	*Powderham Castle*
4084	*Aberystwyth Castle*
4085	*Berkeley Castle*
4086	*Builth Castle*
4087	*Cardigan Castle*
4088	*Dartmouth Castle*
4095	*Harlech Castle*
4096	*Highclere Castle*
5004	*Llanstephen Castle*
5007	*Rougemont Castle*
5008	*Raglan Castle*

The last three were received direct from Swindon as part of the 1927 batch of construction. Following the arrival of the extra Castles the remaining Stars moved away, the last two to go were 4070 *Neath Abbey* in March 1928 and 4014 *Knight of the Bath* later in the same year.

The Castles played second string to the Kings but they were more reliable. A comparative analysis of pre-war visits to Swindon Works over a five year period for the original batches 4073 to 5012, produced an average of 5.85 visits per annum, which, compared to the Kings, is even better than the 6.80 for the Wolverhampton based members of the class.

Castles were equally well at home on the top link jobs as the Kings, although with a lower permitted tonnage behind the tender, and were very much at home working the Boat Trains. They did not get the standard of grooming that the Kings received, especially after they were relegated from the top link work, so that those long out of shops were often in a very grubby state as they pottered around on local services and parcels. There were two converted Stars in the area, sometimes based at Laira and sometimes at Newton Abbot. They were 4009 *Shooting Star* and 4032 *Queen Alexandra.* 4009 was renamed and renumbered as 100A1 Lloyds in January 1936 when it left the West of England sheds for good. Apart from a short spell at Paddington in the mid thirties 4032 was always in the Newton Abbot Division. Those two engines did not appear to be very popular judging by their infrequent appearance on top link turns.

The Castles had a wide distribution so that those allocated to South Wales and in the Worcester Division were very rare indeed in Plymouth. On the other hand, the Castles moved around much more than the Kings so that there were only extended absences from the Plymouth scene compared with the permanent transfer of Kings to Wolverhampton. London based engines only made erratic visits to Plymouth, usually appearing in lieu of unavailable Kings, or on boat trains or summer week-end extras. They could often be seen on the Sunday 9.45am from Millbay to London. There were no regular rosters and, of course, it was normally those in better condition, not so long out of Swindon Works.

What may appear surprising was the infrequent appearance of the Bristol engines, for they would have been principally employed on the London trains. By reference to page H16 of the RCTS *Locomotives of the Great Western Railway* Bristol Bath Road only had two Castles on the books in 1932, four in 1935 and seven in 1938. On the other hand, there were 13 Stars in 1932 and still 12 in 1938.

Table 2 depicts the monthly appearance in Plymouth of Castles numbered 5000 to 5029 for the calendar years 1932 to 1939. Without exception, the extended gaps all refer to engines allocated to sheds in South Wales, i.e. Cardiff Canton, Swansea Landore and Carmarthen. Carmarthen usually had one or two on the books between 1932 and 1936. The table also depicts the arrival on the scene of new construction 5013 to 5022 in 1932 and 5023 to 5029 in 1934. Conversely, it shows the departure of what were additional engines to South Wales leading to the relegation of Stars from top link duties.

To assist in the interpretation of the detail, certain features are highlighted. The four undermentioned engines were allocated to Paddington for the whole of the period under review:

5005	*Manorbier Castle*
5018	*St. Mawes Castle*
5027	*Farleigh Castle*
5029	*Nunney Castle*

Their erratic appearance in Plymouth will be noted. By way of contrast, the Laira and Newton Abbot engines had a continuity that confirms the reliability of the newly constructed engines. These can be identified as:

5013	*Abergavenny Castle*
5019	*Treago Castle*
5024	*Carew Castle*
5028	*Llantilio Castle*

Also 5014 *Goodrich Castle* until transferred to Paddington in 1935 and moving on to Bristol Bath Road in 1938. 5006 *Tregenna Castle* and 5025 *Chirk Castle* were also at Bristol in 1938/9.

As far as the Welsh engines were concerned it will be seen that 5004 *Llanstephan Castle* paid one visit to Plymouth in August 1934 whilst based at Cardiff, prior to moving to Paddington in 1935. A second example is 5020 *Trematon Castle* which paid one visit in July 1937 whilst based at Landore. In both cases they probably arrived on the one annual excursion from Cardiff and Swansea respectively.

Then there is 5012 *Berry Pomeroy Castle*, which after nearly six years absence in South Wales returned to the Westcountry in 1939, working from Exeter, no doubt, taking its turn rostered for the Penzance to Paddington TPO.

Table No. 2

MONTHLY RECORD OF CASTLES VISITING PLYMOUTH

	1932 (JAN–DEC)	1933 (JAN–DEC)	1934 (JAN–DEC)	1935 (JAN–DEC)	1936 (JAN–DEC)	1937 (JAN–DEC)	1938 (JAN–DEC)	1939 (JAN–DEC)
5000	12345678---12	--3456789 10 11 12	12-456789 10-12	123456789 10 11 12	12-4-6789 10 11	89	--78910--	--4567-9 10 11-
5001	123456789---	-2345-7-9 10 11 12	234 678910-12	-2-4-6789-11		CARDIFF	1---6-8---	1234
5002	123456789 10 11-	123456789 10 11-			CARDIFF			78
5003	123456789 10 11 12	---4-6789 10 11-	1-34	CARDIFF	1-3456789 10 11 12	123456-89 10 11 12	123456789 10 11 12	12345-7-9--12
5004	123456789 10 11 12	1 CARDIFF	8	9--12	1--45---- 10 11-	----5678910-12	--3--678910 11 12	--4567
5005	1234-6--9 10 11-	-2345678910--	--3456789 10 11 12	1--45678910--	1234-67-9-11-	1-3-567----	--3--6789-11 12	-23---78-10 11-
5006	12--56789 10 11 12	1--4-6789 10 11 12	1234 LANDORE	8----	123456-89-11 12	---5--89 10 11-		12-2 10 11 12
5007	12345678-10 11 12	-234-678-10 11 12	---456789-11 12	1234--7---11 12	-2345--8---12	1-345-78910 11 12	-2-----8-10	LANDORE
5008	CARMARTHEN	9 10 11 12	12---6789 10 11 12	1234-6--9--12	123456789 10 11 12	1---567----	12---78----	1---67---11-
5009	123 LANDORE	10 11 12	12345678910--	123456789--12	123456789 10 11 12	1234-6789 10 11 12	123456789 10 11 12	1-3456789 10 11 12
5010	1234567-9 10 11 12	123456789 10 11 12	1		CARDIFF			
5011	CARDIFF	23-56789 10 11 12	--3456789 10 11 12	1234--789 10 11 12	123456789 10-12	123456789 10 11 12	12--56789 10 11 12	12345678-10-12
5012	123456789---	-23-5-78		CARDIFF			67	89 10 11 12
5013	6789 10 11 12	12345-789 10 11 12	12345-789 10 11 12	12345678910--	123456789 10 11 12	123-56789 10 11 12	1234567-9 10 11 12	12345678-10 11 12
5014	789 10 11 12	12345678910-12	123456789 10 11 12	123456789 10 11-	1234--7-9---	1--45--89--	-23-5---9---	-345----10--
5015	CARDIFF	9 10 11 12	12-4--789 10 11 12	12345678910-12	12345678910-12	1234-6789 10 11 12	12345678910-12	-----78----
5016	8-10 11-	-2345678910-12	123456789-11 12	12-456789 10 11 12	12845678910 11-	123456789 10 11 12	12--5	12
5017	78 CARDIFF		123456-89---	123456789 10 11 12	1-3456789 10 11 12	12345-789 10 11 12	123456789 10 11 12	1 WORCESTER
5018	8 9 10 11-	123456789--12	--345678910--	12345678---12	1--45--8----	12-4--7-9 10--	1-3--6-8-10---	---56-8-10 11 12
5019	89 10 11 12	123456789-11 12	123456789 10 11 12	--345678910 11 12	1234-678910 11 12	123456789 10 11 12	123456789 10 11 12	-----67-9 10 11 12
5020	89 10 11 12	123456789 10 11 12		CARDIFF	CARMARTHEN	LAN 7 DORE	6---10 11 12	12
5021	89 10 11 12	12345678910-12	123456789 10 11--	-23456789 10 11 12	1-3456789 10 11 12	123456--9 10 11 12	12345678910	7-9
5022	9 10 11 12	-234-678	2-456789 10 11 12	12-456-89 10-12	-23--6-89 10 11 12	--3--6-89---	2--5-7--10--	1--456-8--11 12
5023			5678910 11 12	-234567-9 10-12	-2 CARDIFF		3-5-78-10--	12345---9-11-
5024			6789 10 11 12	123456789 10 11 12	-23456789 10 11 12	123456789 10 11 12	123456789 10 11 12	1-3456789 10 11 12
5025			5--8910-12	12-456789 10-12	-3456789 10 11 12	12345678	89	34
5026			5678910-12	123456789 10 11 12	123-56789 10 11 12	123-56789 10 11 12	1234-6789 10 11 12	123-5678-10 11 12
5027			5678-10-12	1-34-67-9-11-	12-4567---11 12	1-3-56-89---	1-3--6789--12	12---6-----12
5028			56789 10 11 12	123456789 10 11 12	12-456789 10 11 12	123456789 10 11 12	123456789 10 11 12	123456789 10 11-
5029			789--12	123456789 10 11-	---4567-9 10--	-----789-11-	------7-9 10 11-	12---67----

Finally, the extraordinary case of 5017 *St. Donat's Castle* one of the 1932 new construction. It went initially to Taunton, a shed which did not normally have a Castle on its books. It was only there for July and August before moving on to Cardiff. No doubt, it was there to assist with the summer traffic off the Barnstaple and Minehead branches.

During the 1920s and 1930s much railway publicity centred around the prestigious named trains and the engines which hauled them. Thus, there was the LMS *Royal Scot* and 6100 of similar name. Then there was the *Flying Scotsman* with 4472 of similar name, followed by the SR's *Atlantic Coast Express* with 850 *Lord Nelson*. The GWR's contribution was the *Cornish Riviera Express* headed by 6000 *King George V*. Much public discussion revolved around traction effort and which engine was the most powerful of the four.

When the *Torbay Express* was introduced in 1928 12noon out of both Paddington and Torquay (11.25 Kingswear) prestige demanded that the train had to be hauled by a member of the King class. In anticipation of the train's introduction a number of bridges on the Torquay branch were identified as in need of strengthening. Unfortunately, the work had not been completed on time and the Kings were prohibited to work beyond Torquay. To overcome that little difficulty the authorities of the day decided to take the appropriately named 4088 *Dartmouth Castle*, repaint it, and transfer it from Laira to Newton Abbot to just haul the up and down Torbay Expresses for the nine miles between Torquay and Kingswear until such time as the strengthening had been completed. In all probability that was a complete day's work for *Dartmouth Castle*. Every Sunday a resplendent 4088 could be seen in Plymouth.

In 1933 the Great Western introduced a through engine working between Wolverhampton (Low Level) and Plymouth on the existing 10.40am to Penzance. That introduction brought for the first time rostered Wolverhampton based Castles and Stars to Plymouth. The corresponding up train left Penzance at 10.45 and Plymouth at 1.40pm, worked by Laira and Wolverhampton men on alternate days as a lodging turn.

In July 1937, newly constructed 5063 *Thornbury Castle* was officially allocated to Laira. It would appear that it did some work locally (earning six recorded points) before being transferred away almost immediately to Worcester. At Worcester it was renamed *Earl Baldwin* in honour of the elevation of the erstwhile Prime Minister (Mr Stanley Baldwin) to the peerage, Worcester was his former Parliamentary constituency.

At the end of our period under review, 31st December 1939, Laira had thirteen Castles on its books, plus one Star, compared with twelve Castles and two Stars back in 1927. They were:

4012	*Knight of the Thistle* (Star Class)
4032	*Queen Alexandra* (Castle Class)
4088	*Dartmouth Castle*
4090	*Dorchester Castle*
4093	*Dunstar Castle*
4098	*Kidwelly Castle*
5009	*Shrewsbury Castle*
5011	*Tintagel Castle*
5024	*Carew Castle*
5041	*Tiverton Castle*
5057	*Earl Waldegrave*
5078	*Lamphey Castle*
5090	*Neath Abbey*
5095	*Barbury Castle*

5041 *Tiverton Castle* was an exceptionally long stayer having been a Laira engine since newly constructed in July 1935. The last three on the list were among the 1939 new construction. 5057 was formerly *Penrice Castle*, 5078 was subsequently renamed *Beaufort* and 5090 was a rebuilt Star.

4012 *Knight of the Thistle*, transferred from Taunton in January 1939 was the first Star on Laira's books since the departure of 4014 *Knight of the Bath* in 1928.

THE HALLS

Back in 1928, and no doubt prior to that, there was a mystery engine, 2925 *Saint Martin*, shedded at Penzance. The mystery was its disappearance for long periods of time. Where it went and what it did remained a mystery, but we now do know that it was a prototype for the new Hall class which eventually numbered no less than 330 examples.

On Christmas Eve 1928, 4902 *Aldenham Hall* appeared at the coaling stage at Laira, the first of the class to appear in Plymouth. On New Year's Eve *Saint Martin* appeared on the scene, now renumbered 4900. It had been renumbered on 7th December*, but where had it been in the interim? By the end of January 1929, engines up to 4909 were at work except 4902 *Aldenham Hall*. that engine promptly disappeared for about three months with no information as to its whereabouts. Was it moving around the system on widespread test runs? No! It was back in Swindon Works.**

The first fourteen of the new construction, together with 4900, all came to the West of England, shared between Penzance and Laira. It seems that some members of the class may have been tried out elsewhere as they did not arrive in strict numerical order. The whole story is illustrative of the paucity of information available to young enthusiasts in those days.

When 4983 *Albert Hall* appeared on the scene in 1931 there were facetious suggestions that one be named *Henry Hall* after the popular dance band leader of the day. By the end of the decade there were 200 Halls on the road and just part of the every day scene.

THE MOGULS

Right at the end of 1927 there appeared 8300 and 8335, alias 4351 and 4385, both sheded at Penzance. The original intention was to convert numbers 4351 upwards and to renumber them 8300, upwards in strict numerical sequence. Those original two disappeared within weeks

*Locomotives of the Great Western Railway, part eight
**PRO RAIL 254/88

Bulldog 3441 *Blackbird* at Laira shed 1938. *R C Riley*

Hall 4911 *Bowden Hall* at Laira in the 1930's. The rarest Hall which spent most of its short life in the West of England being scrapped as a result of enemy action at Keyham in 1941. *Authors collection*

Duke 3256 *Guinevere* at North Road station August 1938. *H. W. Adams*

because of a change of plan. Instead, 65 assorted engines from the 53XX series, which when converted, became 83XX merely by changing the first digit from 5 to 8. The rate of conversion was so rapid that all 65 engines were done within the first three months of 1928, so rapid that some engines appeared with chalked cabside numbers until proper numberplates could be supplied. With the exception of 8315, 8365 and 8368 which went to Wolverhampton Oxley, the whole of the 83XX were initially allocated to sheds in the Bristol and Newton Abbot Divisions. Dispersion followed upon arrival of the Halls. By 1934, 23 members of the class had left the West of England, although there were still 33 working from sheds in Devon and Cornwall. The conversion was no more than the fitting of a heavy casting behind the buffer in order to reduce flange wear over tracks abounding in sharp curvature in Devon and Cornwall.

In 1932 further Moguls were constructed at Swindon and the first five went to Truro. Their initiation was on the 7.35am stopping train from Truro to Millbay where it arrived exactly two hours later for the $54^1/_4$ mile journey, calling at ten stations, but omitting Probus and Ladock Halt, Menheniot and Keyham. The engine went to Laira to recover from its exertions and returned home on the 1.15pm from Millbay. Those two trains were the last long distance Cornish services in and out of Millbay, surviving until the outbreak of war.

The sojourn of 9300-4 in Cornwall was short lived for the whole class of twenty had congregated within the London Division before the end of 1934.

THE 4-4-0s

COUNTIES

In my time there were never any regular rosters for Counties working to Plymouth. Swindon based members of the class made occasional visits, particularly on the stopping trains from Newton Abbot arriving at Millbay at 8.36am or 5.41pm. There were also occasional visits when Counties arrived with summer week-end holiday extras. The last visit of the Class to Plymouth would appear to be on an unspecified train on an unspecified date, believed to be in July 1930, when 3802 *County Clare* was photographed approaching Mutley station piloted by nameless Duke 3289 and carrying Class A express headlamps. 3289, formerly *St Austell* lost its nameplates in July 1930, which helps to date the photograph.

THE CITIES

The only two recorded visits to Plymouth were the two Reading pilots taking over from Kings which had failed on the down 1.30pm West of England train from Paddington – both in 1928.

3707	*Malta*
3716	*City of London*

2912 *Saint Ambrose* at Laira Shed sometime between April 1931 and July 1936 and fitted with the Great Bear's tender.
M J Dart collection

FLOWERS
Two single visits have been recorded:

4161	*Hyacinth*
4168	*Stephanotis*

I have no remembrance of the circumstances surrounding 4161, but 4168 arrived in June 1929 on the down stopping train due to arrive at Millbay at 3.36pm, returning on the up 4.20pm back to Newton Abbot. The trains in question were the regular preserve for Taunton's Saints.

BULLDOGS
The 1927 allocation was:

3357	*Trelawney*
3368	
3416	*John W. Wilson*
3424	

3357 left in 1928 and there were no more changes until 1932 when 3368 and 3416 were transferred away. Thereafter there was a gradual increase in the Bulldog allocation as the demand increased for pilot engines over the hilly section to Newton Abbot. Two of the original four donated their frames to the new Dukedogs i.e.

3416 became part of 3202 *Earl of Dudley*
3424 became part of 3203 *Earl Cawdor*

The most significant event during the period was the collapse of the sea wall at Dawlish during the early days of January 1930 with all traffic diverted over the Southern Railway via Okehampton. Weight restrictions were imposed by the Southern which meant that only Dukes and Bulldogs were permitted, so trains were double headed by vintage 4-4-0s, but no more vintage than the Southern's own Greyhounds.

To deal with the emergency, extra Bulldogs were drafted in and those noted were:

3302	*Sir Lancelot*	Reading
3311	*Bulldog*	Cardiff (ex works)
3326	*Laira*	Reading (ex works)
3336	*Titan*	Swindon
3371	*Sir Massey Lopes*	Bristol Bath Road
3373	*Sir William Henry*	Bristol Bath Road
3404	*Barbados*	Salop (Shrewsbury)
3430	*Inchcape*	Swindon
3454	*Skylark*	Didcot (ex works)
3373	even worked on a boat train!	

Although not part of the Laira allocation, it is worth noting that 3348 *Launceston* was the last Bulldog to be shedded in Cornwall, at Truro. It had a regular duty in bringing up from Cornwall the through Penzance to Wolverhampton (Low Level) train, due off North Road at 1.40pm

DUKES
In August 1928, 3270 *Earl of Devon,* appeared at Laira, the first of a Class, once familiar in Plymouth, to be allocated

there since 3253 *Roscawen* departed in 1926. It stayed only a couple of months, but in November 1929 there arrived:

3284	*Isle of Jersey*
3289	*St. Austell*

followed in the following April by:

3272	*Fowey*

A fourth member of the class, 3282, worked in to Plymouth from mid July 1930 when it was allocated to Newton Abbot, but they had all gone by the middle of 1932. In the meantime 3272 and 3289 had lost their nameplates for fear that passengers would confuse them with the destination of their train. One of the Laira engines was regularly used as station pilot and the other two mainly for piloting duties.

There were at least two occasions later in the decade when Dukes were seen in Plymouth, both of them were recorded in the *Railway Observer*. The first occasion was on Friday, 14th August 1936 when 3273 *Mounts Bay* arrived. Bearing in mind that it was allocated to Shrewsbury, it could have worked a relief service the whole way.

The second occasion was on 11th August 1938 when 3256 *Guinevere* of Didcot arrived doing piloting duty. It is regretted that no more information is available, H.W. Adams had a photograph of it standing at North Road station. (see page 22)

DUKEDOG

Extraordinary was the arrival of 4-4-0 Dukedog 3226 at Laira, first noted on 15th June 1939, newly constructed and officially allocated to Laira in period 6/39. During the same period 6/39 it was reallocated to Oswestry and the author travelled behind it between Llanymynech and Oswestry on 12th July.

DEAN 0-6-0s

These were only occasional visitors to Plymouth, often appearing on down goods services at times of pressure such as holiday periods or returning broccoli empties.

One notable appearance was 2377, a double framed member of the twenty strong 2361 class. It first arrived in Plymouth at the head of a summer only North to West express during the early evening of Monday 27th August 1928, following an engine change at Newton Abbot, the other portion of the train having taken the Torquay branch. It worked the train for five consecutive days through to the following Friday; the more extraordinary because in the RCTS publication *Locomotives of the Great Western Railway*, part four, it is stated that the 2361 class rarely appeared on passenger trains.

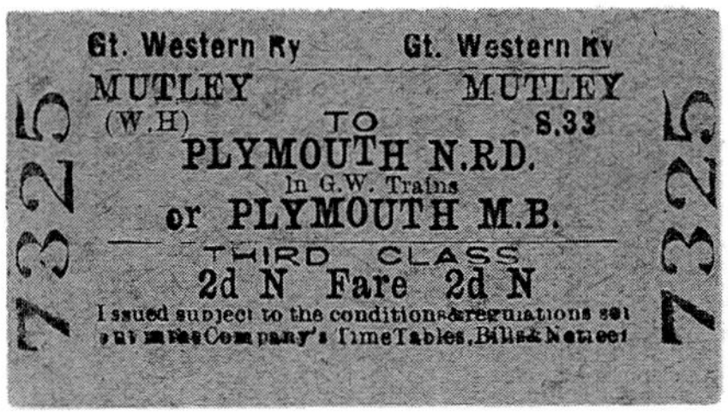

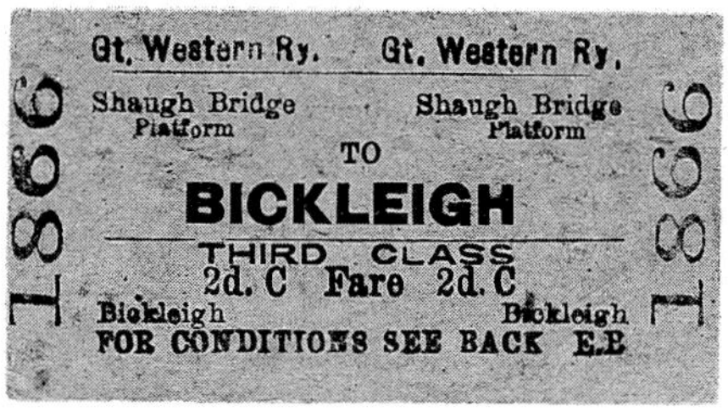

5. THE TANKS

Laira had three large 2-6-2T's at the 31st December 1927, namely 3141/73/81, three being the normal allocation. 3141 departed to the Midlands late in 1928 having been renumbered 5141 and was replaced by 3188. The 31s were mostly based at sheds where banking duties were the principal activity, Severn Tunnel Junction being the prime example. Of the Laira engines, one was at Tavistock Junction to assist goods trains up the two mile 1 in 42 Hemerdon Bank. The daily roster started with the 2.30pm Laira to Bordesley Sidings, Birmingham.

The second duty started with an early morning passenger trip at 6.15am from Millbay to Liskeard, arriving back in Millbay at 8.14am. The next duty was the mid-morning St. Austell goods, due to pass through North Road at 9.50am. That was one of the few trains of the day when the North Road West distant signal was pulled off to give the train a clear run through North Road station.

There was quite an allocation of the small 45XX 2-6-2Ts and of the smaller 44XX series. Their presence was required principally for both the passenger and goods services on the Tavistock Branch. There were constant changes in the allocation over the years which were usually between sheds within the Newton Abbot Division, i.e. Taunton and west thereof. On 31st December 1927 the Laira allocation was 4403/8/9/10, 4530/1/5/ 42/60/98 and 5501. There was a preponderance of the older small tank variety throughout the 1930s (4500-74). Very much against the trend, 4598, which arrived newly constructed from Swindon in 1927 stayed at Laira for the whole of the twelve years under review.

At one time it was possible to identify from a distance, say from the height of Mount Gold, down to Lipson Vale, each individual engine on Laira's books – clean, dirty, large or small tanks, with or without outside steam pipes, copper top, polished brass safety valve cover etc.

Of the smaller 44XX variety, it was during the late twenties and the early thirties that all eleven members of the class were working from Laira or from sheds west thereof, St Blazey or Penzance, hence the four at Laira. There were normally always two at Laira for use on the Princetown branch with 4402 as the regular engine from 1931 forward. When not required for the Princetown Branch, the spare engine(s) shared duties with their larger 45XX brethren.

1398 Constructed in 1873. The last of the Cornwall Mineral Railway's 0-6-0ST's to be allocated in the West of England. Laira July 1925. *M J Dart collection*

Of the 0-6-0Ts in residence, not all were panniers. Of the saddle tanks, 1398, vintage 1873, was the last of the Cornwall Minerals Railway engines to be working in the West of England. It can clearly be remembered shunting at the west end of Laira Yard shortly before it left for Swindon Works in December 1927, never to return. It was transferred to the Swindon Running Shed in March 1928 for further service. 1932 was one of the few remaining saddle tanks of the 850 class which survived at Laira until withdrawal in 1930. Finally, there were the five dock tanks 1361-5, all of which were at Laira in 1928. Two members of the class stabled at week-ends in a small shed situated within Millbay Docks. Over the years one could often be found working at Newton Abbot.

Of the pannier tanks, the most hard working were the eight members of the 1076 class which were fitted for auto working. (see Chapter 6). The remaining pannier tanks fitted broadly into the larger 1854 Class and the smaller 850 Class. In the main they pottered around on transfer trips and shunting in the various yards. At holiday times, the 1854s were sometimes pressed into service to work relief trains on the Tavistock Branch, but rarely beyond Yelverton. To complete the picture, the pannier tank allocation on 31st December 1927 was:

1076 Class	– auto fitted 738 1235/52/65/9/84 1600
	not auto fitted 1575
1854 Class	1895/7 1900
850 Class	854 1905/9/27/30/52/85/99
	plus saddle tank 1932

Of those the following still had open cabs:
1575 1897 1900 1909/30/32

In Plymouth's speciality of driving rain, protection was provided by draping a tarpaulin from the cab roof over to the back of the bunker.

There was another shed at Harwell St. (Millbay) which officially closed before my time, but nevertheless was still used for servicing purposes. Well into the 1930s there were still engines (panniers and Class 1361 Dock Tanks) allocated to Harwell St., recorded as PLY, in the official engine registers. The transfers between the two sheds were usually for a few months at a time and too numerous to have any relevance here.

The West of England was very slow to receive an allocation of the new modern 57XX pannier tanks. Construction commenced in 1929 and the first to arrive were 7715/6 in 1930, but they went on to St. Blazey. Laira's first arrival were 7760 in early January 1931, followed by 8709 in March, only to lose it to St. Blazey later in the year. So, 7760 remained Laira's sole example until 1934.

61XX 2-6-2Ts

These large 61XX tanks were shedded wholly within the London Division for use on Thames Valley suburban commuter services. Nevertheless, 6160-4, then newly constructed, passed through Plymouth in late 1935 for temporary work between Penzance and Truro whilst the Penzance turntable was out of action for a few weeks undergoing maintenance. 6162 was at Laira on the way down on 23rd October and 6164 passed through North Road on its way back to London on 19th December.

1932 of 850 class. One of the few surviving open cab shunting saddle tanks seen on active service in Laira Yard in 1927. It was withdrawn in 1930. *M J Dart collection*

6. THE RAIL MOTORS

In 1927, Laira housed nine 0-6-0 pannier tanks of class 1076, eight of which were fitted for working auto trains, better known as rail motors. Those tanks were 738, 1168, 1235, 1265, 1269, 1284 and 1600. All eight were of 1873-9 vintage. Thus 738, the oldest, already had 54 years to its credit by 1927. Two of them, 1235 and 1252, were originally constructed as broad gauge convertibles and both saw service on the broad gauge. Over the next few years 1168, 1269 and 1600 departed and were replaced by 1167, 1271 and 1570. 1570 also ran as a broad gauge convertible. 1570 arrived in January 1929, followed by 1167 in the following month, both ex Swindon Works after being newly fitted with auto gear. 1167 carried the letters GWR above the number on the numberplate, indicating an engine absorbed at the grouping of 1923. It had been Rhondda and Swansea Bay Railway's no. 34 from 1907 until the grouping, following which it reverted to its original number.

The rail motors maintained an irregular but all day intensive suburban service between Millbay and Saltash on the Cornish side of the River Tamar from about 6am until nearly midnight. The journey distance was 4¼miles with originally six intermediate stations, platforms or halts. Devonport and Keyham were stations, St Budeaux was a Platform, Ford and Dockyard Halts. Wingfield Villas halt closed in June 1921. The through single fare from Millbay to Saltash shown in Brendon's local timetable for June 1929 was 7½d (3p) first class and 4½d (2p) third class. Day return fares were available at 8d (3½p) first class and 6d (2½p) third class. As the rail motors were third class only, first class passengers (if there were any) would have needed to patronise the rather infrequent main line Cornish trains that called at Saltash.

There being no road bridge across the Tamar, the Great Western had a virtual monopoly of the passenger traffic from Saltash and west thereof into Plymouth. For Saltash residents the only alternative was the slow chain ferry to Saltash Passage on the Devon side of the river, followed by an equally slow tram ride into town. Returning foot passengers had to face the formidable hill from the waterside up to the Saltash town centre.

Saltash Station was fully staffed, the premises and platforms maintained in a spotless condition. The station even had a bookstall so that commuters could purchase their morning papers. Three quarters of a mile beyond Saltash was Defiance Platform. It was constructed in 1905 for the benefit of naval personnel who were ferried in for shore leave from warships anchored out in the Hamoaze, the Hamoaze being a wide and deep stretch of water, a part of the River Tamar

1570 of 1076 class at Dockyard Halt on an Saltash to Millbay rail motor train. September 1929.

M J Dart collection

A four car Saltash Motor train leaving the Cornwall side of the Royal Albert Bridge in April 1931. Engine is 1570 of class 1076.
Authors collection

Down service from Plympton to Millbay with 1076 class 1269 sandwiched between four Rail Motors in September 1925.
F H C Casbourne/Stephenson Locomotive Society

The Saltash Ferry circa late 1930's. This was a chain ferry which ceased operation on the opening of the Tamar Road Bridge in October 1960. *Authors collection*

south of the Royal Albert Bridge. Even the name Defiance has naval connotations.

An account of the construction of the Platform, with assistance from naval ratings from HMS Defiance appeared in the *GWR Magazine* for May 1905. The Platform officially closed on 27th October 1930. Notwithstanding the official closure and its disappearance from the public timetable, trains continued to call at the Platform. The following footnotes appeared in the Working Timetable for the summer of 1938:

1. The 12.45pm from Menheniot to Millbay called to pick up.
2. The 4.40pm from Millbay to Saltash was extended to Wearde Sidings and called at Defiance to set down, if required.
3. The 11.15pm from Millbay to Saltash was extended to Liskeard WThSO and called at Defiance on Saturdays only, if required.

Prior to closure, there were in 1929 no less than twenty rail motors serving the Platform, including three early morning arrivals at 7.3, 7.43 and 7.50 and, not unexpectedly, the two last trains of the day were at 11.3 and 11.38pm. There were six trains on Sundays, the last arrival was at 6.38pm – no Sunday jaunts for sailors in those days. During the last month of the service there were still 15 trains to Defiance.

Wearde Sidings were a further quarter of a mile beyond Defiance and used mainly for the storage of passenger rolling stock, but they also provided a convenient turn round point for the terminating Defiance motors. The sidings were on the original alignment of the main line to Cornwall until the deviation of 1908.

According to traffic requirements, the rail motors were formed with either two or four suburban type trailers, in the latter case with the engine sandwiched in the middle. In the two car situation it was most unusual for the engine to be running bunker first when at the head of the train. That four cars were even necessary is indicative of the volume of traffic generated for only a 4¼ mile maximum journey. The trailers were stabled at Laira on the opposite side of the main line to the engine shed. They were permanently coupled in pairs, their numbers being remembered as 3 and 4, 5 and 6, 9 and 10, 71 and 74, 72 and 73, 95 and 96, 126 and 127, 134 and 135. The first three and the last two pairs were permanent residents. They are remembered as very commodious vehicles with seats reversible to the direction of travel. The trailers were of the suburban type with doors at each end as compared with the branch line type which had only one door positioned one third of the way along the car side.

Rail motor services also operated from Millbay Station to Plympton, Yealmpton and Tavistock. The first

PLYMOUTH, PLYMPTON AND SALTASH SUBURBAN SERVICE.

Week Days.

Miles	Station	a.m. (Mons. only)	M a.m.	a.m.	a.m.	M a.m.	M a.m.	a.m.	M a.m.	a.m.	M a.m.	M a.m.	M a.m.		a.m.	M a.m.	a.m.	a.m.	a.m.	M a.m.	a.m.	M a.m.	M a.m.	a.m.
—	Plympton dep.																8 39				9 22			
—	Marsh Mills										7 52				8 39								10 17	
3½	Mutley		5 38			6 30					7 57				8 44		8 48				9 28		10 22	
4	North Road	4 40	5 40			6 33				7 40	7 59				8 46		8 51	9 15	9 23		9 30		10 24	10 30
5	Millbay arr.										8 4				8 52		8 58		9 27		9 33		10 30	
	Millbay dep.			5 45	6 15		6 42	7 10	7 25			8 10	8 37			8 55				9 33		10 12		
6¼	Devonport		5 44	5 51	6 20	6 37	6 47	7 18	7 30	7 45		8 15	8 42			9 0		9 19		9 38		10 17		10 35
6¾	Dockyard Halt		5 46		6 22	6 39	6 49		7 32			8 17	8 44			9 2				9 40				
7	Ford Halt						6 51		7 34			8 19	8 46			9 4				9 42				
7½	Keyham	4 47	5 48	5 56	6 25	6 41	6 53	7 22	7 36	7 48		8 21	8 48			9 6				9 44		10 19		
8½	St. Budeaux Platform		5 51	5 59	6 28		6 56	7 25	7 39			8 24	8 51			9 9				9 47		10 22		
9½	Saltash arr.		5 55	6 3	6 32		7 0	7 29	7 43	7 55		8 28	8 55			9 13				9 51		10 26		10 42

Station	M a.m.	a.m.	M a.m.	a.m.	M a.m. (Saturdays excepted)	M p.m.	p.m. (Saturdays only)		M p.m. (Saturdays excepted)	p.m.	M p.m.	p.m.	p.m.	M p.m.	M p.m.	M p.m.		M p.m.		p.m.		M p.m.
Plympton dep.		10 27											1 15									
Marsh Mills				11 34										1 21						2 42		
Mutley		10 33		11 39	11 53								1 21	1 28						2 47		
North Road		10 35		11 41	11 57					12 36			1 25	1 30						2 49		
Millbay arr.		10 42		11 47									1 30	1 35						2 54		
Millbay dep.	10 37		11 10			12 5			12 25		1 5	1 15			1 45	2 10		2 25				3 15
Devonport	10 42		11 15		12 1	12 10	12 25		12 30	12 40	1 10	1 21			1 50	2 15		2 30				3 20
Dockyard Halt	10 44		11 17			12 12			12 32		1 12				1 52	2 17		2 32				3 22
Ford Halt	10 46		11 19		12 3	12 14			12 34		1 14				1 54	2 19		2 34				3 24
Keyham	10 48		11 21		12 5	12 16	12 30		12 36		1 16	1 25			1 56	2 21		2 36				3 26
St. Budeaux Platform	10 51		11 24		12 8	12 20	12 34				1 19				1 59	2 24		2 39				3 29
Saltash arr.	10 55		11 28		12 14	12 24	12 37			12 50	1 26	1 30			2 3	2 28		2 43				3 33

Station	M p.m.	p.m.	p.m.	p.m. (Saturdays excepted)	M p.m.	p.m. (Fris. and Sats. only)	M p.m.	p.m. (Saturdays only)	M p.m.	p.m.	M p.m.	M p.m.	p.m. (Saturdays excepted)	M p.m.	p.m. (Saturdays only)	M p.m.	M p.m.	p.m.	M p.m.	p.m.	p.m.	M p.m.	p.m.	p.m. (Saturdays only)
Plympton dep.				3 55				4 28					5 19		5 38								7 7	
Marsh Mills		3 36									5 7									6 46				
Mutley		3 42		4 3				4 34			5 13		5 25		5 44					6 52	7 8		7 13	
North Road		3 44	3 57	4 5		4 16		4 36		5 15	5 17		5 27		5 46			6 45		6 54	7 10		7 15	7 28
Millbay arr.		3 55		4 10		4 25		4 45			5 22		5 37		5 55					7 0	7 16		7 23	7 33
Millbay dep.	3 26				4 17		4 40		5 8			5 35		5 50		6 15	6 30		6 58			7 20		
Devonport	3 31		4 2		4 22		4 45		5 13	5 20		5 41		5 55		6 20	6 35	6 50	7 3			7 25		
Dockyard Halt	3 33				4 24		4 47					5 43				6 22	6 37		7 5			7 27		
Ford Halt	3 35				4 26		4 49					5 45				6 24	6 39		7 7			7 29		
Keyham	3 37		4G 5		4 28		4 51		5 16	5 23		5 47		5 58		6 26	6 41		7 9			7 31		
St. Budeaux Platform	3 40		4G 8		4 31		4 54		5 20	5 26		5 50		6 1		6 29	6 44		7 12			7 34		
Saltash arr.	3 44		4 12		4 35		4 58		5 24	5 31		5 54		6 5		6 33	6 48		7 16			7 38		

Station	M p.m.	p.m.	p.m.	M p.m.	M p.m.	M p.m.	p.m.	M p.m.		M p.m.	M p.m.	M p.m.	M p.m.	p.m.	M p.m.	p.m.		M p.m. (Saturdays excepted)	p.m. (Saturdays only)	M ng't.		ng't
Plympton dep.							8 42															
Marsh Mills		7 46								9 4						10 43						
Mutley		7 51					8 48			9 9						10 49						
North Road		7 53	8 15				8 50			9 11				10 20		10 51				12 23		12 40
Millbay arr.		7 59					8 57			9 17				10 24		10 57				12 28		12 45
Millbay dep.	7 40			8 25	8 35	8 55		9 15			9 35	10 0	10 15		10 50			11 15	11 15			
Devonport	7 45		8 20	8 30	8 40	9 0		9 20			9 40	10 5	10 20		10 55			11 20	11 20			
Dockyard Halt	7 47				8 42	9 2		9 22			9 42	10 7	10 22		10 57			11 22				
Ford Halt	7 49				8 44	9 4		9 24			9 44	10 9	10 24		10 59			11 24				
Keyham	7 51			8 33	8 46	9 6		9 26			9 46	10 11	10 26		11 1			11 26	11 26			
St. Budeaux Platform	7 54			8 36	8 48	9 9		9 29			9 49	10 14	10 29		11 4			11 29	11 29			
Saltash arr.	7 58		8 27	8 40	8 52	9 13		9 33			9 53	10 18	10 33		11 8			11 34	11 34			

Sundays.

Station	a.m.	a.m.	M a.m.	a.m.	a.m.	M a.m.	M a.m.	M a.m.	a.m.	p.m.	M p.m.	p.m.	M p.m.	M p.m.	p.m.	M p.m.
Plympton dep.									11 50							
Marsh Mills										12 26		1 28			3 54	
Mutley			8 51							12 31		1 33			3 59	
North Road		7 50	8 53		10 0				12 5	12 33		1 35			4 1	
Millbay arr.			8 56						12 10	12 38		1 40			4 6	
Millbay dep.	7 5		9 6	9 35		10 8	11 0	11 55			12 55		2 0	3 0		4 15
Devonport	7 12	7 55	9 10	9 40	10 4	10 13	11 5	12 0			1 0		2 5	3 5		4 20
Dockyard Halt			9 12			10 15	11 7	12 2			1 2		2 7	3 7		4 22
Ford Halt			9 14			10 17	11 9	12 4			1 4		2 9	3 9		4 24
Keyham	7 15	7 58	9 16	9 43		10 19	11 11	12 6			1 6		2 11	3 11		4 26
St. Budeaux Platform	7 19	8 0	9 19	9 46		10 23	11 14	12 9			1 9		2 14	3 14		4 29
Saltash arr.	7 24	8 5	9 23	9 49		10 27	11 18	12 13			1 13		2 18	3 18		4 33

Station	p.m.	M p.m.	p.m.	M p.m.	p.m.	M p.m.	M p.m.	p.m.	p.m.	p.m.	p.m.	p.m.	M p.m.	p.m.	M p.m.	p.m.	p.m.	M p.m.
Plympton dep.	4 50											8 34		9 22				
Marsh Mills					6 43					8 18						9 59		
Mutley					6 48					8 23		8 40		9 28		10 4		
North Road	4 56		5 26		6 50			7 50	8 17	8 25		8 42		9 30		10 6	10 18	10 25
Millbay arr.	5 5		5 30		6 57			7 58	8 25	8 32		8 48		9 36		10 11	10 27	
Millbay dep.		5 17		5 55		7 5	7 55				8 45		9 0		9 50			
Devonport		5 22		6 0		7 10	8 0				8 50		9 5		9 55			10 29
Dockyard Halt				6 2			8 2						9 7					10 31
Ford Halt				6 4			8 4						9 9					10 33
Keyham		5 25		6 6		7 13	8 6				8 53		9 11		9 58			10 35
St. Budeaux Platform		5 28		6 9		7 16	8 9				8 56		9 14		10 1			10 38
Saltash arr.		5 32		6 13		7 20	8 13				9 0		9 18		10 5			10 42

G—Saturdays excepted. M—Rail Motor Car, one class only. S—Saturdays only.

A frequent 'bus service is operated by the Western National Omnibus Company between Plympton and Plymouth.

Week Days.

	M a.m.	M a.m.	a.m.	a.m.	M a.m.	a.m.	a.m.	M a.m.	a.m.	M a.m.	M a.m.	a.m.	a.m.	M a.m.	a.m.	M a.m.	a.m.	M a.m.	a.m. (Fris. and Sats. only)	M a.m.	a.m.	a.m.	a.m. (Saturdays only)	M a.m.	M a.m.
Saltash dep.		6 16	6 36					7 19	7 56		8 10			8 30		9 3	9 19	9 30		9 55	10 1				10 30
St. Budeaux Platf'rm		6 22	6 40					7 23	8 0		8 14			8 34		9 7		9 34		9 58					10 34
Keyham		6 26	6 44		7 4			7 26	8 4		8 17			8 37		9 10		9 37		10 2	10 8				10 37
Ford Halt			6 46		7 6			7 28			8 19			8 39		9 12		9 39		10 4					10 39
Dockyard Halt			6 48		7 8			7 30			8 21			8 41		9 14		9 41		10 6					10 41
Devonport		6 29	6 51		7 10			7 32	8 9		8 23			8 43		9 17	9 26	9 43		10 8	10 14				10 43
Millbay arr.		6 34	6 56		7 15			7 37	8 14		8 30			8 48		9 25	9 35	9 48		10 13	10 19	10 18			10 48
Millbay dep.	6 20			7 0		7 20	7 33			8 25		8 35	8 45		9 20				10 0				10 30	10 40	
North Road	6 27			7 4		7 25	7†48			8 30		8 42	8 52		9 25				10 5				10 35	10 44	
Mutley	6 29			7 6		7 27	7 50			8 32					9 27							10 21		10 46	
Marsh Mills arr.	6 35			7 12			7 56			8 40														10 52	
Plympton arr.						7 34									9 34										

Station	a.m.	a.m.	M a.m.	M a.m.		p.m.	p.m.	M p.m. (Saturdays only)	p.m. (Saturdays only)	M p.m. (Saturdays excepted)	M p.m.	M p.m.	p.m. (Saturdays excepted)		M p.m.	M p.m.	p.m. (Saturdays excepted)	p.m. (Saturdays only)	M p.m.	M p.m.	p.m.	M p.m.
Saltash dep.		11 10	11 15	11 48							12 39	1 8				1 53			2 23	2 36		3 0
St. Budeaux Platf'rm			11 19	11 52							12 43	1 12				1 56			2 27	2 40		3 4
Keyham			11 22	11 55				12 32		12 40	12 47	1 16				1 59			2 31	2 43		3 7
Ford Halt			11 24	11 57				12 34			12 49	1 18				2 1			2 33	2 45		3 9
Dockyard Halt			11 26	11 59							12 51	1 20				2 3			2 35	2 47		3 11
Devonport		11 21	11 28	12 0				12 36		12 43	12 53	1 22				2 5			2 37	2 50		3 13
Millbay arr.			11 33	12 6				12 41		12 48	12 58	1 27	1 29			2 10			2 42	2 57		3 18
Millbay dep.	10 55					12 8	12 30		12 45						2 6		2 15	2 35			3 3	
North Road	11 1	11 25				12 14	12 35		12 49						2 10		2 20	2 40			3 8	
Mutley	11 4					12 16	12 38		12 51				1 33		2 13		2 22	2 42			3 10	
Marsh Mills arr.						12 22			12 57						2 19						3 15	
Plympton arr.	11 12						12 45										2 29	2 49				

Station	p.m.	M p.m.	p.m.	p.m.	M p.m.			p.m.	M p.m.	p.m.		p.m.	p.m.	M p.m.	M p.m.	p.m.	p.m.	M p.m.	p.m.	M p.m.	p.m.	M p.m.	M p.m.	M p.m.	M p.m.
Saltash dep.	3 27	3 57			4 15				4 53	5 9				5 15	5 45			6 25		6 44			7 0	7 12	
St. Budeaux Platf'rm		4 0			4 19				4 57					5 19	5 49			6 29		6 48			7 4	7 16	
Keyham		4 3			4 22				5 0	5 15				5 22	5 52			6 32		6 51			7 7	7 19	
Ford Halt					4 24				5 2					5 24				6 34		6 53			7 9	7 21	
Dockyard Halt					4 26				5 4					5 26				6 36		6 55			7 11	7 23	
Devonport	3 36	4 6			4 28				5 6	5 20				5 28	5 55			6 38	6 45	6 58			7 13	7 26	
Millbay arr.		4 11			4 35				5 12					5 33	6 0			6 43		7 2			7 18	7 31	
Millbay dep.			4 23	4 33				5 10				5 25				6 10	6 20				7 10	7 14			7 42
North Road	3 40		4 28	4 37				5 15		5 23		5 30	5 40			6 16	6 26		6 48		7 15	7 17			7 46
Mutley			4 30	4 33				5 17				5 32	5 42			6 18					7 17	7 19			
Marsh Mills arr.				4 45								5 38				6 24						7 25			
Plympton arr.			4 37					5 24					5 49								7 24				

Station	p.m.	M p.m.	M p.m.	M p.m.	M p.m.	p.m.	p.m.	M p.m.	M p.m.	M p.m.	p.m.	M p.m.		M p.m.	p.m. (Saturdays only)	p.m.	M p.m.	M p.m.	M p.m.	p.m.	M p.m. (Weds., Thurs., and Sats. excepted)	nig't (Weds., Thurs., & Sats. only)
Saltash dep.	7 43	7 48	8 0	8 32	8 44			9 8	9 25	9 40	9 55	10 5		10 25		10 32		10 50	11 19		11 58	12 42
St. Budeaux Platf'rm		7 52	8 4	8 35	8 48			9 12	9 29	9 44		10 9		10 29				10 54	11 23			
Keyham		7 54	8 7	8 38	8 51			9 15	9 32	9 47		10 12		10 32				10 57	11 26			
Ford Halt		7 56	8 9	8 40				9 17	9 34	9 49		10 14						10 59				
Dockyard Halt		7 58	8 11	8 42				9 19	9 36	9 51		10 16						11 1	11 28			
Devonport	7 49	8 2	8 13	8 44	8 54			9 21	9 38	9 53	10 3	10 19		10 36		10 41		11 3	11 30	11 59		
Millbay arr.		8 7	8 18	8 50	8 59			9 26	9 43	9 58		10 27		10 41				11 8			P 12 11	P 12 55
Millbay dep.						9 5	9 20								10 45		10 55					
North Road	7 53					9 10	9 25				10 8				10 48	10 50	10 59		11 35	12 2		
Mutley						9 12	9 27								10 52		11 1		11 37			
Marsh Mills arr.						9 18											11 7					
Plympton arr.							9 34								11 0							

Sundays.

Station	a.m.	a.m.	a.m.	M a.m.	a.m.	a.m.	M a.m.	a.m.	a.m.	M a.m.	M p.m.	p.m.	p.m.	M p.m.	p.m.	p.m.	M p.m.
Saltash dep.		9 5		9 30		10 5	10 37			11 30	12 30		1 34	1 40			2 30
St. Budeaux Platf'rm		9 9		9 34		10 10	10 41			11 34	12 34			1 44			2 34
Keyham		9 15		9 37		10 13	10 44			11 37	12 37			1 47			2 37
Ford Halt				9 39			10 46			11 39	12 39			1 49			2 39
Dockyard Halt				9 41			10 48			11 41	12 41			1 51			2 41
Devonport		9 23		9 43		10 18	10 50			11 43	12 43			1 53			2 43
Millbay arr.		9 27		9 48		10 23	10 55			11 48	12 48		1 42	1 58			2 48
Millbay dep.	7 0		9 45		10 15	10 35		11 0	11 25			1 10			2 5	2 25	
North Road	7 5		9 50		10 20	10 40		11 4	11 30			1 15	1 45		2 10	2 30	
Mutley						10 42		11 6	11 32						2 12	2 32	
Marsh Mills arr.						10 48			11 38						2 18	2 38	
Plympton arr.								11 13									

Station	M p.m.	p.m.	M p.m.	p.m.	M p.m.	M p.m.	p.m.	p.m.	M p.m.	p.m.	p.m.	M p.m.	p.m.	M p.m.	M p.m.	p.m.	M p.m.	p.m.
Saltash dep.	3 30		4 35		5 35	6 40			7 25	7 42		8 20		9 25	10 8	10 23	10 52	
St. Budeaux Platf'rm	3 34		4 39		5 39	6 44			7 29			8 24		9 29	10 12	10 27	10 56	
Keyham	3 37		4 42		5 42	6 47			7 32			8 27		9 32	10 15	10 30	10 59	
Ford Halt	3 39		4 44			6 49						8 29		9 34			11 1	
Dockyard Halt	3 41		4 46			6 51						8 31		9 36			11 3	
Devonport	3 43		4 48		5 45	6 53			7 36	7 49		8 33		9 38	10 18	10 34	11 5	11 56
Millbay arr.	3 48		4 53		5 50	6 58			7 41			8 38		9 43		10 39		
Millbay dep.		4 30		5 35			7 15	7 40			8 25		9 20					
North Road		4 35		5 39			7 20	7 43		7 53	8 31		9 25		10 21		11 10	11 59
Mutley		4 38		5 41			7 22				8 33		9 27				11 12	
Marsh Mills arr.		4 45									8 39							
Plympton arr.				5 48			7 29						9 34					

M—Rail Motor Car, one class only. P—Calls to set down passengers only.

†—North Road arrive 7.36 a.m.

A frequent 'bus service is operated by the Western National Omnibus Company between Plymouth and Plympton.

The Bridge from bottom of Fore Street, Saltash.
FRITH.
STH 10.

Looking down Fore Street Saltash showing the steep incline from the Ferry terminal up to the town with the Royal Albert Bridge towering above. Circa 1930's. *Authors collection*

two services were early casualties to road transport competition, both ceasing on 21st June 1930. The Plympton trains served both Laira Halt and Lipson Vale Halt, although Plympton remained open for main line services. With the cessation of the rail motors Laira Halt was closed. The stairway from the subway to the downside platform was blocked off, although still insitu to-day and, in due course, the wooden platform was demolished. That was a pity for the platform provided an ideal vantage point to observe movements in the adjoining engine shed. The upside platform was at ground level and all that was needed was a barrier to close it off. The formation is still visible.

Even up to the date of closure there were still nine rail motor services to and from Plympton all of which ran in and out of Millbay and thus became integrated with the main Saltash service. Early morning departures from Plympton were at 5.45, 6.15, 7.13 , 7.50 and 8.10. The first two catered for the Yardees, by which name the Dockyard workers were universally known. Although there were more trains in 1910, the early morning service was little different from 1929 at 5.40, 6.5, 7.24 and 7.50. Interestingly, both the 6.5 of 1910 and the 6.15 of 1929 terminated at Keyham which is adjacent to the Dockyard's North gate. The competing Plympton bus service was operated by the infant Western National Omnibus Company, then trading as the DMT (Devon Motor Transport), who during the 1920s had seen off a number of upstarts who had tried to compete in a ruinous price war. One such upstart can be remembered as Hopper and Berryman.

Turning to the Yealmpton branch – pronounced Yamton – and spelt as such in the small print in some of the Working Timetables (WTTs). An example can be seen in the WTT reproduced on page 115. Yealmpton (or Yampton) was a small village about seven miles east of Plymouth on what is now the A379 road to Kingsbridge and Dartmouth. Before it left Plymouth in 1928, the Branch was worked by steam rail motor 72, that is when it was in good health, although, in fact, it was frequently bailed out by a conventional rail motor. No 72 was a representative of a dwindling class of 0-4-0Ts comprising of engine and coach combined, constructed early in the 20th Century for use on lightly loaded branch lines. The memory is of looking down from the then unobstructed vantage point above Lipson Vale and both seeing and hearing No. 72 going flat out as it came in from Yealmpton on the first train of the day. At about 30mph, its tiny 4'0" wheels revolving at such a rate that its rapid, yet feeble, exhaust made it sound as if it was going at twice the actual rate of progress.

In latter years there was a week-days only service of eight trains in each direction. Ironically, only a few weeks after the official closure the railway tried out an August Bank Holiday Sunday and Monday special service for which handbills were available. Patronage was poor on the only occasion that the train was seen, hauled by a 4-4-0 Bulldog with ordinary coaching stock.

The Branch was an early casualty to road competition, the irony being that the competition came from the Great Western's own buses. The GWR Excursion Timetable for 1929 included details of its own bus services and that indicated that there were 21 services on week-days and 15 on Sundays to Yealmpton and beyond against which the rail service stood little chance, especially as road and rail were roughly parallel for most of the way. The road service operated from the Millbay Station forecourt, but by the summer of 1930 it was operating from the North Road Station forecourt, for by this time Millbay was very much a backwater as far as the railway was concerned.

With effect from 1st January 1934 all the railway operated bus services, country wide, were merged with those of local operators. In the case of Plymouth it was the Western National Omnibus Company. Nevertheless, the bus timetables continued to appear in the railway's annual excursion booklet right up until 1939. However, the 1934 edition contained a caveat "The times are liable to alteration, but particulars of any alterations can be obtained from Current Handbills announcing the services". In the 1935 and following issues the caveat was stronger "Although every endeavour is made to ensure accuracy the Great Western Railway can assume no responsibility for the times of the various Omnibus Services shown in this pamphlet".

The Yealmpton and Plympton rail motors both called at Lipson Vale Halt. When those services ceased the Great Western owned Halt was left to be served only by Southern Railway rail motors to St. Budeaux and by the occasional services to and from Bere Alston and Tavistock.

During 1930 Swindon took small 0-6-0T 2062 of class 2021 out of service, rebuilt it with a new boiler, fitted it with 5'2" wheels and it became the first 5400. Later in the same year the 5'2" wheels were replaced with wheels of 4'7½" diameter and it became the prototype of the 6400 class. In August 1931 there appeared 5400 in Plymouth working the rail motor services. It did not stay very long, but Nemesis was not long in coming. Newly constructed 6406 appeared at Laira on 16th April 1932 and was immediately put to work on the Saltash rail motor services. Within three weeks 6407, 6408 and 6409 were also working the rail motor services. The year 1934 saw the arrival of 6414, 6417 and 6419, followed in 1935 by 6420 and 6421. Prior to the arrival of the final pair 6408 and 6409 had departed for pastures new.

Late in February 1937 auto fitted 0-4-2T 4829 (later 1429) arrived at Plymouth and was put to work on the rail motor services. After two months it was replaced by 4827 (later 1427) but that left in the following July, presumably having been found unsuitable.

As for the old faithfuls, only 1252 went straight from Laira for scrap. All the rest went to sheds in South Wales, the last to leave Laira being 1167 and 1271 in September 1936. None lasted in their new abodes, for all had made their last journeys to Swindon by early 1938.

POSTSCRIPT

The steam operated rail motor service to Saltash and beyond survived until 13th June 1960 when, on that date, British Rail's then new dmus took over. They did not last long because on 24th October 1961 the new Tamar road bridge was opened. Passengers promptly abandoned the railway in favour of their cars and the buses which conveyed them to the city centre instead of the less convenient North Road Station. The rail service just withered away. Of the class 64xx auto fitted engines allocated to Laira 6406/7/14/20/1 spent all their working lives there.

The Yealmpton branch was reopened to passengers as a wartime measure between 3rd November 1941 and 6th October 1947 operating from the Southern Railway's Friary Station instead of Millbay which had already been closed on 23rd April 1941 due to war damage.

The timber Lipson Vale Halt was closed on 22nd March 1942 and subsequently demolished as a wartime fire hazard in a residential area.

6407 of class 6400 collecting two "push" rail motor vehicles from the holding sidings at Laira in January 1934. It will then reverse into the complimentary siding to attach two "pull" vehicles to work sandwich fashion. The trailer visible appears to be no.72. *P D Orton*

Yealmpton Station. *M J Dart collection*

7. THE BRANCH

To railwaymen and enthusiasts alike, it was the Branch. If you said The Branch everyone knew what you meant. Even Bernard Mills entitled his Book *"The Branch"*. The Branch went from Plymouth to Launceston, but to railwaymen and locals alike it went to "Lanson", although posh people called it "Launson". It was even "Lanson" in the small print in the Working Timetable (WTT).

The passenger service worked, basically by a mixture of three or four clerestory non corridor trains behind a 45xx 2-6-2T, or by a two coach auto set with an auto fitted 0-6-0 pannier tank. Only four trains per day worked through to Launceston, the rest terminated at Tavistock. There was an extra evening train to Launceston on Saturdays. The engine on the last train of the day to Launceston stabled there overnight, or over the week-end as the case may be. A peculiarity of the timetable was the morning express from Tavistock which ran non-stop from Yelverton to North Road (arrive 9.23am) except for a call at Bickleigh. It was said that Mr. R.J. Fittall, Town Clerk of Plymouth, travelled into town on that train from Bickleigh.

On Saturdays, the 9.5pm to Tavistock was extended to Launceston. Such was the throng that the train was regularly run in two parts and there is the vague memory that it was sometimes in three parts. Summer and winter, Saturday afternoons and evenings in Plymouth were festive events. The country folk brought their produce to market, and with the proceeds purchased their necessities for the following week. Country folk with their simple ways, broad dialect, superstitions, and often distinctive dress are an extinct breed, as are the carriers. A carrier was a man with a covered lorry, based on a rural village or township, who conveyed goods to the appropriate town on market day. (Market days were always annotated in the index of railway timetables – even Bradshaw). So folk could be seen in the early afternoon, heavily laden, relieving themselves of their burdens at the carrier's vehicle. Two or three such vehicles could be seen each Saturday in an area known as The Back of the Market, an area shared with a variety of cheap jacks disposing of their wares of dubious quality to willing buyers.

The shops on a Saturday night stayed open until at least 8pm (some until 9pm), Woolworths, Fifty Shilling Taylors (a man's suit for £2.50) and departmental stores such as Spooners amongst them. In days prior to refrigeration, meat, fruit and vegetables were sold off cheap during the evening to canny town and country folk who had just waited for that hour. The eating places did a roaring trade, Sellicks in East Street was a popular lower priced venue, always with joints of cooked meat and pans of steaming faggots and peas, seen through the steamed up window. Their Cornish pasties at tuppence or threepence needed no advertising such was their reputation throughout a wide area around Plymouth.

The cinemas were a great attraction with the latest films in "Glorious Technicolour" playing to capacity audiences with invariably long patient queues waiting outside for the front stalls seats, priced at 6d (2½ p). There were two 3000 seat modern city centre houses, Gaumont and Odeon (formerly Regent) to which was added in 1938 the Royal. All three showing the latest releases, none of which would reach the small town cinemas for many months – if at all. The great attraction at the Royal was the young maestro, Dudley Savage at the "Mighty Compton Organ" which at interval time rose from the bowels of the earth in full tune and to great applause.

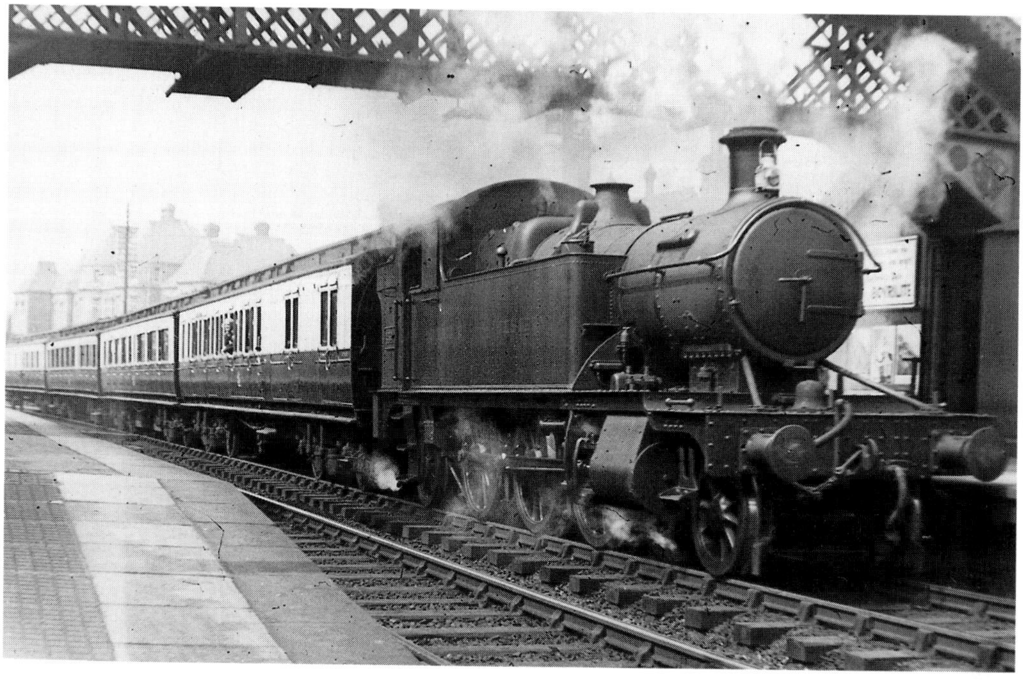

4534 at Mutley station with the 12.8pm to Launceston in August 1937. A typical "Branch" train, four aging clerestory non corridor coaches hauled by one of the early small tank engines of the 4500 series which predominated at Laira.

P D Orton

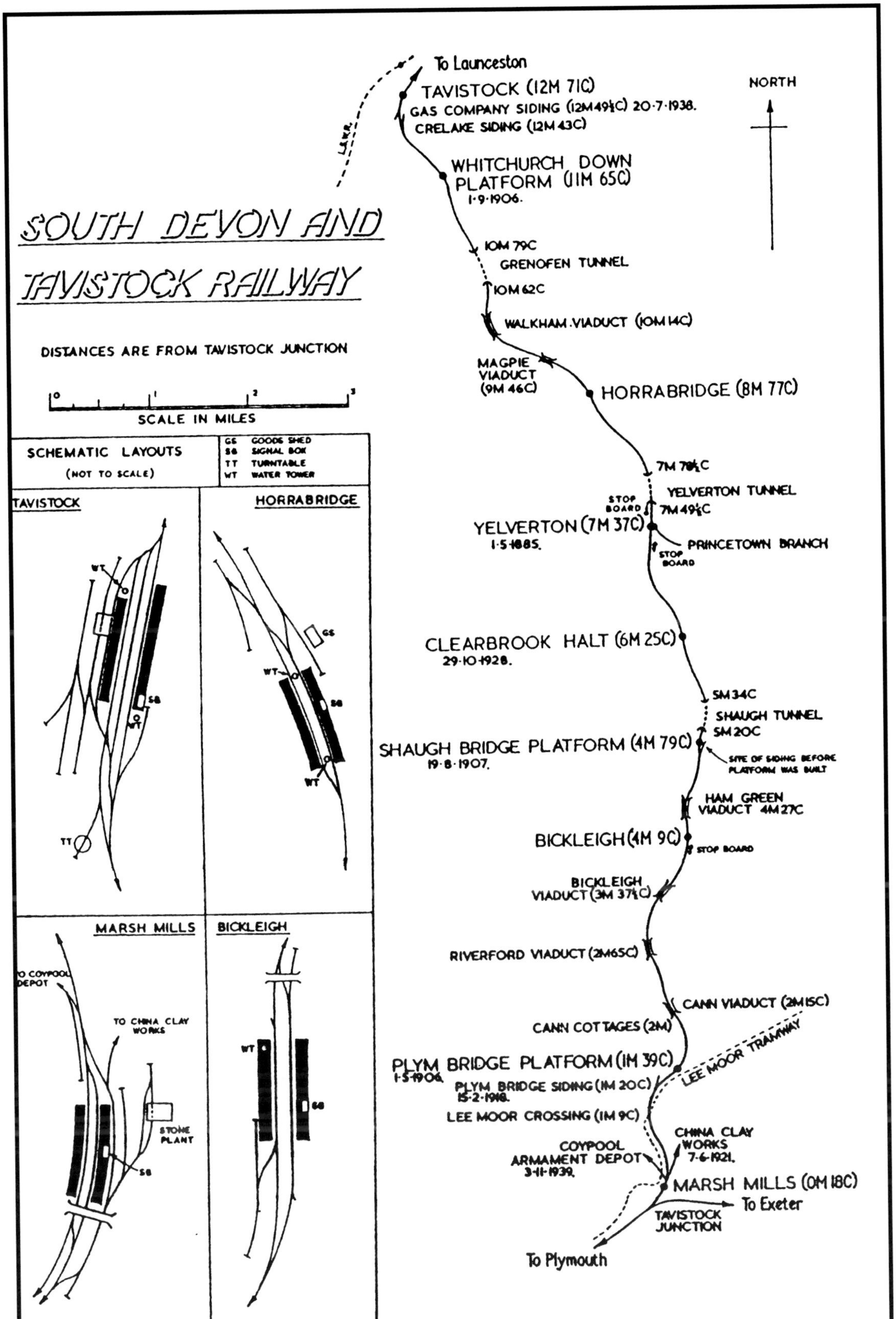

The Launceston Branch. Reproduced courtesty of The Oakwood Press (1997).

After all that, it is not difficult to visualise the need for two five or six coach trains at 9.5pm on a Saturday night in order to get the country folk home at a reasonable time for bed. The first train for Tavistock ran non stop from Millbay to Yelverton, followed by the second through to Launceston calling at all stations, halts and platforms along the way.

The branch only boasted one Sunday train each year through to Launceston, that is in addition to the normal four train service to Tavistock. That was a special laid on for Roman Catholics attending the annual pilgrimage to the shrine of Cuthbert Mayne on the third Sunday in June. Cuthbert Mayne was the first seminary priest to be martyred in England, back in 1577. A feature of the branch in the 1930s was the evening excursion operating daily during the summer months. The fare was 6d(2½p) return valid any station to Yelverton, 9d(3½ p) to Horrabridge, 1/- (5p) to Tavistock and 1/3 (6½ p) to Princetown. Comparatively few passengers travelled beyond Yelverton and, therefore, the majority paid only 6d return. Consequently the trains were known as the "Woolworths" because no article in that well known store cost more than 6d. Of course, one could buy a very nice pair of slippers for 1/- (one shilling – 5p), 6d for the right foot and 6d for the left foot. Many more examples could be quoted, such as a 21 piece china tea service for less than ten shillings (50p), each piece being priced separately.

Tickets for the Woolworths were valid on any train on or after 4.30pm. During the period of their validity there was a train starting from Millbay at 4.30pm every day, including Sundays, terminating at Yelverton. On week-days the motive power was usually a pannier tank of the non auto fitted variety from the 1076 or 1854 classes. During the summer of 1933 the regular performer was vintage double framed 1658 of class 1076 constructed in 1881. That strenuous duty must have taken its toll, for 1658 was withdrawn from service during the following year.

The highlights of the Woolworths were fine summer Sunday afternoons when the timetabled 4.30pm ran in three parts, conveying upwards of two thousand passengers. The first part ran non-stop through North Road and Mutley stations and only the third part stopped at Mutley. Strangely, Laira rarely turned out ancient panniers for their Sunday trains. Halls and Castles were frequent performers and, on at least one occasion a class 47xx 2-8-0 put in an appearance. Moguls and Laira's large 31xx 2-6-2Ts also shared in the work. In fact, with the exception of the Kings, all classes of engine could worked as far as Yelverton, there were weight restrictions beyond.

The first part was normally a large 2-6-2T which, after its return from Yelverton, was used on the year round roster to work the 8.45pm from Millbay to Liskeard and its corresponding return working at 10pm from Liskeard. The second part was nearly always a big engine, and the third part the normal small 2-6-2T which was rostered to work the Branch Sunday service, whatever the weather.

To cater for the crowds returning home, including those who had travelled out on the earlier trains at 10.35am and 2.5pm, the railway provided a lavish return service from Yelverton at 6.25, 7.30, 8.00, 8.35, 9.10 and 9.41. Thus, there were five trains at roughly half hourly intervals, of which only the last originated at Tavistock. The 7.30 and 8.35 did not appear in the public timetable, only running on a as required basis, i.e. when the weather was hot and sunny.

On Bank Holiday Mondays (note not Bank Holiday Sundays) the railway issued a special timetable in the form of a handbill. It was basically the same from year to year. The necessity for such a handbill was to cater for the literally thousands of passengers going mainly to Shaugh Bridge Platform or Yelverton. The normal service of three trains between 8.35am and 11.55am was augmented to nine, two of which were booked non-stop between Millbay and Shaugh Bridge Platform. Shaugh Bridge Platform was a popular destination situated in the middle of nowhere in particular. There was the River Plym with two nearby well patronised tea gardens, or there was the choice of a formidable hill up to the hamlet of Shaugh Prior, the best part of two miles from the railway. Shaugh Prior, on the edge of the Moor was good walking and picnicking country.

The problem that faced the railway on Bank Holidays was that the crowds who had travelled out on the morning and afternoon trains, plus the Woolworths, all wanted to return home during a very limited evening time scale. For example, on Whit Monday 1936 there were departures from Yelverton at 6.5, 6.33, 6.55, 7.33, 7.50, 8.10, 8.40 and 9.16. Eight trains in the space of just over three hours, although only the 7.50 started its homeward journey from Yelverton. Of those eight trains four were worked out from Plymouth as empty stock, one as far as Horrabridge, two to Tavistock and just the one to Yelverton. Bearing in mind that there were also three timetabled evening trains out from Plymouth it meant that the 7½ miles of single track between Marsh Mills and Yelverton, with only a passing loop at Bickleigh accommodated fifteen trains within those three hours. Quite a feat of organisation.

Where did all those crowds go who travelled on the branch on Bank Holiday Mondays and on Sundays? Those who had travelled through to Yelverton, walked

Examples of three part trains are set out below:

	5th September 1937	**12th September 1937**	**24th July 1938**	**11th September 1938**
1st	3180	3180	3180	3180
2nd	6801 *Aylburton Grange*	4991 *Cobham Hall*	4092 *Dunraven Castle*	3186
3rd	4502	4502	5519	5573

Whit-Monday Train Service from PLYMOUTH & DISTRICT to

Princetown, Tavistock and Launceston

For PLYM BRIDGE, SHAUGH BRIDGE, MOORLANDS, LYDFORD GORGE, etc.

Station	a.m.	a.m.	a.m.	a.m.	a.m.	a.m.	a.m.	a.m.	a.m.	a.m.	p.m.	p.m.	p.m.	p.m.	p.m.	p.m.	p.m.	p.m.	p.m.	p.m.
SALTASH dep.	6 36	7 56	8 30	9 3	9 19	9 35	9 55	..	11 0	..	12 32	..	1 8	2 36	4 10	5 0	6 15	7 12	8 44	10 30
St. Budeaux "	6 40	8 0	8 34	9 7	—	9 40	9 58	..	11 4	..	12 36	..	1 12	2 40	4 14	5 4	6 19	7 16	8 48	10 34
Keyham "	6 44	8 4	8 37	9 10	—	9 44	10 2	..	11 7	..	12 40	..	1 16	2 43	4 17	5 7	6 22	7 19	8 51	10 37
Devonport "	6 51	8 9	8 43	9 16	9 26	9 50	10 8	..	11 10	..	12 46	..	1 22	2 50	4 23	5 13	6 28	7 26	8 54	10 41
PLYMOUTH Millbay "	**7 5**	**8 25**	**9 5**	**9 35**	**10 5**	—	**10 45**	..	**11 30**	**11 50**	**1 20**	..	**2 5**	**3 5**	**4 30**	**5 20**	**6 40**	**8 0**	**9 5**	**11 10**
PLYMOUTH North Road "	**7 9**	**8 31**	**9 10**	**9 40**	—	**10 25**	—	**11 0**	**11 35**	**11 54**	**1 25**	**2 2**	**2 11**	**3 10**	**4 36**	**5 25**	**6 47**	**8 5**	**9 10**	**11 14**
PLYMOUTH Mutley "	7 11	8 34	9 13	9 44	—	10 28	—	11 3	11 37	11 56	1 28	2 5	2 15	3 12	4 40	5 28	6 50	8 8	9 12	11 16
Marsh Mills "	7 17	8 40	9 18	9 49	—	10 34	—	—	11 42	12 2	1 36	—	2 21	3 18	4 46	5 34	6 56	8 14	9 18	11 22
Plym Bridge Platform "	—	8 44	9 23	—	—	—	—	—	11 45	12 5	1 41	—	2 26	3 22	4 51	5 37	7 1	8 18	—	—
Bickleigh "	7 28	8 51	9 30	—	—	—	—	—	11 53	12 14	1 52	—	2 38	3 32	5 2	5 47	7 12	8 25	9 29	11 31
Shaugh Bridge Platform "	—	8 55	9 36	10 3	10 30	10 50	11 13	11 30	11 56	12 17	1 57	2 22	2 44	3 36	5 6	5 51	7 16	8 29	9 32	11 35
Clearbrook Halt "	—	9 0	9 41	—	—	10 58	—	11 40	12 0	12 23	2 5	—	2 50	3 43	5 13	5 58	7 23	8·34	9 38	11·40
YELVERTON arr.	7 37	9 4	9 45	10 10	10 40	11 5	11 26	11 45	12 5	12 26	2 10	2 30	2 55	3 48	5 18	6 3	7 28	8 38	9 41	11 44
Yelverton dep.	—	9 10	..	11 0	11 0	—	—	..	..	12 40	—	..	3 0	—	5 25	—	7 40	..	9.47	—
Dousland "	—	9 16	..	11 6	11 6	—	—	..	..	12 46	—	..	3 6	—	5 31	—	7 46	..	9 53	—
Burrator Platform "	—	9 22	..	11 12	11 12	—	—	..	..	12 52	—	..	3 12	—	5 37	—	7 52	..	—	—
Ingra Tor Halt "	—	9 34	..	11 24	11 24	—	—	..	..	1 4	—	..	3 24	—	5 49	—	8 4	..	—	—
King Tor Halt "	—	9 45	..	11 35	11 35	—	—	..	..	1 15	—	..	3 35	—	6 0	—	8 15	..	10 14	—
PRINCETOWN arr.	—	9 55	..	11 45	11 45	—	—	..	..	1 25	—	..	3 45	—	6 10	—	8 25	..	10 25	—
YELVERTON dep.	7 40	9 5	..	10 15	10 44	11 10	11 30	11 50	..	12 29	2 14	..	2 58	3 52	5 20	6 6	7 30	8 39	9 42	11 45
Horrabridge "	7 44	9 9	..	10 20	10 50	11 16	11 36	12 0	..	12 33	2 20	..	3 3	3 58	5 26	6 12	7 36	8 43	9 46	11 49
Whitchurch Down Platform "	7 51	9 15	..	10 25	10 57		11 43	12 7	..	12 40	2 27	..	3 10	4 5	5 33	6 19	7 43	8 48	9 53	11 55
TAVISTOCK "	7 54	9 20	..	10 30	11 0	..	11 50	12 10	..	12 49	2 30	..	3 15	4 11	5 40	6 25	7 49	8 55	9 56	12 0
Mary Tavy and Blackdown "		9 29	..			..			..	12 57		..		4 19			7 57			
Lydford "	..	9 39	..	..	..	..	..	..	..	1 6	..	..	..	4 28	..	..	8 6	..	..	..
Coryton "	..	9 49	..	..	..	..	..	..	..	1 15	..	..	..	4 38	..	..	8 16	..	..	..
Litfon "	..	10 0	..	..	..	..	..	..	..	1 25	..	..	..	4 49	..	..	8 27	..	..	..
LAUNCESTON arr.	..	10 10	..	..	..	..	..	..	..	1 35	..	..	..	5 0	..	..	8 40	..	..	..

NOTE—Passengers from Stations West of Plymouth change either at Millbay or North Road.

For particulars of Cheap Fares by the above Trains, see page 4.

Monthly Return Tickets at pre-War Fares—Any Day—Any Train—Anywhere

AVAILABLE FOR ONE MONTH, FOR FULL DETAILS, ENQUIRE AT G.W. STATIONS AND OFFICES.

Whit-Monday Train Service from LAUNCESTON, PRINCETOWN & TAVISTOCK

To PLYMOUTH and DISTRICT

Station	a.m.	a.m.	a.m.	a.m.	p.m.	p.m.	p.m.	p.m.	p.m.	p.m.	p.m.	p.m.	p.m.	p.m.	p.m.	p.m.	p.m.	night
LAUNCESTON dep.	7 22	..	..	11 0	..	..	2 10	..	..	..	..	..	..	7 0	..	..	..	..
Lifton "	7 31	..	..	11 11	..	..	2 19	..	..	..	..	..	..	7 10	..	..	..	..
Coryton "	7 38	..	..	11 18	..	..	2 26	..	..	..	..	..	..	7 17	..	..	..	..
Lydford "	7 50	..	..	11 34	..	..	2 39	..	..	..	..	..	..	7 32	..	..	..	..
Mary Tavy and Blackdown "	7 57	..	..	11 42	..	..	2 46	..	..	..	..	..	..	7 40	..	..	..	..
TAVISTOCK "	8 5	9 30	..	11 50	12 50	..	2 53	4 30	5 50	..	6 33	7 10	..	7 50	8 20	9 0	10 10	12 5
Whitchurch Down Platform "	8 8	9 33	..	11 53	12 54	..	2 56	4 33	5 53	..	6 38	7 14	..	7 54	8 24	9 3	10 13	12 8
Horrabridge "	8 17	9 40	..	12 0	1 2	..	3 5	4 41	6 1	6 25	6 48	7 22	..	8 2	8 32	9 11	10 21	12 16
YELVERTON arr.	8 21	9 45	..	12 4	1 5	..	3 10	4 44	6 4	6 30	6 53	7 27	..	8 7	8 35	9 14	10 25	12 20
PRINCETOWN dep.	7 40	—	10 0	—	11 45	1 30	—	4 0	—	—	—	6 28	..	—	—	8 25	—	—
King Tor Halt "	7 45	—	10 6	—	11 51	1 36	—	4 6	—	—	—	6 34	..	—	—	8 31	—	—
Ingra Tor Halt "	7 54	—	10 15	—	12 0	1 45	—	4 15	—	—	—	6 43	..	—	—	8 40	—	—
Burrator Platform "	8 6	—	10 27	—	12 12	1 57	—	4 27	—	—	—	6 55	..	—	—	8 52	—	—
Dousland "	8 11	—	10 33	—	12 18	2 3	—	4 33	—	—	—	7 1	..	—	—	8 58	—	—
Yelverton arr.	8 16	—	10 40	—	12 25	2 10	—	4 40	—	—	—	7 10	..	—	—	9 5	—	—
YELVERTON dep.	8 22	9 46	..	12 5	1 7	..	3 15	4 47	6 7	6 33	6 55	7 33	7 50	8 10	8 40	9 16	10 26	12 21
Clearbrook Halt "	8 25	9 49	..	—	1 11	..	3 20	4 51	6 12	6 38	—	7 38	—	—	8 45	—	10 29	—
Shaugh Bridge Platform "	8 28	9 52	..	12 10	1 16	..	3 25	4 56	6 20	6 46	7 5	7 46	8 0	8 20	8 53	9 25	10 33	—
Bickleigh "	8 31	9 58	..	12 15	1 20	..	3 32	5 1	—	—	7 12	—	—	8 24	8 57	9 29	10 36	12 29
Plym Bridge Platform "	8 36	10 3	..	12 20	1 26	..	3 37	5 7	—	6 52	—	—	8 8	—	—	9 35	—	—
Marsh Mills "	8 39	10 7	..	12 23	1 29	..	3 41	5 11	—	6 56	—	7 56	8 11	8 32	—	9 38	10 44	—
PLYMOUTH Mutley arr.	8 45	10 13	..	12 28	1 36	..	3 46	5 16	6 40	7 1	7 27	8 1	8 15	8 37	9 10	9 43	10 51	—
PLYMOUTH North Road "	**8 48**	**10 15**	..	**12 32**	**1 40**	..	**3 50**	**5 18**	**6 42**	**7 5**	**7 32**	**8 6**	**8 20**	**8 40**	**9 14**	**9 47**	**10.54**	**12 45**
PLYMOUTH Millbay "	**8 52**	**10 40**	..	**12 36**		..	**3 55**	**5 25**	—	**7 19**	**7 37**	**8 11**	**8 25**	**8 45**	**9 20**	**9 52**	**10 58**	**12 50**
Devonport "	9 0	10 35	..	1 10	..	..	4 22	5 41	6 50	7 30	7 45	8 22	8 40	9 0	9 40	10 5	11 20	
Keyham "	9 14	10 47	..	1 16	..	..	4 28	5 47	7 9	7 36	7 51	8 25	8 46	9 6	9 46	10 11	11 26	..
St. Budeaux "	9 18	10 50	..	1 19	..	..	4 31	5 50	7 12	7 39	7 54	8 28	8 48	9 9	9 49	10 14	11 29	..
SALTASH "	9 15	10 42	..	1 26	..	..	4 35	5 55	7 16	7 43	7 58	8 33	8 52	9 13	9 53	10 18	11 34	..

NOTE.—Passengers to Stations West of Plymouth change either at Millbay or North Road. **For particulars of Cheap Fares by the above Trains, see page 4.**

For Attractive Sunday Half-Day Excursions

SEE ANNOUNCEMENTS

pre-War Fares refer to the 1914-18 War

4402 of class 4400 the regular Princetown Branch engine at Yelverton in 1931. Note flange oiling device equipment fitted to side of smokebox.
F H C Casbourne/Stephenson Locomotive Society/ M J Dart collection

An early photograph of the Princetown train approaching Yelverton. This illustrates how the train ran round the engine, ready to return to Princetown. The engine propelled the coach to the position shown, then retired into the siding visible in the foreground, whilst the coach ran back into the platform under gravity, but under the control of the guard.
Authors collection

up the hill from the station, and promptly sat on the nearest empty space available on the moorland greensward to watch the wild Dartmoor ponies. There was some similarity with the density of those on the beach at a popular seaside resort.

Go to Yelverton to-day and the greensward that was at the top of the hill is a road complex of roundabouts. Again, go to Yelverton to-day and all that can be seen will be a few cars parked at the roadside, their elderly occupants dozing in the warm seasonal sunshine. Even the buses are nearly empty. Where have the crowds gone?

They are all in Majorca.

The branch off The Branch at Yelverton went to Princetown, a well known village throughout the land because of the adjacent prison. Indeed, Princetown was, and still is, a very small village. Inevitably, traffic was sparse and it would probably have disappeared long before 1956 but for usage by the prison authorities. As it was, come the 1930s, the Southern Railway's station at Tavistock was seeing increasing use for the transfer of prisoners and for the departure station for those who had served their time. Therefore, the one coach train was adequate for day to day requirements. Princetown Station enjoyed the privilege of being the highest station on the Great Western at 1395 feet above sea level.

The branch was distinctive in a number of respects:

1. It was the preserve of the small 44xx 2-6-2Ts from the date of their construction in 1905 until their ultimate demise in 1955. During the early part of 1928 4402 was transferred to Laira from St Blazey. 4402 became the permanent resident at Princetown coming into Laira only for maintenance. Only occasionally was it seen in traffic in Plymouth.
2. There being no running loop at Yelverton there was the unusual procedure of the train running round the engine. The modus operandi was for the engine to propel the coach back up the bank from the platform, uncouple and reverse, then run forward into the engine spur. The guard then released the brake and the empty coach ran back into the platform under gravity. That was, of course, long before the days of the Health and Safety Executive.
3. There is a well known delightful fact that a passenger could alight at Ingra Tor Halt, walk across the moor, wait for and rejoin the same train at King Tor Halt. That highlighted the snail's progress of the train as it laboriously wound its way around the Tor gaining height as it went. The train took 45 minutes for 10½ miles (14mph), rising 900ft between Yelverton and Princetown on a ruling grade of mostly 1 in 40.
4. In the days when the branch functioned the weather was much harsher than to-day and it was not unusual for the line to be blocked at some time during the winter months. That gave editors the opportunity to fill their newspapers with tales of snowbound passengers, the heroics of railwaymen, together with pictures of the snow plough in action.
5. If the branch existed to-day it would be a tourist attraction of the first order, shorter in length, but equalling the Settle and Carlisle for grandeur taking in Plymouth Sound, the Tamar (pronounced Tamer) Valley, and the Cornish Hills beyond. Like the Settle and Carlisle – weather permitting.

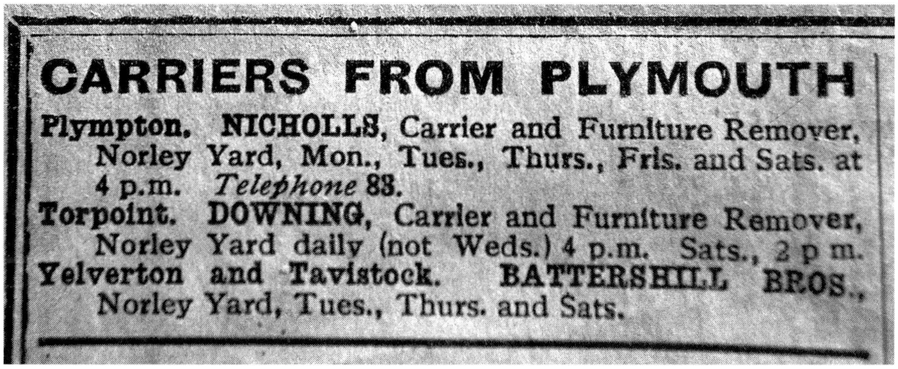
CARRIERS FROM PLYMOUTH
Plympton. NICHOLLS, Carrier and Furniture Remover, Norley Yard, Mon., Tues., Thurs., Fris. and Sats. at 4 p.m. Telephone 83.
Torpoint. DOWNING, Carrier and Furniture Remover, Norley Yard daily (not Weds.) 4 p.m. Sats., 2 p m.
Yelverton and Tavistock. BATTERSHILL BROS., Norley Yard, Tues., Thurs. and Sats.

Carriers advertisements in Brendon's Plymouth local timetable guide in 1930's.
Authors collection

8. MAIN LINE TRAIN SERVICES

WINTER SERVICE
UP TRAINS

It was not until the winter timetable of 1935/6 that a 7am train from Millbay to Paddington was introduced, due to arrive at its destination at 11.35am. It was Saturdays Excepted during the currency of the summer service. Prior to that, the first up train to London did not depart Millbay until 8.35am and did not arrive in Paddington until 1.15pm It was a six coach formation which included a dining car and a slip coach for Reading, effectively four coaches to accommodate passengers from Plymouth and intermediate stations to London. A second slip coach was attached at Taunton which slipped at Westbury providing a connection for Trowbridge, Chippenham and Swindon.

After 8.35, there was nothing more until 11.22am (8.50 from Penzance) and not into Paddington until 3.45pm as part of the Torbay Limited Express. That is illustrative of the paucity of demand for long distance travel in pre-war days, including business travel. The next through train from Cornwall departed Penzance at 10 o'clock, the Cornish Riviera Limited Express, 12.30 off North Road and into Paddington at 4.45pm. It was an eleven coach formation, including a Luncheon Car. As an aside, only seven minutes were allowed to change engines at North Road.

Two further trains at 11.10am and 1.15pm from Penzance (North Road at 2pm and 4.10pm) completed the quota of five day time trains to Paddington. However, mention must be made of the 6.20pm from Millbay which did not make its weary way into Paddington until 2.40 next morning. During the summers of 1929 and 1931 it was routed via Westbury instead of Bristol. From 1932 forward the train continued to run via Bristol, but was diverted to run via Westbury on summer Saturdays only.

Finally, there was the up Midnight, 9pm off Penzance and 12.15 from North Road which had sleeping cars in its formation. It was known to railwaymen from Bristol towards Paddington as "The Waker".

DOWN TRAINS

The first arrival at North Road at 4.32am was the 9.50pm the previous night from Paddington. This was a time honoured train which survived until rationalisation of

A summer Saturday holiday extra in August 1937 gathering speed through Mutley Station with 4940 *Ludford Hall* and 4948 *Northwick Hall*, both with small tenders. A clerestory non-corridor coach leading. Note period clothes of waiting passengers.

P D Orton

the timetable following dieselisation. It included sleeping cars through to Cornwall. The down midnight passenger train, with sleeping car accommodation as far as Plymouth arrived at 7.20am. That train was known to railwaymen in the Westcountry as "The Owl".

The 5.30am from Paddington was another time honoured train which can be found in the earliest of Working Timetables at the Public Record Office, dating back into the early 1870s. It was into North Road at 12.26pm and eventually ambled into Penzance at 3.40pm. It was known to railwaymen as "The Paper Train". The train included in its formation somewhat elderly passenger accommodation in the shape of Dreadnought coaches, notable because the corridor changed sides at the half way point. The original "Paper Train" terminated at Plymouth (Millbay) at 2.58pm on broad gauge metals, quite late in the day for the latest London news.

The 7.15am was an extraordinary train. It left Paddington 3¼ hours before the 10.30 departure and terminated at Plymouth half an hour before the 10.30's arrival. During 1939, at least, a lot of time was lost changing engines en route. In that year the procedure was as follows:

To Swindon	Paddington King or Castle
To Bath	Carmarthen Hall
To Bristol	45XX 2-6-2T!!
To Plymouth	Alternative days
	Landore (Swansea) Castle or Hall
	Taunton Star or Hall

Quite extraordinary!

The 10.30am referred to in the previous paragraph was the prestige Cornish Riviera Express, non-stop to Plymouth in the summer, doing the journey in the level four hours, seven minutes later in the winter with a stop at Exeter, where a through coach for Kingsbridge was detached. It will be observed that it was the first realistic through service to Plymouth and Cornwall for the day, albeit not getting into Plymouth until 2.30pm and Penzance until 5pm.

The 1.30pm was the second, and last, day train through to Penzance. The 3.30pm finished at Truro, but even that was cut back to Plymouth in the winter months during the dark days of the depression.

The last two day time trains to the West of England, both routed via Bristol were the 4.30pm and 6.30pm and not into Millbay until 10.20pm and 12.45am respectively, a tedious six hour journey. In the winter timetable of 1935 the 4.30pm was accelerated to leave Paddington at 5.5pm with the same arrival time at Plymouth.

SUNDAYS

Bradshaw for May 1934 shows the undermentioned trains from Plymouth to Paddington:

Millbay dpt	7am	Paddington arr	3.35pm
	9.45am		4.10
	1.10pm		8.15
North Road	2.40		7.50
	8pm		3.05am
	12.15am		7.10

The 7am from Millbay had a restaurant car from Plymouth for Liverpool, but the through Liverpool passenger accommodation started out from Paignton and the restaurant car was attached at Newton Abbot.

The 9.45am from Millbay was an interesting train because it often produced a Paddington based Hall class engine, which were otherwise quite rare in Plymouth. For a train routed via Bristol it was reasonably fast doing

2806 These 2-8-0's of class 2800 were pressed into service for peak summer weekend holiday traffic. At North Road Station in August 1937. *P D Orton*

the journey in 6hrs 25mins, aided by travelling via Badminton instead of Bath and Chippenham.

The 1.10pm from Millbay was worked by a Paddington King off the previous night's down 6.30pm. It was a rare example of a King working an up London bound train on two successive days.

It will be noted that the 2.40pm (11.10am Penzance) was the only decent train of the day and was rostered for a Laira King. It was routed via Westbury, whereas all the others were via Bristol.

Why anybody from Plymouth, or anywhere in the West of England for that matter, would want to arrive in London at 3 o'clock on a Monday morning is a mystery. One would have thought it more convenient to use the up midnight train and arrive at Paddington at the more civilised time of 7.10. However, people did use that train. A footnote in the timetable indicated that the 8pm from Plymouth would call at Ivybridge (a mere village) at 8.20pm to pick up passengers for Paddington if notice was given by 7.15pm.

The only improvements during the decade to the winter timetable were (1) The 7am was re-directed to the North West, thus providing Plymouth with a day service in that direction, and (2) The summer 10.15am to Paddington became a year round service.

In the down direction, Brendon's local timetable for June 1929 only lists three day time departures from Paddington for Plymouth (nothing beyond) at 9.10am, 2.30 and 4.30pm. The 9.10am wandered around Bristol and took 15 minutes short of eight hours to reach its destination at 4.55pm. The 2.30pm was the opposite service to the 2.40pm up service and did the journey in a not very exciting 5½ hours. The 4.30pm was the equivalent of the down week-day train at that time.

Only one significant improvement took place during the winters of the 1930s. During the winter of 1932/3 the summer 10.30am from Paddington became a year round service, but only to Plymouth where it terminated at 3.20pm. There was a "connection" for principal stations to Penzance at 6.55pm. On the other hand, passengers could have travelled on the earlier 9.10am from Paddington and then there was only a two hour wait at Plymouth. However, all was not lost, the 10.30am was extended to Penzance three years later, during the winter of 1935/6.

SUMMER SERVICE

The Monday to Saturday basic main line service applied throughout the year upon which the week-end holiday trains were superimposed. Pages 44 to 46 list the Great Western main line passenger trains to, from and passing through Plymouth, providing a comparison between 1932 and 1938. Even over the short period of six years there is good evidence in the growth of the holiday trade. Salient points from those timetables are set out below.

1. The 1938 timetable was more finely aligned to the holiday season in as much as many of the down Saturday Only Trains had ceased to run by the middle of September.
2. Pressure was eased on the limited accommodation at the Penzance terminus by starting some trains from St. Erth, the stock coming from Ponsandane sidings.
3. An interesting train which appeared in the 1938 Working Timetable was a Fridays Only 12.8pm train of empty diners setting out from Paddington, and not from Old Oak Common as may be expected. Perhaps, that was to facilitate the loading of dry goods, crockery etc. from the central stores.
4. It was normal practice to run extra trains as 'parts' of a timetabled service, therefore, in 1932 the Cornish Riviera Express ran in two parts. By 1938, the train ran in four parts, departing from Paddington at five minute intervals, albeit only two parts were scheduled to run throughout the summer timetable.

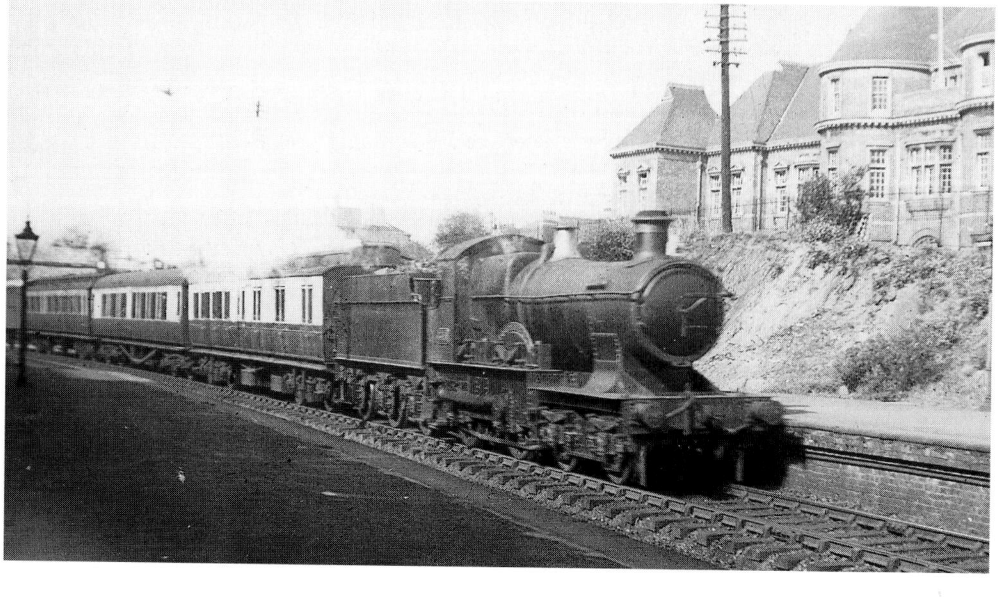

Bulldog 3449 *Nightingale* on an up stopping train at Mutley Station April 1938.
P D Orton

5. Falmouth had a through train to London in 1932 and a through train from London in 1938. Perranporth had no through service in 1932, but in both directions by 1938. Perranporth no longer has either a station or even a railway.

6. Some trains were not timetabled to call at North Road and, therefore, changed engines at Devonport in the down direction or at Laira Junction in the up direction.

7. In 1932, the Saturday 10.55am from Paddington was, apparently, non-stop to Par without an engine change. In 1938, the up 9 o'clock from Perranporth was, apparently, non-stop from Liskeard to Paddington without an engine change, there being no mention of one in the Working Timetable.

8. The trains shown as 'Excursions' in the 1932 Working Timetable did not always appear in the public timetable, and where they did, they were described as Holiday Ticket Trains. Such trains were provided for the benefit of holiday makers travelling with reduced fare tickets which had restrictive travel conditions, often involving overnight travel. The year 1932 was the last year that the trains ran as such because the Summer Tickets which were introduced in 1933 permitted unrestricted travel by any train. (See below). Some of the trains continued to run as normal timetabled services, e.g. the 4am from Bristol Midland Section, due at North Road at 7.45am in 1932 appears in 1938 as the 7.50am arrival from Bradford.

9. Surprisingly, even by 1938 there was no through Saturday service from Cornwall and Plymouth to the North Midlands via Bristol and the LMS. The only trains were those provided by the Great Western to Birmingham Snow Hill and to Wolverhampton Low Level.

10. Finally, there was a significant imbalance between the up and down trains on Saturdays which was, in part, corrected by an imbalance in the opposite direction on Sundays.

All the foregoing information has been extracted from the Working Timetables and, therefore, the times shown may vary by the occasional minute or two from the public timetable. Cross country trains rarely gave any indication of travel the other side of Crewe. Trains conveying the through Aberdeen coaches made no reference to that facility.

The Cornish Riviera Express Limited was often referred to as 'The Limited' because that was part of its official title, the train being limited to reserved seat holders only – hence the reference in the 1932 WTT to the first and second parts of the Ltd.

With the introduction of the 1934 summer timetable the Great Western introduced a systematic numbering of Saturday holiday trains. A metal frame was attached to the engine's smokebox door into which were slotted three single digit numbers. The first digit represented the point of origin of the train, followed by the train number which always ended in 0 or 5. The terminal numbers 1, 2, 3, 4, and 6, 7, 8 and 9 were reserved for use in the event that the train was running in more than one part, for example, the down Cornish Riviera was number 125, but the third part would be 127. The first digits representing the point of origin of the train were:

1. Paddington
2. Shrewsbury
3. Wolverhampton and Birmingham
4. Bristol
5. Exeter and Torbay
6. Plymouth and Cornwall
7. South Wales
0. Special train

Within the system the up Cornish Riviera was 615 and the down 3.30pm to Plymouth and Cornwall was the 175. The large numerals were white on black and could be read from a quarter mile distant and proved to be of great assistance in identifying trains to signalmen and platform staff, especially if they were running out of sequence.

Initially, the system was only used during the period of the summer service but was the forerunner of the more sophisticated train identification system that is still in use to-day.

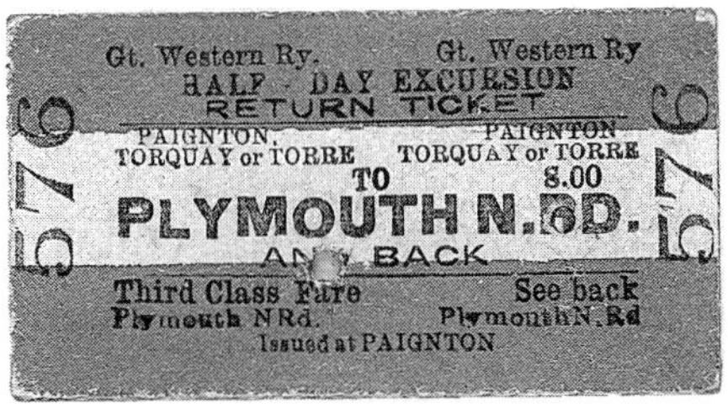

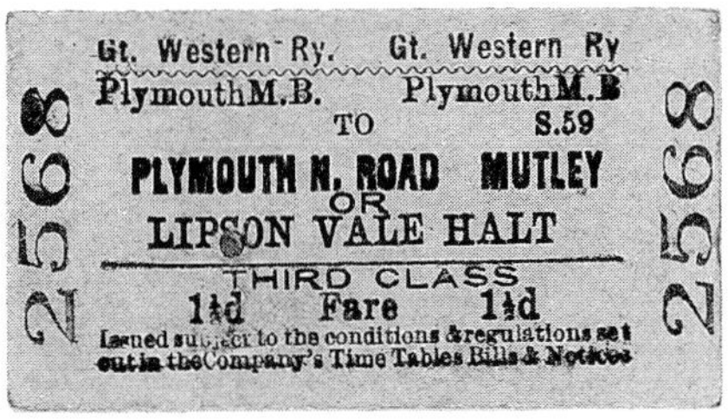

SUMMER SATURDAYS 1932
DOWN MAIN LINE TRAINS AT PLYMOUTH NORTH ROAD

Arrive				From	To	
4.32am			9.50pm*	Paddington	Penzance	
4.43		FSO	6.25pm*	York	Penzance	
5.0		SO	11.0 pm*	Paddington	Penzance	Excursion Holiday Ticket Train
5.25		SO	9.30pm*	Wolverhampton L.L.	Truro	23rd/30th July 6th August only Not in public timetable
6.5			1.40am	Paddington	Penzance	
6.48		SO	11.35pm*	Shrewsbury	Penzance	Excursion Not in public timetable
7.22			12ngt*	Paddington	Penzance	
7.45		SO	4.0am	Bristol Midland Section	Penzance	Excursion Not in public timetable
10.3			2.35	Shrewsbury	Penzance	North Mail
11.20		SO		Avonmouth Dock	North Road	Not 30th July Excursion Not in public timetable
12.25pm			5.30	Paddington	Penzance	
1.17		FSO	8.25	Paddington	Penzance	Excursion Holiday Ticket Train
1.53			10.5	Bath	North Road	Extended to Truro RR
	RR	SO	10.25	Paddington	Penzance	Calls Devonport 2.28-2.34 to change engines
2.30			10.30	Paddington	Penzance	Cornish Riviera Limited
2.32	RR	SO	10.30	Paddington	Penzance	2nd part Limited
3.8		SO	9.3	Wolverhampton L.L.	Penzance	
(3.21)		SO	10.55	Paddington	Newquay	Apparently non stop to Par
3.43			11.5	Paddington	Penzance	
4.26		FSO	9.45	Swansea	Penzance	Daily to Kingswear
4.44		SO		Sheffield	Millbay	All stations from Exeter
4.53			10.40	Wolverhampton L.L.	Penzance	Starts from Bristol SO
5.4		FO	12.5	Paddington	Millbay	Excursion Holiday Ticket Train
5.46		SO	12.10	Paddington	Millbay	All stations from Exeter
6.14			10.32	Crewe	Truro	
6.36			1.30	Paddington	Penzance	
7.26		SO	11.43	Crewe	Millbay	
8.8			3.30	Paddington	Penzance	
9.37		SO	4.38	Paddington	Penzance	Excursion Holiday Ticket Train
10.14			4.30	Paddington	Millbay	
12.31am			6.30	Paddington	Millbay	

*Previous night

SUMMER SATURDAYS 1932
UP MAIN LINE TRAINS AT PLYMOUTH NORTH ROAD

Depart			From	To	
8.42am			Millbay	Paddington	
8.52			Millbay	Crewe	
10.2	FSO		Millbay	Crewe	Manchester S0
10.30		7.45	Penzance	Crewe	FSO Birmingham Snow Hill
10.40	SO		Millbay	Cardiff	
11.50		9.15		Falmouth	Paddington
12.25pm	RR	10.46	Truro	Paddington	When this train does not call at North Road it will stop specially at Laira Junction to change engines. Train not in the public timetable.
12.30		10.0	Penzance	Paddington	Cornish Riviera Limited
12.35	SO		North Road	Paddington	When up 'Limited' is divided from Truro the second part to run as shown.
1.10		10.15	Penzance	Crewe	
1.23	SO	10.40	Falmouth	Bristol	
1.42		10.45	Penzance	Wolverhampton L.L.	
1.52	FSO	12.0	Truro	Edinburgh	
2.5		11.10	Penzance	Paddington	

2.30	SO	12.20	Newquay	Paddington	
3.55		12.30	Penzance	Crewe	North Mail
4.10		1.30	Penzance	Paddington	
4.25	SO	1.40	Penzance	Paddington	Excursion Holiday Ticket Train
6.20			North Road	Paddington	Via Westbury SO
8.0		5.5	Penzance	Crewe	
8.25	SO		North Road	Avonmouth	Excursion Not 30th July Not in public timetable
9.25	FO	5.55	Penzance	North Excursion	Holiday Ticket Train
11.25	FO	8.10	Penzance	Paddington	Holiday Ticket Train
12.20am		9.0 pm*	Penzance	Paddington	
12.50	FO	10.50pm*	Truro	LMS Midland Excursion	Not in public timetable

SUMMER SATURDAYS 1938
DOWN MAIN LINE TRAINS AT PLYMOUTH NORTH ROAD

Arrive			From		To	
4.4am		SO	11.0pm*	Paddington	Penzance	Sleepers Newquay & Penzance Until 10th September
4.20			9.50pm*	Paddington	Penzance	Sleepers to Penzance
4.33		SO	6.25pm*	York	Penzance	Through Aberdeen Coaches
6.10			1.35pm*	Paddington	Penzance	
6.51		SO	11.35pm*	Shrewsbury	Truro	Colne, Manchester & Liverpool Until 27th August
7.22		MX	12Ngt	Paddington	Penzance	Sleepers to North Road
7.50		SO	8.25pm*	Bradford	North Road	Until 3rd September
10.3			1.35am	Crewe	Penzance	North Mail
11.0		SO	6.41	Clifton Down	North Road	Excursion 9th July to 6th August Not 30th July. Not in public timetable
12.26pm			5.30	Paddington	Penzance	"Paper train"
12.50		SO	9.40	Bristol	Penzance	Also Newquay Until 10th September
1.37		SX	7.30	Paddington	Millbay	
1.50		SO	9.30	Paddington	Perranporth	Until 27th August
2.32		SX	10.30	Paddington	Penzance	Cornish Riviera Limited
		SO	10.25	Paddington	Newquay	Calls Devonport to change engines 2.32-2.37 Until 3rd September
2.47		SO	10.30	Paddington	Penzance	Also Helston until 27th August Falmouth from 3rd September
3.0		SO	10.40	Paddington	Falmouth	Until 27th August
3.16		SO	9.5	Wolverhampton L.L.	Penzance	
3.25		SO	11.0	Paddington	Penzance	
3.43			11.10	Paddington	Penzance	Detach Exeter for Kingsbridge
4.17		SO	8.0	Sheffield	Millbay	From Leeds in public timetable
4.28		SO	8.5	Manchester	Penzance	Also Newquay until 10th September
4.52			10.40	Wolverhampton L.L.	Penzance	Starts from Bristol SO
5.24		SO	12.10pm	Paddington	Millbay	All stations from Dawlish except Mutley
5.50			9.10am	Liverpool	Penzance	
6.9		SO	10.20	Manchester	Truro	Not after 10th September
6.10	RR	FO	12.8pm	Paddington	Penzance	Empty diners
6.33			1.30	Paddington	Penzance	
7.25		SO	11.3	Crewe	Millbay	Train went to Kingswear Coaches from Birkenhead attached Shrewsbury for Plymouth Not after 3rd September
8.3			3.30	Paddington	Penzance	
8.47			1.10	Crewe	Millbay	
10.24			5.5	Paddington	Millbay	
11.24		FSO	4.7	Crewe	Millbay	
12.28am			6.30	Paddington	Millbay	

*Previous night

SUMMER SATURDAYS 1938
UP MAIN LINE TRAINS PLYMOUTH NORTH ROAD

Depart			From	To	
7.5am	SO	7.0am	Millbay	Crewe	To Cardiff 10th, 17th, 24th September
7.20	SX		North Road	Paddington	
8.42		8.35	Millbay	Paddington	
8.52		8.45	Millbay	Crewe	
10.0	SO	9.55	Millbay	Liverpool & Manchester	
10.32		7.45	Penzance	Crewe	Birmingham Snow Hill SO
	SO	9.0	Perranporth	Paddington	Calls Par and Liskeard only No mention of an engine change
	SO	9.30	Newquay	Paddington	Calls Laira Junction to change engines 11.25-11.35
11.50		9.0	Penzance	Paddington	
	SO	10.0	Penzance	Paddington	Calls Laira Junction to change engines 12.15-12.21
12.30pm	SX	10.0	Penzance	Paddington	Cornish Riviera Limited
12.32	SO	10.20	St. Erth	Paddington	Also St. Ives. Helston & Falmouth
1.10		10.15		Penzance	Crewe
1.23	SO	10.15	Ponsandane	Cardiff	
1.42		10.45	Penzance	Wolverhampton L.L.	
1.52		10.25	Ponsandane	Edinburgh	Conveys through Aberdeen coaches
2.5		11.10	Penzance	Paddington	
2.40	SO	12.32	Newquay	Paddington	
3.55		12.30	Penzance	Crewe	North Mail
4.10		1.30	Penzance	Paddington	
6.18		6.15	Millbay	Paddington	Via Westbury SO
8.2		5.0	Penzance	Crewe	
11.20	SO		North Road	Birmingham Snow Hill	
12.30am		7.50	Penzance	Paddington	

Trains from Ponsandane Sidings commenced their public service at St. Erth

The reference to the down Friday Only empty diners to Cornwall prompts some comment concerning on train catering. All the main line day time London trains (except the down 5.30am Paper Train and the awful up 6.20pm) had a restaurant car, as did the four cross country trains at 8.52am, 10.30am 1.10pm and 1.40pm, plus many of the Saturday extras for returning holiday makers. This was, as much as anything, a reflection on the class of clientele that the railway catered for and the standards to which they adhered. The procedure was for a steward to go through the train about 11am inviting passengers (1st and 3rd class) to take a ticket as a reservation for luncheon, having first been given the option of first or second sitting. There would then be a call about 12 noon and another about an hour later. Earlier in the morning there would have been a call to the restaurant car to take morning coffee.

Similarly, there was later in the day a call to the restaurant car to take afternoon tea, and still later, the procedure for first and second sittings for dinner. The standard of catering was high, akin to that of a good hotel, which was also reflected in the price of the meal, as indeed is generally the case to-day.

SUMMER TICKETS

In order to boost travel during the time of the great depression of the 1930s 'Summer Tickets' were introduced on 1st May 1933 until the end of September of that year, subject to a minimum fare of 4/- (20p) first class and 2/6 (12½ p) second class. The tickets were valid for one month on any train at the rate of single fare and one third, equivalent to one penny per mile. In conjunction with the LMS and LNER the tickets were valid for return by any alternative recognised route, with break of journey permitted. That was a tremendous advance on anything available before. *The Great Western Railway Magazine* for April 1933 listed the advantages for the new tickets as:

1. Available by any train.
2. The use of restaurant or sleeping cars, where available.
3. A reserved seat upon payment of the usual fee of one shilling. (5p)

Summer tickets came to stay as Monthly Return Tickets and they lasted well into the British Rail era, although it must be said at substantially more than one penny per mile.

9. CROSS COUNTRY SERVICES

Apart from the one through train each day in both directions between Wolverhampton Low Level and Penzance there were no cross country trains at all out of Plymouth: they were all made up of through coaches to assorted destinations. Furthermore, they were all routed via the Severn Tunnel and Wem to Crewe over Great Western metals or jointly owned track with the LMS between Hereford and Shrewsbury. Wem was only a wayside station, but strategically placed, between Shrewsbury and Crewe which prevented passengers routed that way using any other route. Really, it was a bit of an anachronism because it was possible to purchase tickets at the same price via the LMS route, but that involved changing trains at both Bristol and Birmingham (New Street).

Through coaches were available to four destinations, Birkenhead, Liverpool, Manchester and Glasgow, but not always to all four on the same train. To say that is very simple, as applied to Plymouth but to follow the train through the Bradshaw Timetable a different story emerges. To illustrate the point we will follow the 7.45am from Penzance to its destinations. It set out from Penzance with portions for Liverpool (Lime Street), Birkenhead (Woodside) and Birmingham (Snow Hill). This is what followed:

At Newton Abbot a portion from Kingswear to Manchester (London Road) was added.

At Bristol the Birmingham portion was removed.

At Pontypool Road coaches from Cardiff, destined for Liverpool and Birkenhead were attached.

At Shrewsbury the Birkenhead portions were detached and coaches from Swansea (Victoria – Central Wales line) were attached. Finally, at Crewe, the Liverpool and Manchester portions were separated. The train started out with a Luncheon Car and completed its journey to Liverpool as a Restaurant Car.

Through coaches for Birkenhead (detached at Shrewsbury) will probably seem strange to many readers, but it was GWR all the way, although jointly with the LMS (formerly LNWR) beyond Chester. Passengers alighting at the terminus, Birkenhead (Woodside), walked off the platform on to the gangway for the Mersey ferry to Liverpool Landing Stage, i.e. Pier Head. Alternatively, they could change at Rock Ferry on to the Mersey Railway trains to Liverpool (Central) Low Level.

Journeys were unbelievably slow, the best train of the day took almost nine hours for the 316 miles from Liverpool (Lime Street) to Plymouth, approximately 35mph. The interesting trains were the up and down North Mails which included in the consists a Travelling Post Office (TPO) between Bristol and Plymouth. Those trains were the slowest of all because of lengthy station stops for mail and parcel traffic. On those trains there was no public access between the Liverpool, Manchester and Glasgow portions for they were all separated in the train formation by an assorted collection of vans for parcels and Royal Mail traffic. That arrangement facilitated the shunting at Crewe and the transfer of portions from the incoming train on to the connecting service. With that sort of arrangement the provision of refreshment facilities was a non starter.

ABERDEEN

Perhaps, the most well known of all cross country services was the 785 mile trek between Aberdeen and Penzance, first introduced in October 1921.* Two Gresley teak liveried coaches were provided by the LNER for each service and they ran attached to other trains as set out below:

dpt	Aberdeen	10.20am	arr York	6.14pm
	York	6.25pm	Swindon	11.30
	Swindon	12ngt	Penzance	7.40am

The 10.20am from Aberdeen was bound for Kings Cross and the 12ngt from Swindon was the 9.50pm from Paddington to Penzance. Reservations for sleeping car accommodation from Swindon could be made en route until 3pm. By the date of the 1932 summer timetable, the 6.25pm from York was running as a through train from York to Penzance on Thursday/Friday nights, i.e. Friday/Saturday mornings only, running twelve minutes behind the 9.50pm from Paddington. By 1938, that had been cut back to Friday nights/Saturday mornings only.

The up coaches left Penzance on the rear of the 11.10am departure for Paddington and timings were as under:

dpt	Penzance	11.10am	arr Westbury (Wilts)	5.3pm
	Westbury	5.20pm	York	11.13
	York	11.25	Aberdeen	7.30am

From Swindon to York the train conveyed a buffet car but by the time the train reached York, the vehicle had been elevated to a restaurant car. Sleeping accommodation was available from York. On early Sunday mornings the coaches were attached to the Night Scotsman with timings as follows:

dpt	York	1.9am	arr Edinburgh	6.6am
	Edinburgh	7.35am	Aberdeen	11.3am

A few minutes short of 24 hours after setting out from Penzance!

During the currency of the summer timetable, in most years it ran as a separate train ten minutes in advance of the 11.10am from Penzance, although in 1932 and 1933 it was Fridays and Saturdays only, starting out from Truro. In 1938 the train started from St. Erth, the stock setting out from Ponsardane Sidings at 10.55. This was to relieve pressure at Penzance, for the train was sandwiched between the 10.45 departure for Wolverhampton and the 11.10 to Paddington. The train,

*Great Western Railway Magazine November 1921

itself, was made up with more vans than passenger accommodation.

Motive power for both the up and down trains throughout the year was GWR and LNER in alternate years between Swindon and Leicester (Central) and, when seen, the LNER used Ivatt Atlantics.

Indicative of the standard of timekeeping, it will be observed that only 11 or 12 minutes was allowed at York to transfer the two Aberdeen coaches between the connecting services.

MIDLANDS

There were no through trains from Plymouth on to the LMS Midland line to Leeds, Bradford, York and the North East. True, York and the North East were served by the through Aberdeen service, but the arrival in the North East in one direction, and the West of England in the other were both in the middle of the night. Passengers from Plymouth out of the up 8.45am could transfer at Newton Abbot into a train from Paignton to Leeds and Bradford; a forerunner of the Devonian.

There were only two through trains each day to and from Birmingham (Snow Hill), the 7.45am and 10.45am from Penzance which became the 10.30am and 1.40pm respectively to Snow Hill and Wolverhampton (Low Level). The equivalent down trains left Wolverhampton LL at 7.25am and 10.40am. All four trains ran via Birmingham (Snow Hill), Stratford on Avon and Cheltenham (Malvern Road), then exercising running powers between Yate and Standish Junction over LMS (formerly Midland Rly) metals. The trains did not call at Gloucester, but used the Great Western avoiding line rather than use the LMS Gloucester station. To use the GWR's own Gloucester station would have involved a reversal and engine change. Because of weight restrictions on the LMS, the GW used 4-4-0s as far as Bristol until 1933. After that through working of Laira and Wolverhampton Stafford Road engines and men was introduced as lodging turns on an alternative day basis, up on the 1.40pm from North Road and down on the 10.45am from Wolverhampton. Castles formed the normal motive power, although Wolverhampton often used the smaller Star Class. As this was the first occasion that Wolverhampton engines would be seen in Plymouth there was great anticipation as to which engine would turn up. It was a complete let down, for it was a resplendent, ex works, 4096 *Highclere Castle* newly transferred from Newton Abbot to Wolverhampton!

6800 *Arlington Grange*, newly constructed and within a few days of its allocation to Newton Abbot, on what was to be its regular duty, the 7.45am from Penzance, 10.30am. North Road to Liverpool (Lime Street) and Birkenhead (Woodside) approaching Mutley Station September 1936. *P D Orton*

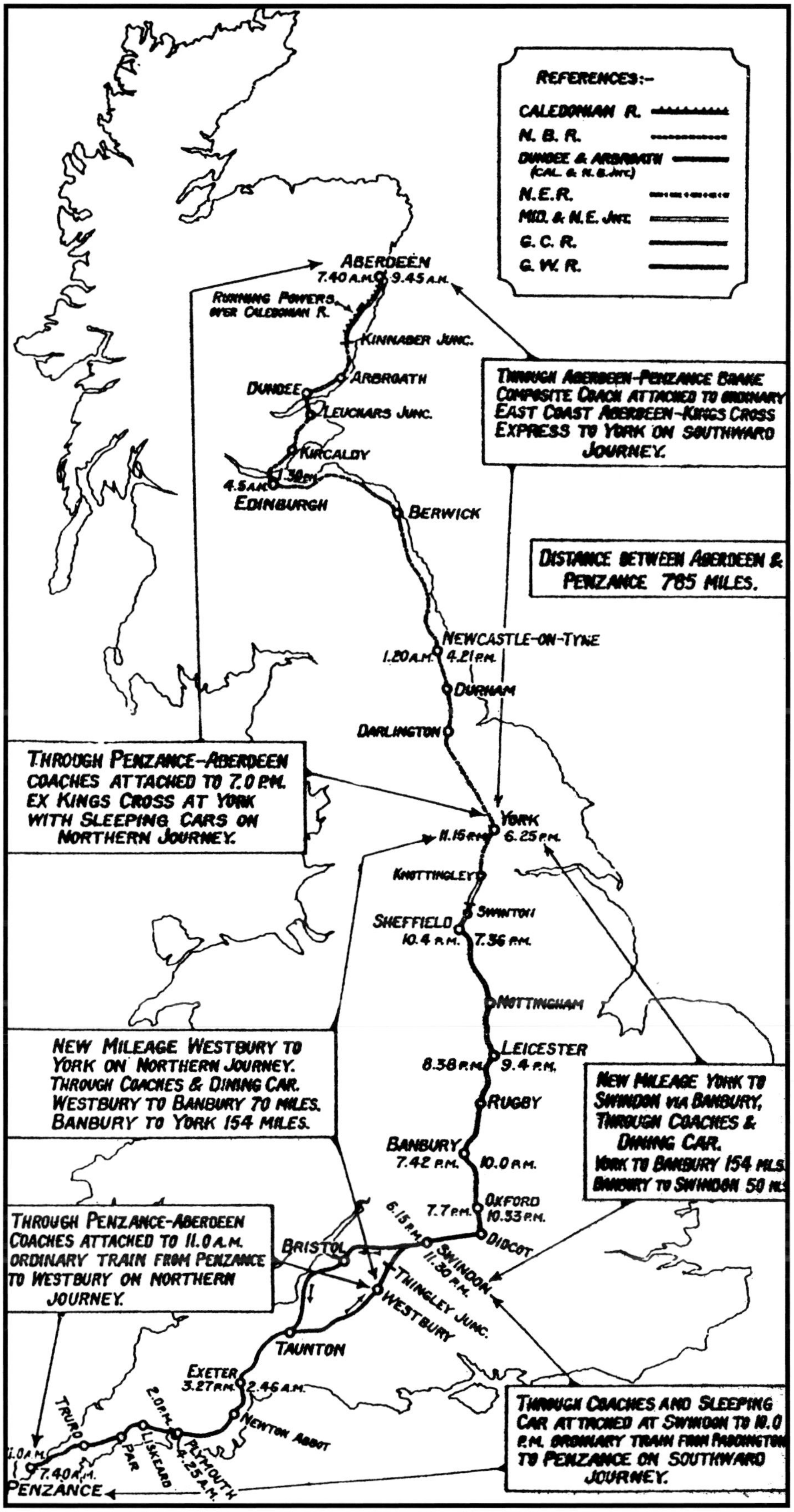

REFERENCES:-
CALEDONIAN R.
N. B. R.
DUNDEE & ARBROATH (CAL. & N. B. JNTC)
N.E.R.
MID. & N. E. JNT.
G. C. R.
G. W. R.
ABERDEEN
7.40 A.M.
9.45 A.M.
RUNNING POWERS OVER CALEDONIAN R.
KINNABER JUNC.
ARBROATH
DUNDEE
LEUCHARS JUNC.
KIRCALDY
4.5 A.M.
EDINBURGH
BERWICK
THROUGH ABERDEEN-PENZANCE BRAKE COMPOSITE COACH ATTACHED TO ORDINARY EAST COAST ABERDEEN-KINGS CROSS EXPRESS TO YORK ON SOUTHWARD JOURNEY.
DISTANCE BETWEEN ABERDEEN & PENZANCE 785 MILES.
NEWCASTLE-ON-TYNE
1.20 A.M.
4.21 P.M.
DURHAM
DARLINGTON
THROUGH PENZANCE-ABERDEEN COACHES ATTACHED TO 7.0 P.M. EX KINGS CROSS AT YORK WITH SLEEPING CARS ON NORTHERN JOURNEY.
YORK
11.15 P.M.
6.25 P.M.
KNOTTINGLEY
SWINTON
SHEFFIELD
10.4 P.M.
7.36 P.M.
NOTTINGHAM
LEICESTER
8.38 P.M.
9.4 P.M.
RUGBY
NEW MILEAGE WESTBURY TO YORK ON NORTHERN JOURNEY. THROUGH COACHES & DINING CAR. WESTBURY TO BANBURY 70 MILES. BANBURY TO YORK 154 MILES.
NEW MILEAGE YORK TO SWINDON VIA BANBURY, THROUGH COACHES & DINING CAR. YORK TO BANBURY 154 MLS. BANBURY TO SWINDON 50 MLS.
BANBURY
7.42 P.M.
10.0 P.M.
OXFORD
7.7 P.M.
10.33 P.M.
DIDCOT
6.15 P.M.
SWINDON
11.30 P.M.
THINGLEY JUNC.
WESTBURY
BRISTOL
THROUGH PENZANCE-ABERDEEN COACHES ATTACHED TO 11.0 A.M. ORDINARY TRAIN FROM PENZANCE TO WESTBURY ON NORTHERN JOURNEY.
TAUNTON
EXETER
3.27 P.M.
2.46 A.M.
NEWTON ABBOT
2.0 P.M.
PLYMOUTH
4.25 A.M.
LISKEARD
PAR
TRURO
1.0 A.M.
7.40 A.M.
PENZANCE
THROUGH COACHES AND SLEEPING CAR ATTACHED AT SWINDON TO 10.0 P.M. ORDINARY TRAIN FROM PADDINGTON TO PENZANCE ON SOUTHWARD JOURNEY.

Route of the New Aberdeen–Penzance Through Service

CROSS COUNTRY SERVICES

via Severn Tunnel & Wem

UP TRAINS

From		To	
8.45am Millbay		Liverpool Lime Street	arr 5.21pm
		Birkenhead Woodside	5.29
		Glasgow Central	9.35
7.45am Penzance	10.30am North Road	Liverpool Lime Street	7.5pm
		Birkenhead Woodside	7.20
1pm Millbay		Manchester London Road	8.58pm
		Liverpool Lime Street	9.6
		Birkenhead Woodside	9.10
12.30pm Penzance	3.55pm North Road	Liverpool Lime Street	1.5am
		Manchester Exchange	3.22
5.5pm Penzance	8pm North Road	Liverpool Lime Street	5.55am
		Manchester London Road	6.3
		Glasgow Central	7.43

DOWN TRAINS

Arrive North Road 10.5am	Penzance 1.20pm	dpt Glasgow Central	5.40pm
		Manchester London Road	11.45 *
		Liverpool Lime Street (previous day)	11.50 *
Millbay 6pm		Liverpool Lime Street	9.10am
		Birkenhead Woodside	9.43
** Millbay	9.3pm	Birkenhead Woodside	11.55am
		Liverpool Lime Street	12 noon
		Manchester London Road	12 noon
*** Millbay	12.40am	Glasgow Central	10.5am
		Birkenhead Woodside	2.40pm
		Liverpool Lime Street	3pm
		Manchester London Road	3.5pm

* Not Sunday nights
** All stations from Exeter
*** Combined with the 6.30pm from Paddington at Bristol

SUNDAYS

UP TRAINS

7am Millbay		Manchester London Road	5.30pm
		Liverpool Lime Street	5.50pm
4.45pm Penzance	8pm North Road	Manchester London Road	6.3am

Passengers could travel on the 1.10pm from Millbay, change at Bristol and arrive Manchester 1.30am and Liverpool at 3.15am!

DOWN TRAINS

arr North Road 11.56**	dpt Glasgow Central	5.40pm*
	Manchester London Road	11.45*
	Liverpool Lime Street	11.50*
arr Millbay 8.25pm	Liverpool Lime Street	10.40am
	Manchester London Road	11.45

* Previous day
** Bradshaw for May 1934 showed on arrival at Penzance as 9.30pm, almost 28 hours after leaving Glasgow. From the summer of that year the train was extended through to Penzance. During the winter it reverted to terminate at Plymouth – next train to Cornwall at 6.55pm. Things improved the following winter when the "connecting" service was at 3.23pm, the extended 10.30am from Paddington.

10. SUNDAY TRAINS IN CORNWALL

Cornwall in 1930, aided by a strong tradition of Methodism, still enjoyed the peace of a Victorian Sunday and, for that matter, it was also largely true of Plymouth. As a child, a Sunday afternoon visit to the Municipal Art Gallery and Museum in Tavistock Road was considered an appropriate educational experience. That Victorian peace was truly mirrored by the railway: the last day time winter train to Cornwall beyond Liskeard left North Road at ten o'clock in the morning. Liskeard was only marginally better for the one and only later train left Millbay at 8.25pm.

During the winter there was no day time train service to Cornwall from London or anywhere east of Plymouth except for the 12.30am sleeping car service which left North Road at 8 o'clock in the morning. That was hardly a day time service, but it did have a restaurant car!

In the opposite direction there were only three departures from Penzance, at 11am, 4.45pm and 8.50pm, all for Paddington, leaving North Road at 2.25pm, 8pm and 12.30am Monday morning. The 4.45pm from Penzance conveyed through coaches for Manchester with an arrival at 6.3am next morning.

Of the branch lines, only the Truro to Falmouth operated throughout the year. There was an advertised road connection from either Redruth or Camborne to Helston and another to St. Ives from St. Erth. Both at that time were probably operated by the Great Western Railway's own omnibuses. To and from Newquay it could be by rail via Chacewater and Truro when the branch was open during the summer months, or by road via St. Austell.

The winter Sunday train service remained pretty dismal throughout the decade and the improvements are easily summarised as under:

1. For the summer of 1932 there was a new train leaving Penzance at 9.50am for Plymouth North Road, returning to Penzance at 6.55pm. From the summer of 1933 it became a regular summer and winter service, except for the summers of 1938 and 1939, when for the 6.55pm alternative arrangements were made (see later).
2. For the winter of 1932/33 a 10.30am from Paddington to Plymouth was introduced, arriving at 3.23pm. That provided a "connection" for Cornwall at 6.55pm until the 10.30 was extended to Penzance in the winter of 1935/36.

All the Cornish branches, except Falmouth, remained closed throughout the winter months throughout the decade.

SUMMER SERVICE
The day time Sunday summer service in Cornwall is summarised below, detailing the year in which the service was introduced. Sufficient to say that by the end of the decade the traditional Cornish Sunday was no more in the Duchy's principal seaside resorts.

10am	North Road to Penzance	
10.15am	North Road to Newquay	1933
11.35	North Mail extended to Penzance	1934
3.23pm	10.30am from Paddington (Initially non stop North Road to Truro)	
5.30	10.50am from Wolverhampton LL extended to Penzance	1938
6.55	North Road to Penzance Not summers of 1938/9 when it was replaced by the 5.30pm and the 7.55pm	1933
7.55	2.30pm from Paddington extended to Penzance	1938
9.50am	Penzance to North Road arr. 12.30pm	1933
10.50	Penzance to Paddington dpt North Road 1.55pm	
12.30pm	Penzance to Paddington 3.15	
12.45	Penzance to Wolverhampton 3.30	1934
1pm	Newquay to Paddington 3pm	1933
5pm	Penzance to Paddington 8pm	
7.30pm	Newquay to North Road arr 9.35pm	1933
7.45	Penzance to North Road 10.35pm	1934
9pm	Penzance to Paddington dpt North Road 12.15am	
10pm	Penzance to Paddington (Sleeper) 1.30am	c1937

Notes

1. Where no date for introduction of the service is shown, the train was already in the timetable for 1929.
2. The introduction of a train for Newquay in 1933 at 10.15 in the morning and a corresponding evening return train from Newquay for the benefit of day trippers was a sure sign of the changing attitude to Sunday.
3. The 12.30pm from Penzance conveyed through coaches for Wolverhampton during the summer of 1933. During the winter months the train ran earlier through Cornwall, departing from North Road at 2.25pm for Paddington.

By the summer of 1934 all the Cornish branches were open except Bodmin and Helston, generally from the end of May. Bodmin never had a Sunday service. Helston continued to have a road service from either Redruth or Camborne, largely because of RNAS at Culdrose.

POSTSCRIPT
For the winter of 2000/01 there were 13 Sunday trains from Plymouth to Penzance, commencing at 09.28, another at 10.30 and then at 12.30 and at approximately hourly intervals until 21.55. There were seven Great Western trains from Paddington and three Virgin cross country services. There were no branch line trains, but within the Wales and West pocket timetable there were shown five connecting bus services between Redruth and Helston, three extended to Culdrose RNAS, operated by Truroian route T34.

11. SPECIAL TRAFFICS

SAILOR SPECIALS

Plymouth was very much a Navy town. Pre-war, off duty sailors would be in evidence in the City Centre at week-ends, especially in Union Street, every one in his number one uniform. Especially remembered was the arrival of the First day of May when every sailor's cap appeared with a white top, the regulation summer uniform until the end of September. In those days when tram and bus drivers and conductors were required to wear a headdress they also adopted the First day of May ruling.

When leave came around the railway ran sailor specials. The dockyard had its own internal railway system with a spur off the Great Western down main line just beyond Keyham station. As may be expected, there were heavy gates barring admission to the Dockyard except for authorised rail traffic. Outside the gate and between there and the main line there was a platform from which the sailor specials originated, the naval barracks being situated just across the road. It was on one such an occasion in 1928 when City class 4-4-0 3707 *Malta* returned home after relieving a King which had failed on the 1.30pm Paddington to Penzance express on the previous day in the Reading area. It made a fine sight as it passed non-stop through North Road Station.

For week-end leave when a special train was not warranted, sailors could be seen in significant numbers on Friday afternoons alighting from the trams and making their way along the station approach for the 3.55pm North Mail or the 4.10pm to Paddington.

To cater for sailors returning off leave, the down 9.50pm from Paddington called at Keyham at 4.37am to set down on Mondays only. As for sailors on the 1.40am from Paddington, they had to alight at North Road at 6.10am and use the trams to get back to barracks. The down midnight from Paddington did not run on Sunday nights.

TEA PARTIES

The areas around Plymouth Friary, Millbay, and the two Devonport stations were thickly populated, much of it in sub-standard property, or even slums. The areas concerned were well provided with churches and chapels and, although, perhaps, adult congregations were thinning, the Sunday Schools were still thriving. One of

4702 of class 4700. Laira must have been "hard up" for engines to have used their "47" for banking duties on Hemerdon during the broccoli season. April 1939. *P D Orton*

the highlights of the Sunday School year was the Annual Treat, otherwise known as a Tea Party. The children were taken by train to some rural destination for an afternoon of games or other amusements, followed by tea in a field kindly made available by a local farmer. For many children it was the only outing of the year and certainly their only experience of travel by train. Popular destinations were Bere Alston, Bere Ferrers, Calstock and Turnchapel therefore the Southern had most of the traffic. Normally a three or four coach non-corridor train was provided headed by a T1 0-6-0T with two or more Schools sharing. There were less popular destinations on the Yealmpton branch at Elburton or Yealmpton itself. The author can remember one outing to Cornwood on the GW main line, outward on a strengthened 2.15pm up stopper, returning on the 7.40pm ex Newton Abbot running nearly an hour late.

THE POST OFFICE

The Post Office relied heavily on the railway for the conveyance of mail outside of urban areas. At most country stations the local postman met designated trains for receipt or despatch of mail. A very good illustration appears in the Southern Railway working timetable (WTT) dated 17th July 1932. It relates to the 5.52am passenger train from Plymouth Friary to Salisbury which called at Brentor at 7.1am. Brentor is a very isolated community and the footnote to the timetable states "Calls at Brentor to put out Mails only. A postman will be in attendance to receive the Mails from the Guard, but should he fail to present himself the Mails to be taken through to Lydford and returned by the first train".

The West of England train for the conveyance of overnight mail between major centres was the Postal. The train was made up of six vehicles, partly travelling letter sorting vehicles and partly stowage vans, plus accommodation for the guard. There were two notable features, the public letter box set into the side of a sorting vehicle (for which an extra ½ d stamp was required) and the exterior pick up apparatus for the exchange of mail bags whilst the train travelled at speed. The train left Penzance at 6.38pm and 9.16pm off North Road, a train with an exemplary timekeeping record. It started from North Road on Sunday nights. The train was hauled by Exeter based Star class 4-6-0s on a three day roster, starting in the small hours by taking over the 9.50am overnight passenger train from Paddington at Exeter and going through to Penzance. It is believed that the engine stayed at Penzance all day prior to working the up Postal right through to Paddington. At 326 miles it was the longest through engine working in the country, worked day in and day out until the LMS and LNER commenced through engine working between London and Glasgow/Edinburgh. The Exeter Star (Castle from the mid 30s) returned home from Paddington on the 9.50pm departure, thus completing the circle. The 9.50pm Paddington to Penzance was a time hallowed train which only disappeared from the timetable when the introduction of diesels brought about some rationalisation of the timetable.

The down Postal left Paddington at 10.10pm and was through Plymouth, calling from 3.44am to 3.53am. It was worked through Plymouth to Penzance by a Newton Abbot allocated Hall class 4-6-0 or Grange class 4-6-0 when they became available later in the decade. The engine returned home on the 7.40am from Penzance conveying through coaches to Birkenhead, Liverpool Lime Street and Glasgow Central. During the twelve month period from August 1929 the duty was the preserve of newly constructed 4942 *Maindy Hall* on which the paintwork was maintained in pristine ex works condition throughout its reign, terminated only by its call into Swindon Works for overhaul, and sadly not to return to Newton Abbot.

An article in the *Great Western Railway Magazine* in 1933 quoted a total travelling staff of 25, including the supervisor, of whom five sorters worked through to Truro, eight to Bristol, and the remainder to Plymouth. Additional sorters who joined the train at Plymouth worked through to Penzance. As the up and down trains crossed at Bristol presumably, there was a cross platform partial exchange of London and Plymouth based sorters. The Magazine quotes the make up of the train as five vans A to E, (either sorting or stowage, a brake for the guard and two Siphon Gs. The Siphons were probably left at Bristol, as the Plymouth train comprised only six vehicles.

There was a second mail train service which conveyed one Royal Mail sorting vehicle between Bristol and Plymouth. The trains were known respectively as the up and down North Mails and, although a passenger service, there was a preponderance of assorted vans conveying parcels as well as mails. The originating station for the down train varied in different editions of the working timetable, for example:

Winter 1930	11.20pm from Liverpool
Summer 1932	2.35am from Shrewsbury
Summer 1938	1.25am MO from Crewe
	1.35am MX from Crewe

If we take the 11.20pm from Liverpool as the real origin, then it picked up through coaches from Manchester and Glasgow en route, undoubtedly at Crewe. The train was booked to arrive at North Road at 10.3am next morning, almost eleven hours after leaving Liverpool, moving off to Penzance at 10.23am. The length of the journey is indicative of long station stops, the twenty minutes at North Road being a good example.

The up train was the 12.30 from Penzance conveying through coaches for Liverpool (arr. 1.05am), Manchester (arr. 1.35am) and Glasgow (arr 6.45am). It stood at North Road from 3.40pm for fifteen minutes, during which time the mail sorting vehicle off the down train was attached. It should be noted that through coaches were something different to through trains, they were merely attachments to other trains enroute, involving much shunting and often significant delays waiting for the connecting service train to arrive. Although there were the three passenger portions included in the up North Mail they were not inter connected but separated from each other in the train's make up by one or more vans.

PERISHABLES

The railway has lost completely to road transport a significant traffic which was known as perishables, i.e. vegetables, fruit and flowers. There were three such trains passing through Plymouth each week-day and even one on Sundays (via Millbay) from Penzance, running throughout the year. Because of the perishable nature of the traffic (in days long before freezers were thought of) the trains ran later in the day with arrival at destinations in time to catch the early morning wholesale markets. The first train through North Road was the 4.35pm from Millbay to Cardiff, regularly worked by one of Bristol's run down and unwashed Saints, mostly from the early constructed series such as 2971 *Albion*, 2977 *Robertson* or 2987 *Bride of Lammermoor*. The train exchanged traffic with the 1.20pm Perishables from Penzance to Crewe at Tavistock Junction between 5.10pm and 5.40pm. It then waited at Tavistock Junction for, and then followed the 2.30pm Perishables from Penzance to Paddington. In 1932 that train was accelerated with its departure from Penzance put back to 4.33pm with arrival in London at 2.30am as previously. That last train was the preserve of a Paddington based King class engine which had spent the day at Laira following an early morning arrival on the down Newspaper train. The footplate men were top link Paddington men who had spent the daylight hours catching up on their sleep in lodgings.

BROCCOLI

The far West of Cornwall developed a lucrative trade in broccoli during the late 1920s and the 1930s following a new variety introduced from France in 1925. The traffic by rail increased from 13481 tons in 1928 to 41474 tons ten years later, for which no less than 450 special trains were called for. The season was comparatively short, from early March for about 10-12 weeks. Traffic built up during the week so that it peaked on Thursdays and Fridays in anticipation of the week-end market. Sometimes there would be as many as twelve special trains in one day. In order to cope with the vast increase in traffic extra engines were drafted in from all over the system, placed on loan mainly to Laira or Penzance, for most of the traffic originated within the Penzance catchment area. For the 1938 season it was reported in the *GWR Magazine* that 20240 wagons were required for the 450 trains run.

The broccoli were cut fresh early in the day, carted to the local railhead, with the trains passing through

Loading broccoli at Penzance cica 1930's *Authors collection*

Plymouth in quick succession from mid afternoon into the mid evening. Destinations were widespread, to London, Midlands and the North. Corresponding 'Broccoli Empties' were worked back to Cornwall at all times of the day and night. These brought many visiting engines from all parts of the system, some of which were appropriated to work down to Cornwall after coaling and maintenance at Laira shed.

One very unusual visitor on down empties in March 1938 was Dean Goods 2439. All sorts of covered wagons were used, favourites being those with open slat such as cattle trucks and milk vans, but sometimes open wagons were used with tarpaulins slung over the top.

Engines of up trains sometimes worked through whilst others changed engines at Tavistock Junction, but one destined for London went up in the afternoon almost invariably worked through hauled by a Castle. Up trains were hauled by all kinds of larger engines, whatever was available, excluding Kings, from Moguls to Castles, goods engines included, and if they were really hard up, a Bulldog 4-4-0 would be produced.

All this traffic severely taxed the resources of Laira shed and regular goods traffic was on occasion worked by 45xx prairie tanks or 0-6-0 pannier tanks since nothing else was available. The shortage of engines was not helped by the necessity to augment the afternoon banking facility from one engine to two in providing assistance for the ascent of Hemerdon bank. The extra engine could be of any suitable type, Bulldogs, pannier tanks, 28xx 2-8-0s prior to their rostered goods turns, or the large 47xx 2-8-0 prior to its regular up London night express goods. Those supplemented the normal large prairie 31xx tank, although there is no remembrance of the two 31xx tanks at the same time, one being regularly used on the morning down St. Austell goods.

Such was the desperate situation that Laira shed in the early evening would be almost empty of usable engines.

OTHER PERISHABLE TRAFFIC

Cornwall being predominately an agricultural community, it provided a lot of traffic for the railway. Most of it was conveyed by the GWR and much of it was concentrated into the early months of the year. The flower traffic started just before Christmas with early blooms of daffodils, originating from the Isles of Scilly, and transhipped from sea to rail at Penzance. The season lasted right through to Easter, augmented by flowers cultivated on the Mainland in the far South West. Special trains were run for flower traffic when required. The tonnage for 1938 was quoted as 4891, which was triple that for 1931.

Strawberries were a speciality of the Tamar Valley. The GWR traffic was centred on Saltash, but the bulk of the produce was railborne via the Callington Branch on the Southern. (See Chapter 17). During the 1938 season the GWR despatched 120,000 packages, some of which would have been French produce landed at Millbay Docks. French strawberries emerged in the early thirties as highly competitive with local crops, much to the chagrin of the farming community. During the

Derry's Clock with the Royal Hotel on left and the Lockyer Hotel on right. Most buildings in this area were gutted by fire during the Plymouth blitz. *Authors collection*

period from the end of May through to mid July there were 3361 tons landed. It was reported that five special trains were run in one day in June 1931.

Finally, within the general heading of perishables, there the special trains conveying the early varieties of potato, again from West Cornwall.

CHRISTMAS

To-day we have been indoctrinated by the Post Office with their widespread publicity "Post Early for Christmas". Before the first week in December is out the first Christmas card will have appeared through the letter box. In the last week before Christmas the deluge will have been reduced to a trickle from last minuters. Not so before the War, indeed, for many years after, the correct thing to do was to aim for your missive, or your parcel, to arrive at its destination, if not on Christmas Day itself, certainly not more than two or three days previous. To the recipient it all added to the excitement and expectations of the festive season, but not to the heavily overburdened Post Office.

On Christmas Eve additional parcel and mail trains were still arriving well loaded and station platforms were still piled high with mail bags the down North Mail, due in North Road at 10.3am, rarely arrived on time during the Christmas period and could be anything up to two hours late. The Post Office worked miracles to get everything delivered by Christmas morning, that is except for the occasional van which ran hot which the railway lost, which would be found some weeks later parked in some isolated siding and well recorded in the newspapers of the day.

The Post Office hired large delivery vans from haulage firms and extra personnel for the parcel traffic and extra men to cope with letter delivery, drawn largely from the ranks of the unemployed – no poverty stricken students in those days. The author can well remember the postman, loaded down with mail, doing his Christmas morning round, collecting his tips and the occasional glass of sherry en route. There was also the parcels van doing its round with, perhaps, a couple of turkeys hanging off the tailboard.

Those were the days when league football matches were played on Christmas morning and when trains, trams and buses operated a revised Sunday service. In Plymouth, the trams and buses terminated around 6pm in the early evening.

A Christmas supplement to the Working Timetable (WTT) for 1932 provides an interesting insight into the mammoth scale of activity leading up to the great day. Christmas Day in 1932 it was on a Sunday.

Special Parcels and Parcel Post trains ran from Paddington as follows:

1am	to Penzance	December 22 23 24
4.30am	Plymouth or Penzance	20 21 22 23 24 25
9am	Plymouth	22 23 24
12.15pm	Penzance	20 21 22 23 24
9pm	Plymouth or Penzance	19 20 21 22 23 24

It will be observed that one train was scheduled to run late on Christmas Eve and a second one in the early hours of Christmas Day itself. Vans were detached, as required, at Bristol, Taunton, Exeter and Newton Abbot from all services.

Friday, 23rd December appears to have been a peak day for passenger traffic, geared very much to the end of the working day. The 4.30pm from Paddington to Plymouth ran in four parts:

First:	Swindon to Plymouth with a restaurant car.
Second:	Paddington to Bristol.
Third:	Paddington to Taunton via the Bristol Relief Line, i.e. not calling at Bristol Temple Meads.
Fourth:	4.38pm to Plymouth.

At 6.45pm there was a special service from Clapham Junction to Penzance, made up as follows:

One brake compo plus three third class for Kingswear.

One brake compo plus two third class for Plymouth.

One brake compo plus three third class and a diner for Penzance.

Whether the train actually conveyed passengers from Clapham Junction is a moot point, more likely Kensington Addison Road.

Finally, there was a further special train from Paddington at 8.5pm made up by:

One brake compo plus six third class for Kingswear.

One brake compo and three third class for Plymouth.

All this extra traffic necessitated the provision of empty stock workings and these were listed as under:

Friday 23rd	10.45pm	Plymouth to Old Oak Common
	11pm	Penzance to Old Oak Common
Tuesday 27th	9.25am	Old Oak Common to Penzance
	3.30pm	Old Oak Common to Plymouth
	7.15pm	Old Oak Common to Tavistock Junction
Thursday 29th	3.30pm	Old Oak Common to Plymouth
	7.15pm	Old Oak Common to Tavistock Junction.

CORNISH BRANCHES

During the currency of the summer timetable there was a 11.10 sleeping car train from Paddington to Penzance on Friday nights calling at North Road from 4.4am until 4.12am on Saturday mornings. That train also ran on Christmas Eve and Maundy Thursday at 11pm from Paddington. Now on Christmas Day and Good Friday it was Sunday service over the whole system and, normally there was no winter Sunday service on any of the Cornish

Notes

1. The 11pm from Paddington via Westbury

Christmas mail on the platform at Paddington on Christmas eve. All will be despatched by train and delivered to its recipients Christmas morning. Consignia take note!
Authors collection

Mr W Clatworthy in his Royal Hotel livery alongside his model T Ford flatbed. *Authors collection*

branches except Falmouth. However, on those two days early morning connections were provided out of the overnight trains from London, as shown below. Special steaming of the engines and double time payment for the train crews would be necessary. Timings are as per the 1938/39 winter timetable.

11pm from Paddington							
Liskeard	arr	4.42am	Set down only				
Par		5.15	Set down only				
Truro		5.55	Set down only				
Gwinear Road		6.34	dpt	6.55am	arr	Helston	7.20am
St. Erth		6.45		7.10		St Ives	7.25
9.50pm from Paddington							
Liskeard	arr	5.14am	dpt	5.20am	arr	Looe	5.45am
Par		5.50		5.55		Newquay	6.45
* Truro		6.37		6.45		Falmouth	7.15
Gwinear Road		7.15		8.00		Helston	8.25
St Erth		7.30		7.45		St Ives	8.5
12ngt from Paddington							
Par	arr	9.10am	dpt	9.20am	arr	Newquay	10.15am
* Truro		9.45		9.55		Falmouth	10.25

*Service train

overtook the 9.50pm from Paddington via Bristol.

2. There were two connecting trains for each branch except Looe. On the other branches time had to be allowed for the engine to run around at the branch terminus and to get the train back to the main line junction for the second train, therefore there was a longer wait at Gwinear Road off the 9.50pm and the Newquay train could only get back to Par in time to connect with the midnight from Paddington.

3. Connections for Falmouth were on normal timetabled trains.

4. Except for Christmas Day and Good Friday, Helston never had a Sunday service, road transport being provided from either Redruth or Camborne.

5. For some reason Bodmin never enjoyed a summer Sunday train service neither did it enjoy Christmas Day and Good Friday main line connections.

TRAVELLERS

No! Not the 1990s variety. The terminology has been upgraded. Although often known as just Travellers, the full title was a Commercial Traveller. With the upgraded terminology they are now Representatives.

The smartly dressed gentlemen arrived by train, and if employed in the clothing trade would be accompanied by armfuls of dresses, suits etc, enclosed in those days' equivalent of the modern plastic or whatever. Many of those people either stayed at, or displayed their wares, at the City Centre Royal Hotel, who thoughtfully provided a Model T Ford flatbed, registration CO 5002 to wait upon them at North Road station. The driver was an old man with a beard, attired in the Royal's brown livery. He must have been an old man, for to youngsters only old men grew beards. He was a Mr. W. Clatworthy.

THEATRICALS

In Plymouth, including Devonport, there were a number of theatrical establishments, some like the Royal Theatre pure theatre and others variety, such as the Palace in Union Street, with a weekly change of programme. There being no practical alternative to the railway, scenery vans appeared in the North Road station sidings at week-ends to cover the change over of programmes. Presumably, the cast travelled on the same trains. (As an aside, it is only in comparatively recently that the Plymouth buses ceased to use 'Theatre' on the destination blinds).

THE TRAVELLING CIRCUS

The train usually arrived in Plymouth on a Sunday afternoon for a week's visit conveying all the animals and equipment necessary for the twice daily performances. There was also passenger accommodation for the supporting clowns, trapeze artistes, cashiers and other supporting staff. After detraining there was a procession to the venue for the week, led by the elephants. A free form of advertising.

NEWSPAPERS

During the period we are considering there was a 5.30am passenger train due Plymouth at 12.25pm which was always known to railwaymen as the Paper Train. The 5.30am was another of those time hallowed trains from Paddington because it appeared in Working Timetables during the 1870s, although it did not reach Plymouth until 2.58pm on Broad Gauge metals of course.

By the 1930s the West of England Newspaper train left Paddington at 1.40am, timed to arrive in Plymouth at 6.5am. On 12th March 1934, and with a great flourish, the Great Western Railway introduced an accelerated 12.50am departure, timed to be in Plymouth by 4.50am. That was seven minutes faster than the winter Cornish Riviera Express which called at Exeter. The train was in Penzance at 8am, "Thus, residents in the far West have their London newspapers on their breakfast tables". The accompanying newspaper picture showed 6015 *King Richard III* with Driver Parsons – his own engine.

Parcels traffic handed in at Paddington before midnight was conveyed to places in Cornwall in time for delivery on the first round next morning.

PIGEONS

To finish off this Chapter on the slightly ridiculous there were the pigeon specials. They were special trains run for the benefit of pigeon fanciers, made up with a number of vans conveying crates of homing pigeons. At the train's destination the station staff released the birds in accordance with instructions, the most important being a record of the exact time of release.

Bottom Crates of Cornish broccoli ready for despatch labelling for Belgium and Germany, Circa 1930's
Authors collection

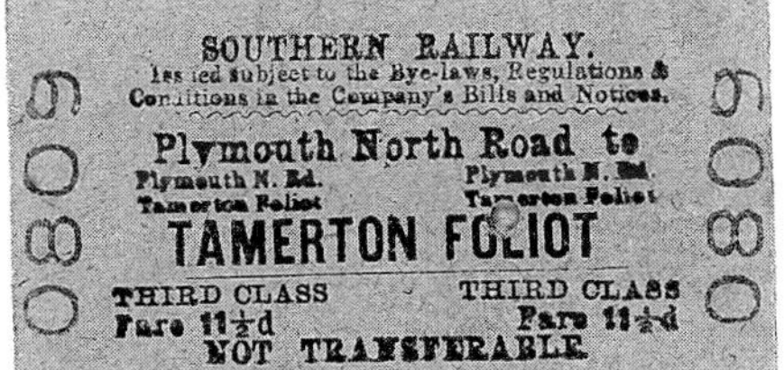

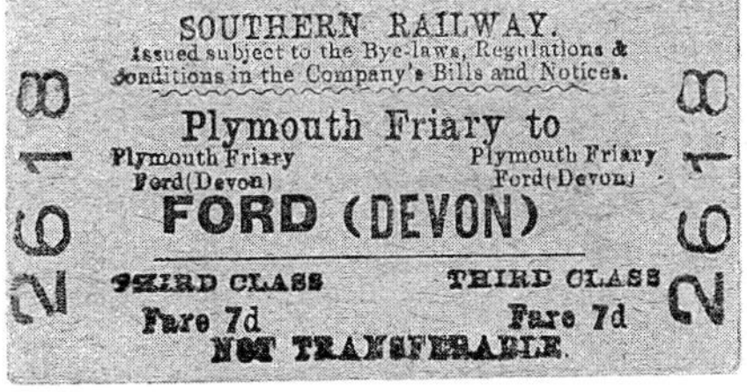

12. THE BOAT TRAINS

Boat trains were very much a feature of the railway scene at Plymouth, but in order to put the subject into perspective, some background information is desirable.

Plymouth was at the height of its prosperity as a port of call for ocean liners during the inter-war years. First and foremost was the Trans-Atlantic traffic from New York, for that was where the money was made. Competition between the various national shipping lines was intense. Film stars, statesmen and V.I.P.s * of all kinds landed at Plymouth and travelled by the Great Western Railway to their ultimate destinations. Cunard and White Star sailings from New York made somewhat infrequent calls at Plymouth as their first port of call was usually Cherbourg or Havre (now known as Le Havré) before crossing the English Channel to Southampton. It was, therefore, often quicker to use "foreign" lines and disembark at Plymouth. In fact, the sales patter was "Land at Plymouth and save a day". Rich Americans predominated on the passenger list, notwithstanding that they had to suffer the not inconsiderable inconvenience of landing at Plymouth to save that day. The ocean going liner dropped anchor in Cawsand Bay where it was met by up to four tenders (according to traffic requirements) coming out from Millbay Docks. That would not be too bad on a warm sunny day, but it could be in the cold light of dawn, or a freezing winter's day, or in Plymouth's speciality of driving rain, or worst of all, in a howling gale when the whole exercise could be called off.

Passengers had to clamber down the open gangway of the towering ocean liner and then find themselves huddled into the lounge of a seemingly miniscule tender for the 15 minute journey to the dockside. Then followed the reverse procedure of clambering off the tender to await the arrival of the baggage and the kindly attention of His Majesty's Customs and Excise Officers. To be fair, passengers were not expected to carry their own baggage, the porters even unpacked and repacked the trunks and suitcases after Customs' examination. All that achieved, the travellers then made for the waiting train where many of them, no doubt, collapsed with exhaustion into the nearest seat. All that to save a day.

In 1931, for the greater comfort of those rich Americans, the Great Western introduced their luxury saloons which HM The King had graciously permitted to be named after himself and members of his family. For the privilege of riding in luxury the railway charged a supplement of 10s 0d (50p) on top of the first class single fare of £2.6s11d (£2.34½p). For those who still had the energy to walk to the front of the train, many were fascinated by the cute little engine which was to haul their train to London.

Normally, the time taken from when the liner dropped anchor in Cawsand Bay to departure of the boat train from the Ocean Terminal was between two and three hours. There then followed a train journey of approximately another four hours to London.

A record was achieved on 5th July 1934 when five Trans-Atlantic liners called and landed 1300 passengers, for which five special trains had to be laid on. That sort of situation placed a great strain on the catering side for a fully staffed kitchen car and restaurant car had to be provided for each train.

The liners calling were:

Columbia	Royal Netherlands Line
Columbus	North German Lloyd Line
Leviathan	United States Line
Paris	French Line
Statenham	Holland America Line (their flagship)

The Columbia was homeward bound from the West Indies, but the other four were all from New York thus illustrating the intense competition on the North Atlantic route.

On 12th June 1935, the French Line's new 79,000 ton *Normandie* arrived at Plymouth on her maiden voyage, having made a record crossing of the Atlantic by passing Bishop Rock lighthouse, off the Isle of Scilly, in four days, three hours and twenty five minutes after passing the Ambrose Lightship, New York and thus becoming the proud holder of the prestige Blue Riband. The Great Western, not to be outdone, also created a record that day with the fastest time ever from Plymouth to Paddington for the almost 227 miles from the Ocean Terminal or only 3 hours 33 minutes from passing North Road station. That compared with the fastest timetabled train of the day which was allowed 4 hours 15 minutes with just one stop at Exeter. The engine on that occasion was Laira's 4094 *Dynevor Castle*. The log of the train is reproduced from the GWR Magazine for July 1935. It will be observed that the GWR lost no time in publicising their achievement. It will also be seen that the train was first class only: the rest would have followed in a second train at a somewhat more leisurely rate of progress.

A local newspaper report in 1953 quoted the Cunard White Star flagship *Queen Mary* as calling at Plymouth regularly every fortnight for one spell in the thirties. It continues "That was the time when she was in keen competition with the French liner *Normandie* for the Blue Riband of the Atlantic. The *Normandie* from the moment she came into service used Plymouth as her first homeward port of call, and the Cunard Line, impressed by the short time taken by *Normandie* passengers to reach London from New York immediately followed the lead. Thus, one or other of these two great liners reached Plymouth every Monday morning. After one complete season the *Normandie*, for some reason never publicly explained, ceased calling regularly at Plymouth and the *Queen Mary* followed the lead yet again".

* The acronym VIP is, strictly speaking, not in context here. It was not known before World War 2. It was introduced to hide the identity of Winston Churchill – a Very Important Person.

SS Ile de France anchored in Cawsand Bay with tender Sir Richard Genville approaching to collect mailbags.
Richard Taylor

Boat train off "Ile de France" 30 June 1931 about to pass through North Road Station. 4946 *Moseley Hall* piloting 4095 *Harlech Castle*. First vehicle is a Dreadnought Ocean Mail van.
W H Adams

The railway issued detailed instructions regarding the provisions of Boat Trains, together with point to point running times. The running times were governed by the Class of engine hauling the train, the tonnage behind the tender and the stopping points along the journey. The running of the individual train was governed by a telegraphic code passed from one signal box to the next as the train progressed on its journey.

Liners from all parts of the world called at Plymouth including such an unlikely candidate as the Johnson Line from Vancouver, San Francisco and the Panama Canal, going forward to Hull and Gothenburg. Some Lines, such as Elder Dempster from West Africa, sailed on to Liverpool, others to Southampton or London, and the rest to Continental ports. When traffic was insufficient to require a special train, a Class 1361 dock tank, proudly carrying Class A express head lamps, would bring two coaches up to North Road Station to await attachment to the next convenient London bound train.

Outward bound traffic was seasonal, with only the weekly French Line traffic during the summer months warranting a regular special train from Paddington. An interesting incident was recorded in the GWR Magazine for February 1930 concerning two outward bound passengers who missed the 11.30pm special sleeping car train at Paddington. They were put on the midnight train which was not due into Plymouth until 7.20am the next morning. From North Road station they were rushed by taxi to the dockside where a high speed motor boat was waiting to get them to the *Paris* just as it was weighing anchor.

In the other direction, it was in 1932 that the White Star *Majestic* made a special call so that Americans could attend the Grand National the next day. Later in the same year, the Cunarder *Berengaria* called to permit passengers to attend the Derby on the following day.

During the 1930s there were upwards of 450 inward calls per annum by ocean going liners, but only a small fluctuating number outward bound. New Zealand Line vessels called outward bound throughout the year en route from London to New Zealand via the Panama Canal. French Line en route to New York called weekly according to the brochures for 1930 and 1931, but had ceased completely by 1936.

Each Shipping Line had its own Plymouth based agent, although Cunard and Orient Steam Navigation had their own branch offices. Cunard catered largely for their weekly arrival from Montreal and Quebec. Orient Steam Navigation were from Australia and the Mediterranean.

Statistical detail published for the year to mid November give some idea of the scale of the operation:

	1935	1938
Calls homeward bound	416	412
Passengers landed	32,572	29,742
Mail bags landed	189,318	132,628
Bullion (tons)	–	225

1935 was the Silver Jubilee Year for King George V and Queen Mary

THE LOG OF THE FIRST SPECIAL TRAIN FROM PLYMOUTH TO PADDINGTON, WITH PASSENGERS FROM THE "NORMANDIE," JUNE 12th. 1935

	Distance point to point. m.	ch.	Times. arr.	pass.	dep.	Minutes occupied point to point.	Speed point to point, m.p.h.
Plymouth Docks	—	—	—	—	p.m. 1.20	—	—
North Road	1	20		1.25		5	
Ashburton Junction	23	28		1.54		29	48.3
Newton Abbot	8	38		2. 5		11	46.3
Exeter	20	18		2.27		22	55.2
Taunton	30	60		2.55		28	65.8
Castle Cary	27	45		3.16		21	78.7
Heywood Road	20	63		3.34½		18½	67.3
Bedwyn	28	12		3.59		24½	68.9
Newbury	13	26		4. 9		10	79.9
Reading	17	9		4.25½		16½	62.2
Slough	17	42					
Paddington	18	36	4.58			32½	66.4
	226	77				218	

Average speed throughout :—62.4 miles per hour.

Formation of train :—

Engine No. 4094.
Stowage Van.
2 Special Saloons.
Kitchen Car.
2 Special Saloons.
Brake First.

Weight of train excluding engine :—

247 tons.

RMS Queen Mary passing Eddystone Lighthouse inward bound to Plymouth 16th March 1937. *Western Morning News/Plymouth Library*

Via CASTLE CARY & FROME and WESTBURY AVOIDING LINES.

	NON-STOP.						CALLING EXETER.						CALLING TAUNTON.					
Telegraphing ⇒	PLYM. A.		PLYM. B.		PLYM. C.		PLYM. D.		PLYM. E.		PLYM. F.		PLYM. G.		PLYM. H.		PLYM. K.	
LOAD IN TONS Eng. Nos. 100A1, 111, 4000, 4016, 4032, 4037 „ „ 4073–5056 (" Castle " Engines)	Up to 270		271–315		Over 316–400 Max.		Up to 270		271–315		Over 316–400 Max.		Up to 270		271–315		Over 316–400 Max.	
„ „ 6000–6029 (" King " Engines)	—		—		Over 400		—		—		Over 400		—		—		Over 400	
	arr.	dep.	arr.	dep.	arr.	dep.	arr.	dep.	arr.	dep.	arr.	dep.	arr.	dep.	arr.	dep.	arr.	dep.
PLYMOUTH DOCKS	—	0 00	—	0 00	—	0Y 00	—	0 00	—	0 00	—	0Y 00	—	0 00	—	0 00	—	0Y00
Ashburton Junction	0 38		0 39		0Y39½		0 38		0 39		0Y39½		0 38		0 39		0Y39½	
Newton Abbot	0 51		0 52½		0 52Y	0 54	0 51		0 52½		0 52Y	0 54	0 51		0 52½		0 52Y	0 54
Exeter	1 13½		1 15½		1 17½		1 14	1 17	1 16	1 19	1 19	1 22	1 13½		1 15½		1 19	
Taunton	1 43		1 46		1 50		1 49		1 53		1 59		1 44†	1 47	1 50†	1 53	1 55†	1 58
Castle Cary	2 8		2 11½		2 16		2 14		2 19		2 25		2 14		2 20		2 25	
Heywood Junction	2 28		2 32		2 37½		2 34		2 40½		2 46½		2 34		2 41½		2 46½	
Bedwyn	2 54½		2 59½		3 5½		3 0½		3 8		3 14½		3 0½		3 9		3 14½	
Reading	3 23½		3 28½		3 35		3 29½		3 38		3 44		3 29½		3 39		3 44	
PADDINGTON	4 0	—	4 5	—	4 12	—	4 6	—	4 15	—	4 21	—	4 6	—	4 16	—	4 21	—

Via BRISTOL and BADMINTON.

	CALLING BRISTOL.						CALLING EXETER and BRISTOL.					
Telegraphing ⇒	PLYM. L.		PLYM. M.		PLYM. N.		PLYM. P.		PLYM. R.		PLYM. W.	
LOAD IN TONS Eng. Nos. 100A1, 111, 4000, 4016, 4032, 4037 „ „ 4073–5056 (" Castle " Engines)	Up to 270		271–315		Over 316–400 Max.		Up to 270		271–315		Over 316–400 Max.	
„ „ 6000–6029 (" King " Engines)	—		—		Over 400		—		—		Over 400	
	arr.	dep.	arr.	dep.	arr.	dep.	arr.	dep.	arr.	dep.	arr.	dep.
PLYMOUTH DOCKS	—	0 00	—	0 00	—	0Y00	—	0 00	—	0 00	—	0Y00
Ashburton Junction	0 38		0 39		0Y39½		0 38		0 39		0Y39	
Newton Abbot	0 51		0 52½		0 52Y	0 54	0 51		0 52½		0 52Y	0 54
Exeter	1 13½		1 15½		1 17½		1 14	1.17	1 16	1 19	1 19	1 22
Taunton	1 43		1 46		1 50		1 49		1 53		1 59	
Highbridge	2 1		2 4		2 9		2 7		2 11		2 18	
Bristol	2 29	2 33	2 32	2 36	2 39	2 43	2 35	2 39	2 39	2 43	2 48	2 52
Steventon	3 36		3 40		3 50		3 42		3 47		3 59	
PADDINGTON	4 29	—	4 34	—	4 47	—	4 35	—	4 41	—	4 56	—

†—In cases where a portion of the train is detached at Taunton a Special to be run from Taunton to Bristol (Temple Meads) after arrival if traffic warrants and if no ordinary service available. Running time Taunton to Bristol (Temple Meads) 50 minutes.

Y—Assisted Plymouth Docks or Dock Gates to Newton Abbot. These trains must stop at Newton Abbot West Box Home Signal to detach " bank " engine.

P.T.O.]

PRIVATE AND NOT FOR PUBLICATION. NOTICE No. 57.

GREAT WESTERN RAILWAY.

INSTRUCTIONS

RELATING TO

OCEAN SPECIAL TRAINS

FROM

PLYMOUTH.

Running Schedules and Telegraphing. Special trains with mails or passengers landed from ocean liners at Plymouth will, until further notice, be timed in accordance with the schedules shewn on back hereof, and telegraphic advices must shew under which table the train is running.

The actual time of departure from Plymouth, also departure or passing Bristol, and Heywood Junction or Westbury must be wired to Traffic T.M., Divisional T., and Station Master, Paddington.

Route. Specials reaching Taunton during the time the Langport and Castle Cary Line is closed, viz.:—

Sundays	9.45 a.m. to 12.30 p.m.	
	7.50 p.m. to 11.45 p.m.	
Mondays.	4. 0 a.m. to 6. 0 a.m.	

must run via Bristol, unless special arrangements have been made otherwise.

Taunton and Bristol Traffic. When there are passengers or mail bags for transfer at Exeter or Taunton from ocean specials, an advice must be sent to the station concerned, and arrangements made for the train to run via the platform line. Passengers, luggage, and mails for Bristol must be kept separate from London traffic, and, if possible, separate vehicles provided to avoid transfer from the London portion *en route*.

Connecting special trains, Taunton to London. In certain cases coaches will be attached to ordinary trains from Plymouth to Taunton, whence they will be run specially to Paddington. Plymouth must send a telegraphic advice to those concerned and the specials should run under the PLYM schedule applicable as from Taunton, the latter station to advise forward the Box to Box message to Paddington and the approximate departure time.

Tickets. A travelling ticket collector should work on all specials where possible, and in every case if there are 50 passengers or over on the train. When a travelling collector is not provided, ticket collection should follow the ordinary course, and Plymouth must wire the stations concerned.

Refreshments. Where ocean specials are not equipped with restaurant cars, stations at which they call must be so advised. Station Masters must see that the Refreshment Department is informed so that attention may be given to the requirements of the passengers. Orders for refreshment baskets should be telegraphed from Plymouth.

Much importance is attached to the ocean special trains, and all concerned are hereby directed to give special attention to the working. The instructions shewn in the Appendices to the Working Time Tables, etc., are to be observed, and the permanent and temporary speed restrictions in operation strictly adhered to.

Acknowledge receipt to head of Department.

F. R. POTTER,

Superintendent of the Line.

Paddington Station,
August, 1936.

(T.92883/5.M.) P.T.O.

7213.

Prior to the Coronation of King George VI on 12th May 1937 there was a considerable build up of Trans-Atlantic travel. On 26th April the RMS *Queen Mary* landed 528 passengers, include Hon. J.W. Garard representing President Roosevelt at the Coronation. From May 8th to 11th twelve liners landed 1500 passengers and eight special boat trains were run to Paddington.

On 24th March 1938, no less than six liners called at Plymouth within the space of twelve hours. They were not all Trans-Atlantic liners and some of them would not have provided sufficient custom to warrant special trains. Those liners were:

City of Benares	City Line from Bombay
Ile de France	French Line to or from New York
Normandie	French Line to or from New York
President Harding	United States Line from New York
Rajputana	P & O Line from the Far East
Shropshire	Bibby Line from the Far East

One of the French Line vessels would have been outward bound and the other homeward bound.

H.W. Adams. when Station Master's clerk at North Road maintained a record of the boat trains and the engines that worked them for the years 1927 to 1938. It makes fascinating record and is now reproduced in tabular form.

For 4070 *Cleeve Abbey* it was Laira's swan song for the Stars on their allocation, being the top performer in 1927. Their other Star, 4014 *Knight of the Bath* did three trips in 1927 and five in 1928 before finally moving away towards the end of 1928. Laira received three extra Castles from the 1927 new construction (5004/7/8); Paddington and Newton Abbot shared the other nine, hence the significant drop in Star appearances on boat trains. The Stars that did appear in the subsequent years were predominately Paddington or Bristol engines. Paddington lost their last Stars in 1935 and the four that appeared in the Table for 1938 were all Bristol engines.

An analysis of engines by allocation for those working the trains in 1935 gave 187 for Laira, 37 for Paddington and seven purloined from elsewhere. Probably most of the Paddington engines brought down empty stock for the next day's up trains. Such an analysis would not have varied significantly over the years. There is no explanation as to why the most frequent performer's appearances dwindled away from a maximum of 37 in 1930 to nine in 1938. The top performers were all Laira engines.

Details have survived of special trains run during the first half of June 1934 showing the telegraphic codes under which they ran. (See reprint of official instructions on page 64)

June	1	French Line	Ile de France	Plym	C	5000	*Launceston Castle*
	7	United States Line	President Roosevelt	Plym	B	5007	*Rougemont Castle*
	8	Royal Netherlands	Stuyvesant	Plym	E	6015	*King Richard III*
	9	French	Champlain	Plym	B	4095	*Harlech Castle*
	10	Holland America	Volendam	Plym	D	4087	*Cardigan Castle*
	10	Pacific S.N.	Reina Del Pacifico	Plym	E	5028	*Llantilio Castle*
	12	United States	Washington 1st	Plym	C	5021	*Whittington Castle*
			2nd	Plym	?	5001	*Llandovery Castle*
	14	White Star	Olympic	Plym	B	4094	*Dynevor Castle*
	14	United States	Leviathan	Plym	C	4092	*Dunraven Castle*
	15	French	Paris	Plym	B	4094	*Dynevor Castle*

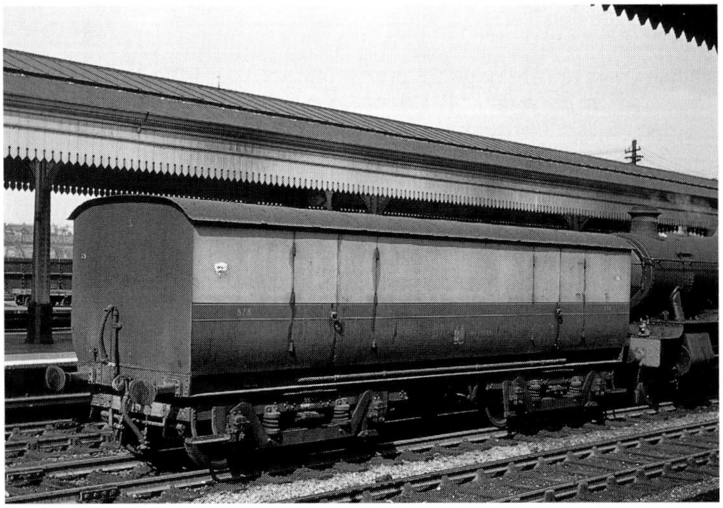

Bullion Van 878 (Diag. M17 Lot 1220). One of a small number built to convey gold bullion to London for the Bank of England. This van is almost identical to the regular ones used on the boat trains from Millbay docks. *T J Edgington*

OCEAN LINERS *via* PLYMOUTH

Date 1938	Steamship Company	Name of Liner	Gross Tonnage	Arriving from	Departing for	Agents in Plymouth
June						
1	*New Zealand*	*Ruahine*	*10870*	*London*	*New Zealand via Panama*	*Cory & Strick, Ltd.*
2	P. & O.	Rawalpindi	17000	Japan, China & Colombo	London	Cory & Strick Ltd.
2	Harrison	Inanda	6000	Demerara, Trinidad and Barbados	London	Fox, Sons & Co., Ltd.
2	United States	President Roosevelt	13869	New York	Havre and Hamburg	Weekes, Phillips & Co., Ltd.
3	Bibby	Yorkshire	10183	Burma, Ceylon and Egypt	London	Weekes, Phillips & Co., Ltd.
3	City	City of Canterbury	8331	Bombay	Liverpool	Weekes, Phillips & Co., Ltd.
3	French	Cuba	11336	West Indies	Havre	Haswell & Co.
3	Royal Netherlands	Costa Rica	8672	West Indies	Havre and Amsterdam	Bellamy & Co., Ltd.
3	Pacific S.N.	Reina Del Pacifico	17707	Valparaiso	Liverpool	Travellers, Ltd.
3	Elder Dempster	Accra	9336	Calabar	Liverpool	Travellers, Ltd.
3	French	Paris	34569	New York	Havre	Haswell & Co.
4	Cunard White Star	Aurania	14000	Montreal and Quebec	Havre and London	Cunard Branch Office
5	American Merchant	American Merchant	7430	New York	London	Weekes, Phillips & Co. Ltd.
5	Holland America	Volendam	15434	New York	Boulogne and Rotterdam	Bellamy & Co. Ltd.
6	Royal Netherlands	Oranje Nassau	3701	Demerara and Madeira	Havre and Amsterdam	Bellamy & Co. Ltd.
7	United States	Washington	24289	New York	Havre and Hamburg	Weekes, Phillips & Co. Ltd.
9	P. & O.	Mooltan	21000	Sydney and Bombay	London	Cory & Strick Ltd.
10	Holland America	Statendam	29511	New York	Boulogne and Rotterdam	Bellamy & Co. Ltd.
11	Cunard White Star	Ascania	14000	Montreal and Quebec	Havre and London	Cunard Branch Office.
11	Elder Dempster	Adda	7816	Port Harcourt	Liverpool	Travellers, Ltd.
12	American Merchant	American Farmer	7430	New York	London	Weekes, Phillips & Co. Ltd.
13	French	Ile de France	43450	New York	Havre	Haswell & Co.
13	Cunard White Star	Queen Mary	81235	New York	Cherbourg & Southampton	Cunard Branch Office
14	Blue Star	Andalucia Star	14943	Buenos Aires	Boulogne and London	Weekes, Phillips & Co. Ltd.
16	United States	President Harding	13869	New York	Havre and Hamburg	Weekes, Phillips & Co. Ltd.
16	P. & O.	Corfu	15000	Japan, China, Colombo and Bombay	London	Cory & Strick Ltd.
18	Holland America	Nieuw Amsterdam	36287	New York	Boulogne and Rotterdam	Bellamy & Co. Ltd.
18	Norddeutscher Lloyd	Columbus	32565	New York	Cherbourg and Bremen	Orlando Davis & Co. Ltd.
18	French	Champlain	28124	New York	Havre	Haswell & Co.
18	British India	Mulbera	9100	Calcutta	London	Weekes, Phillips & Co. Ltd.
18	Cunard White Star	Ausonia	14000	Montreal and Quebec	Havre and London	Cunard Branch Office
19	Bibby	Derbyshire	11650	Burma, Ceylon and Egypt	London	Weekes, Phillips & Co. Ltd.
19	American Merchant	American Banker	7430	New York	London	Weekes, Phillips & Co. Ltd.
20	Royal Netherlands	Simon Bolivar	7906	West Indies	Havre and Amsterdam	Bellamy & Co. Ltd.
21	United States	Manhattan	24289	New York	Havre and Hamburg	Weekes, Phillips & Co. Ltd.
23	Hamburg American	Cordillera	12300	C. America, Trinidad and Barbados	Cherbourg, Ymuiden or Amsterdam and Hamburg	Wm. Muller & Co. Ltd.
23	P. & O.	Strathallan	23500	Sydney and Bombay	London	Cory & Strick Ltd.
23	City	City of Benares	11081	Bombay	Liverpool	Weekes, Phillips & Co. Ltd.
24	British India	Matiana	9045	East Africa	London	Weekes, Phillips & Co. Ltd.
24	*New Zealand*	*Rangitata*	*16737*	*London*	*New Zealand via Panama*	*Cory & Strick, Ltd.*
24	Elder Dempster	Apapa	9332	Calabar	Liverpool	Travellers, Ltd.
25	Cunard White Star	Alaunia	14000	Montreal and Quebec	Havre and London	Cunard Branch Office.
26	American Merchant	American Trader	7430	New York	London	Weekes, Phillips & Co. Ltd.
26	Holland America	Veendam	15450	New York	Boulogne & Rotterdam	Bellamy & Co., Ltd.
27	Royal Netherlands	Stuyvesant	4285	Demerara and Madeira	Havre and Amsterdam	Bellamy & Co. Ltd.
28	French	Ile de France	43450	New York	Havre	Haswell & Co.
28	Harrison	Inkosi	6700	Demerara, Trinidad and Barbados	London	Fox, Sons & Co., Ltd.
30	United States	President Roosevelt	13869	New York	Havre and Hamburg	Weekes, Phillips & Co. Ltd.
30	P. & O.	Chitral	15000	Japan, China, Colombo and Bombay	London	Cory & Strick Ltd.
July						
1	Holland America	Statendam	29511	New York	Boulogne and Rotterdam	Bellamy and Co., Ltd.
2	Pacific S.N.	Orbita	15492	Valparaiso	Liverpool	Travellers, Ltd.
2	Cunard White Star	Aurania	14000	Montreal and Quebec	Havre and London	Cunard Branch Office
3	Bibby	Shropshire	10519	Burma, Ceylon and Egypt	London	Weekes, Phillips & Co. Ltd.
3	American Merchant	American Merchant	7430	New York	London	Weekes, Phillips & Co. Ltd.

A monthly sailing list published by the Great Western Railway

SUMMARY OF BOAT TRAINS FROM MILLBAY DOCKS 1927 TO 1938

	TOTAL	KINGS	CASTLE	STARS	OTHER	TOP PERFORMERS		NUMBER OF TIMES
1927	192		147	45		4070	Cleeve Abbey	25
1928	239	53	170	16		5008	Raglan Castle	28
1929	236	51	170	14	4946	5007	Rougemont Castle	24
1930	257	2	242	12	3373	4094	Dynevor Castle	37
1931	198	2	189	6	2903	5005	Manorbier Castle	27
1932	174	9	162	3		5007	Rougemont Castle	21
1933	172	2	164	6		5020	Trematon Castle	25
1934	224	14	205	5		5021	Whittington Castle	26
1935	231	9	219	3		5009	Shrewsbury Castle	26
1936	166	20	146			4092	Dunraven Castle	18
1937	185	49	136			5041	Tiverton Castle	14
1938	168	53	110	4	2950	6019	King Henry V	9
Total	**2442**	**264**	**2060**	**114**	**4**			

2903 *Lady of Lyons*
2950 *Taplow Court*
3373 *Sir William Henry*
4946 *Moseley Hall*

All the arrivals were from New York, except the *Reina Del Pacifico* which was from Valparaiso and bound for Liverpool and the *Stuyvesant* which was from Demerara and Madeira and bound for Havre and Amsterdam. During the same period there were 15 other arrivals for which special trains were not required. Two trains were required off the *Washington* although the telegraphic code for the second was not recorded.

All the engines were Laira based except 5001 and 6015 which belonged to Paddington. 4094 *Dynevor Castle* unusually worked trains on successive days, June 14th and 15th. No doubt, after servicing at the London end, it returned to Plymouth with the empty stock urgently required for the following day. The boat trains were the preserve of the Castles, although occasionally a Star would be used and sometimes a King.

There was a period when the Kings were prohibited from going beyond the dock gates at Millbay, presumably because of the derailments on the tight curves that had to be negotiated to and from the Ocean Terminal. It would appear from the statistics that the prohibition was imposed in 1929 and relaxed during 1936. The prohibition resulted in the operational inconvenience of having a 1361 dock tank to draw the train forward to the dock gates where the King could take over. Not only was that an inconvenience, it also made a significant increase to the time sensitive journey to the Capital.

Although the passenger side of the business was important, vast quantities of mail were brought ashore. Traffic was particularly heavy at Christmas time when the volume sometimes required a special train for the mail alone. The GWR had a fleet of vans boldly proclaiming on their sides OCEAN MAILS. There were also three bullion vans, miniature Bank of Englands on wheels, whose fleet numbers from memory were 792, 819 and 820. To illustrate the point, the Cunarder *Mauretania*, in July 1928 landed in addition to 258 passengers, 3622 bags of mail and 106 bars of gold valued at £1,250,000, a considerable sum of money in those days.

For a few years the GWR produced brochures advertising "Ocean Liner Luxury". the objective was to entice rail travel to Plymouth, thence to the Continent by ocean liner when all the luxury facilities could be enjoyed which were available to trans-Atlantic passengers. The following destinations were available in the brochures for 1930 and 1931:

Amsterdam	Hamburg American Line
	Royal Nederland Steamship Company
Antwerp	Red Star Line
Bordeaux	French Line

Boulogne	Holland America Line
Bremen	Norddeutscher Lloyd
Cherbourg	United States Line
Hamburg	Canadian Pacific
	Hamburg American Line
	United States Line
Havre	French Line
	Royal Nederland Steamship Company
Rotterdam	Holland America Line
	Jamaica Direct Fruit Line

The fares quoted were all single except for French Line for the very valid reason that the other Lines did not call at Plymouth outward bound. The fares included meals, as appropriate, and a cabin if an overnight journey was involved. Journey times quoted were 8 hours to Cherbourg or Havre, 24 hours to Belgium or Holland, and 36 hours to Germany. Specimen fares are listed below:

Plymouth to Havre by French Line

	Single	Return
First Class	£3.3s 4d (£2.17p)	£5.14s 8d (£5.73p)
Second or Cabin Class	£2.8s 2d (£2.41p)	£4.7s 4d (£4.37p)
Tourist or Third Cabin	£1.13s 0d (£1.65p)	£3.0s. 0d (£3.00p)

Plymouth to Bremen by Norddeutscher Lloyd

	Single	
First Class	£6.10s 0d	Return fare back
Second Class	£3.10s 0d	to Southampton
Tourist Cabin	£3.0s 0d	twice the single
Third Class	£2.10s 0d	fare

The urge to get passengers to "Save a Day" by landing at Plymouth was applied with even greater urgency to the American mails. In the *Great Western Railway Magazine* there was a report of what was, apparently, a regular event when "a bag of mail was dropped into Plymouth Sound on 17th July 1930 from an aeroplane which had been despatched by a catapult apparatus from the French liner *Ile de France* as the vessel sighted the Isles of Scilly. The plane left the ship at 12.20pm and at 12.55pm the bag was dropped. The correspondence was brought to London by the 2.5pm train". That would probably be in time for the last delivery of the day.

To cater for all the ocean liner traffic there were four tenders based at Millbay docks, all with good West Country seafaring names:

Sir Francis Drake
Sir Richard Grenville
Sir Walter Raleigh

Sir John Hawkins

When not required for their main purpose those tenders were used for popular coastal excursions during the summer months to the River Yealm, or westwards along the Cornish coast towards Looe and Fowey, or best of all, provided one was a good sailor, the 28 mile round trip out to the Eddystone lighthouse and back. All for 2/- (10p) or half a crown (12½p)

POSTSCRIPT

Although the liner traffic was revived following the end of hostilities the writing was already on the wall. A report in the Western Evening Herald, dated 20th August 1937 revealed plans for "50 seater" flying boats with four 1500hp engines. The passenger deck was to have private staterooms as well as berths, a public lounge and a dining room!!! Upstairs were the crew quarters. Flying time was projected to be 14 hours. The traffic gradually withered away in the face of competition from the emerging airlines. The last liner called on 18th October 1963, less than twenty years after the end of the war.

CONTINENTAL SAILINGS BY OCEAN LINER VIA PLYMOUTH.

PLYMOUTH to :—

AMSTERDAM	Hamburg American Line, Royal Nederland Steamship Company
ANTWERP	Red Star Line
BORDEAUX	French Line
BOULOGNE	Holland America Line
BREMEN	Norddeutscher Lloyd
CHERBOURG	United States Lines
HAMBURG	Canadian Pacific, Hamburg American Line, United States Lines
HAVRE	French Line, Royal Nederland Steamship Company
ROTTERDAM	Holland America Line, Jamaica Direct Fruit Line

HAVRE to :—

PLYMOUTH - French Line

NORTH SPAIN to :—

PLYMOUTH - French Line

TO CHERBOURG AND HAMBURG.

UNITED STATES LINES.

Leave Plymouth about	Ship	Gross Tonnage
Feb. 8	"American Merchant"	8,000
" 11	"President Roosevelt"	13,869
" 26	"President Harding"	13,869
Mar. 12	"President Roosevelt"	13,869
" 19	"American Shipper"	8,000
" 26	"America"	21,144
April 1	"President Harding"	13,869
" 8	"President Roosevelt"	13,869
" 15	"George Washington"	23,788
" 23	"America"	21,144
" 30	"President Harding"	13,869
May 6	"President Roosevelt"	13,869
" 10	"Republic"	17,910
" 13	"George Washington"	23,788
" 21	"America"	21,144
" 28	"President Harding"	13,869
June 3	"President Roosevelt"	13,869
" 10	"George Washington"	23,788
" 13	"Republic"	17,910
" 16	"America"	21,144
" 21	"President Harding"	13,869
July 2	"President Roosevelt"	13,869
" 8	"George Washington"	23,788
" 13	"Republic"	17,910
" 16	"President Harding"	13,869
" 24	"America"	21,144
" 30	"President Roosevelt"	13,869
Aug. 5	"George Washington"	23,788
" 9	"Republic"	17,910
" 13	"President Harding"	13,869
" 20	"America"	21,144
" 27	"President Roosevelt"	13,869
Sept. 2	"George Washington"	23,788
" 9	"President Harding"	13,869
" 10	"Republic"	17,910
" 17	"America"	21,144
" 24	"President Roosevelt"	13,869
" 30	"George Washington"	23,788
Oct. 8	"President Harding"	13,869

FARES.

PLYMOUTH TO CHERBOURG—	
Cabin Class	£2 0 0
Tourist Third Cabin	£1 10 0
PLYMOUTH TO CHERBOURG AND RETURN TO SOUTHAMPTON—	
Cabin one way and return First Class	£5 0 0
Cabin one way and return Tourist Third Cabin	£3 10 0
Tourist Third Cabin	£3 0 0
PLYMOUTH TO HAMBURG—	
Cabin Class	£3 10 0
Tourist Third Cabin	£3 0 0
PLYMOUTH TO HAMBURG AND RETURN TO SOUTHAMPTON—	
Cabin Class	£7 0 0
Tourist Third Cabin	£6 0 0

LONDON : United States Lines, 14 Regent Street, S.W.1.

PLYMOUTH : Orlando Davis & Co., Ltd., 6 Millbay Road.

13. RAILWAY AIR SERVICES

During the 1920s the railways watched with some apprehension the gradual emergence of commercial air services, both internal and external to destinations such as Paris. To counter the emerging competition the railways obtained permission in their Parliamentary Bill for 1929 to operate air services, both internal and external to most of Europe.

Nothing positive happened until 1933 when the GWR inaugurated Britain's first railway operated air service between Cardiff and Plymouth, calling at Haldon for Torquay and Teignmouth. It was, indeed, an auspicious and historical occasion when the first flight took off from Pengam Moor Airport at Cardiff on 11th April 1933. There was a civic send off at Cardiff and civic welcomes at both Haldon and Plymouth Roborough Aerodromes. At Roborough the welcome gathering was headed by the Mayor, Alderman, R.R. Oke. It will be noted that Cardiff had an Airport whereas both Haldon and Roborough were Aerodromes. The inaugural flight conveyed six senior GWR officials; the public service commenced the following day.

The choice of route was very shrewd because it cut across the Severn Estuary and thus avoided the long way round by rail via Bristol and the Severn Tunnel. Flying time from Plymouth to Cardiff was 80 minutes, although from railway station to railway station was just five minutes short of two hours. The best time by train was four hours twenty six minutes.

The fare from Plymouth to Cardiff was £3.10.0

		First Service.		*Second Service.*	
Cardiff General Station	*dep. by 'Bus*	a.m. 9.0	—	p.m. 1.30	—
Cardiff Air Port	*arr.* ,, ,,	9.10	—	1.40	—
Cardiff Air Port	*dep.* ,, *'Plane*	—	a.m. 9.15	—	p.m. 1.45
Haldon Aero-drome	*arr.* ,, ,,	—	10.5	—	2.35
Haldon Aero-drome	*dep.* ,, ,,	—	10.10	—	2.40
Roborough Aerodrome	*arr.* ,, ,,	—	10.35	—	3.5
Plymouth North Road Station	*arr.* ,, *'Bus*	10.55	—	3.25	—
Plymouth North Road Station	*dep. by 'Bus*	a.m. 11.0	—	p.m. 3.30	—
Roborough Aerodrome	*arr.* ,, ,,	11.20	—	3.50	—
Roborough Aerodrome	*dep.* ,, *'Plane*	—	a.m. 11.25	—	p.m. 3.55
Haldon Aero-drome	*arr.* ,, ,,	—	11.50	—	4.20
Haldon Aero-drome	*dep.* ,, ,,	—	noon 12.0	—	4.30
Cardiff Air Port	*arr.* ,, ,,	—	p.m. 12.50	—	5.20
Cardiff General Station	*arr.* ,, *'Bus*	p.m. 1.0	—	5.30	—

The motor 'bus service between Haldon Aerodrome, Teignmouth and Torquay, is as follows :—

		a.m.	a.m.	p.m.	p.m.
Torquay Station	.. *dep.*	9.0	10.50	1.35	3.20
Torquay Vaughan Parade	*dep.*	9.5	10.55	1.40	3.25
Teignmouth Enquiry Bureau	*dep.*	9.35	11.25	2.10	3.55
Haldon Aerodrome	.. *arr.*	9.55	11.45	2.25	4.10
Haldon Aerodrome	.. *dep.*	10.10	noon 12.0	2.40	4.30
Teignmouth Enquiry Bureau	*arr.*	10.20	p.m. 12.10	2.50	4.40
Torquay Vaughan Parade	*arr.*	10.50	12.40	3.20	5.10

Passengers boarding the Westland Wessex, used by the GWR, for a flight from Cardiff to Plymouth. The pilot looks on as tickets are checked. No doubt they would have been checked at Cardiff General before passengers boarded the connecting road service. 1933. *Authors collection*

Well wishers watching the departure of the inaugural GWR flight from Cardiff, 11 April 1933.

Authors collection

(£3.50p) single and £6 return, compared with £1.16.0 (£1.80p) single first class by train. Passengers holding return tickets had the option of returning first class by train! As some recompense for the high charge for travel, heavy luggage was conveyed Luggage in Advance free of charge, thus saving the passenger two shillings (10p) on each piece conveyed, always provided that it did not exceed the first class limit of 150 lbs.

The aeroplane hired from Imperial Airways was a three engined Westland Wessex monoplane, painted in Great Western chocolate and cream livery, with the following wording:

"Great Western Railway Air Services
Operated by Imperial Airways"

The seating was for six passengers which was upholstered with the same material and braid as used in first class compartments.

DH84 Dragons were used from 1934.

On 22nd May, six weeks after the inaugural flight, the service was extended to the Castle Bromwich Aerodrome, Birmingham and the frequency reduced to one daily flight in each direction, including Sundays. At the same time air fares were reduced consequent upon the introduction of new much reduced Summer Return tickets at one penny per mile for surface travel. Owing to the large number of people using the service the planned closure for the winter on 12th September was extended to the end of the month. 714 passengers were carried during the season.

Overall, the service resulted in a loss of £6526, but that was put down to experience and to the publicity obtained.

	New Fares		Former Fares	
	Single.	Return	Single	Return
Cardiff and Teignmouth Torquay	40/-	72/-	60/-	100/-
Cardiff and Plymouth	45/-	80/-	70/-	120/-
Plymouth and Torquay Teignmouth	12/6	25/-	25/-	40/-

Journey Time

By Rail between Stations	By Air between Aerodromes	Between Birmingham and
170 mins	70 mins.	Cardiff
298 mins.	140 mins.	Torquay
320 mins.	170 mins.	Plymouth

The timetable with the bus connections was:

Birmingham Snow Hill station	.dep.	9.00 a.m.
CASTLE BROMWICH AERODROME	.dep.	9.30 a.m.
Cardiff General station	.dep.	10.30 a.m.
CARDIFF AIR PORT	.arr.	10.40 a.m.
Cardiff General station	.arr.	10.55 a.m.
CARDIFF AIR PORT	.dep.	11.00 a.m.
Torquay Vaughan Parade	.dep.	10.55 a.m.
Teignmouth enquiry bureau	.dep.	11.25 a.m.
HALDON AERODROME	.arr.	11.50 a.m.
HALDON AERODROME	.dep.	11.55 a.m.
Teignmouth enquiry bureau	.arr.	12.10 p.m.
Torquay Vaughan Parade	.arr.	12.40 p.m.
ROBOROUGH AERODROME	.arr.	12.20 p.m.
Plymouth North road station	.arr.	12.40 p.m.
Plymouth North Road station	.dep.	3.30 p.m.
ROBOROUGH AERODROME dep.	.dep.	4.00 p.m.
Torquay Vaughan Parade	.dep.	3.30 p.m.
Teignmouth enquiry bureau	.dep.	4.00 p.m.
HALDON AERODROME arr. 4.25 P.M.		
HALDON AERODROME	.dep.	4.30 p.m.
Teignmouth enquiry bureau	.arr.	4.45 p.m.
Torquay Vaughan Parade	.arr.	5.15 p.m.
Cardiff General station	.dep.	5.10 p.m.
CARDIFF AIR PORT	.dep.	5.40 p.m.
CASTLE BROMWICH AERODROME	.arr.	6.40 p.m.
Birmingham Snow Hill station	.arr.	7.20 p.m.

The service restarted under new management on 7th May 1934. During the course of the previous winter the big four railways decided to work together under the umbrella of Railway Air Services Ltd, each railway, together with Imperial Airways having one director each. The registered office was one room on the top floor of the Imperial Airways Terminal Building, a one time landmark adjacent to London's Victoria Station.

The summer service operated between May and September each year although it took three years to settle down into a regular pattern. The report in the GWR Magazine for June 1934 makes interesting reading and is reproduced on page 74.

Interesting points to note in the report:

1. Cars replaced buses for transport between railway stations and the aerodromes.
2. Cardiff was still the only place to have an airport.
3. Children aged seven or over paid full fare.
4. The fare between Plymouth and Cardiff was further reduced.
5. Torquay disappeared from the timetable.
6. The emergence of KLM, an airline that is still with us to-day.
7. According to Bradshaw for May 1934 it was possible to do the journey by rail from Plymouth to Cardiff in 4 hours 26 minutes by using the 1.40pm, changing at Temple Meads and arriving at Cardiff at 6.6pm. In the reverse direction there was nothing less than 5 hours. Perhaps, the 4hrs 55 minutes was an average time.

Between 1936 and 1939 there was just one flight each day between Plymouth, Haldon, Cardiff, Weston Super

Railway Air Services.

TWELVE months ago the Great Western Company inaugurated Britain's first railway-operated air service over the route between Plymouth and Cardiff, and subsequently extended it to Birmingham. Since then the railway companies in conjunction with Imperial Airways Ltd., have become associated with a new company known as Railway Air Services, Ltd., and the first service to be provided over Great Western territory was introduced on Monday, May 7, between Plymouth, Teignmouth, Cardiff, Birmingham, and Liverpool.

One service daily, Sundays excepted, is being run in each direction, and operated by a De Havilland Dragon 8-seater two-engined aeroplane.

The interesting time table is given below :—

Plymouth, North Road			a.m.
Station	.. dep.	by Car	8.25
Roborough Aerodrome	.. arr.	,, ,,	8.45
,, ,,	.. dep.	,, 'Plane	8.50
Haldon Aerodrome ..	.. arr.	,, ,,	9.10
,, ,, ..	.. dep.	,, ,,	9.15
Cardiff Air Port ..	.. arr.	,, ,,	9.55A
,, ,, ,, ..	.. dep.	,, ,,	10.0 B
Castle Bromwich Aerodrome	arr.	,, ,,	11.0
,, ,, ,,	dep.	,, ,,	11.15
Speke Aerodrome ..	.. arr.	,, ,,	12.0 C
Liverpool, Lime Street			p.m.
Station	.. arr.	,, Car	12.15
,, Adelphi Hotel	.. arr.	,, ,,	12.15
,, 11, James Street	arr.	,, ,,	12.20
			p.m.
Liverpool, 11, James Street	dep.	,, Car	3.0
,, Lime Street			
Station	.. dep.	,, ,,	3.5
,, Adelphi Hotel	.. dep.	,, ,,	3.5
Speke Aerodrome ..	.. arr.	,, ,,	3.20
,, ,, ..	.. dep.	,, 'Plane	3.30
Castle Bromwich Aerodrome	arr.	,, ,,	4.15
,, ,, ,,	dep.	,, ,,	4.20
Cardiff Air Port ..	.. arr.	,, ,,	5.20A
,, ,, ,, ..	.. dep.	,, ,,	5.35B
Haldon Aerodrome ..	.. arr.	,, ,,	6.15
,, ,, ..	.. dep.	,, ,,	6.20
Roborough Aerodrome	.. arr.	,, ,,	6.40
Plymouth, North Road			
Station	.. arr.	,, Car	7.0

A—Connects with Western Airways Ltd. to Bristol and Bournemouth.

B—Connection from Bristol by Western Airways Ltd.

C—Connects with K.L.M. (Royal Dutch Airlines) to Hull and Amsterdam.

Special motor car services operate between the various aerodromes and the railway stations. Passengers taking return tickets by air have the option of making the return journey by rail, and in that case they exchange the return half of their air tickets for a first-class single rail ticket. Passengers holding through air tickets may make part of the journey by air and the rest by rail.

The services connect at Cardiff with Norman Edgar's Western Airway service to and from Bristol and Bournemouth; and commencing on June 1, they will connect with the K.L.M. (Royal Dutch Air Line) at Liverpool, to Hull and Amsterdam.

The comparative times taken by air and rail between the places served show to what extent time is saved by the new means of transport. Nor is the advantage confined to the places mentioned, because passengers are enabled to travel by rail from and to other important centres, and link up with the air services :—

	RAIL.		AIR.	
	Hrs.	Mins.	Hrs.	Mins.
Plymouth—Cardiff	4	45	1	5
,, Birmingham ..	5	20	2	10
,, Liverpool ..	8	0	3	10
Teignmouth—Cardiff ..	3	20	–	40
,, Birmingham	4	25	1	45
,, Liverpool ..	7	30	2	45
Cardiff—Birmingham ..	3	0	1	0
,, Liverpool	4	50	2	0
Birmingham—Liverpool ..	2	0	–	45

The fares, which include transport by special cars between aerodrome and the terminals shown, are given below :—

	Single.	Return.
Plymouth—Teignmouth	12/6	25/–
,, Cardiff	42/–	65/–
,, Birmingham	60/–	90/–
,, Liverpool	85/–	120/–
Teignmouth—Cardiff	40/–	60/–
,, Birmingham ..	55/–	85/–
,, Liverpool	80/–	115/–
Cardiff—Birmingham	30/–	50/–
,, Liverpool	45/–	70/–
Birmingham—Liverpool	30/–	45/–

Children up to three years of age are carried free if not occupying a seat; three and under seven years of age at half the full fares, and seven years of age and over at full fares. Hand baggage up to 35-lb. per passenger is allowed free; excess baggage is charged at the air parcels rates, which vary from 3d. to 6d. per lb., according to distance. The luggage of passengers travelling by railway air services may be collected, conveyed and/or delivered free of charge at any station where cartage facilities exist, provided the weight does not exceed 150-lb. for each passenger.

Air service tickets are on sale at Plymouth (North Road) station, Teignmouth town enquiry office, Cardiff enquiry bureau, Birmingham (Snow Hill) information bureau, Liverpool (11, James Street), Birmingham (New Street), and Liverpool (Lime Street).

Should it be necessary for the pilot to make an emergency landing at any point between Plymouth and Liverpool, road transport to the nearest railway station will be provided free of charge, and rail tickets will be issued to destination.

The inauguration of this service represents the first step in the direction of co-ordinating air travel facilities in conjunction with railway air and rail services.

Mare and Bristol with various connections en route. Business at Haldon must have been rather thin because Haldon became a "request stop" with three hours notice being required by the aerodrome.

On 17th October 1935 Sir James Milne (the GWR General Manager) in an address to the Railway's Lecture and Debating Society commented "The cost of operating an air service in this country was exceedingly high in comparison with the possible revenue which could be obtained. One of the considerable costs was for petrol at the standard rates, no remission of petrol tax being made although the tax revenue largely went to the Road Fund". – T'was always so.

The first ever railway air excursion was on Sunday 15th July 1934 from Plymouth to Cardiff. Departure from North Road was at 8.25am, returning there at 6.30pm. The return fare was £2 which was half the normal fare.

BY AIR MAIL
PAR AVION

NEW AIR MAIL SERVICE

FROM PLYMOUTH TO CARDIFF, BIRMINGHAM, LIVERPOOL

For conveyance of Letters, Packets and Postcards.

BEGINS The new service will commence on 20th August, 1934, leaving Roborough Aerodrome by the Railway Service Airplane at 4.35 p.m. (Sundays excepted).

CHARGES Letters $1\frac{1}{2}$d. for the first 2 oz. and 1d. for each additional ounce, postcards 1d. each.

LATEST POSTING TIME	Plymouth P.O. Blue Air Mail Box	Devonport P.O.	Street letter boxes Plymouth and Devonport
	3.30 p.m.	3.30 p.m.	1.45 p.m. to 2.30 p.m.

BLUE AIR MAIL LABELS These can be obtained at any Post Office and should be affixed to letters for despatch by this service. Failing this a prominent inscription " BY AIR MAIL " is required.

14. THE SOUTHERN

Without a doubt the Southern was the poor relation in Plymouth. It "enjoyed" running powers over the Great Western from Devonport Junction, through North Road and Mutley stations to Friary Junction, and so to its own terminus station at Friary - but at the convenience of the Great Western. It was not unknown at times of pressure, such as a busy summer Saturday, for a Southern train to stand in the platform at North Road for up to a quarter of an hour waiting a path out to Friary.

Friary Station was a modest stone built edifice with two main line platforms, one for arrivals and one for departures together with a middle road. There were also up side and down side bay platforms. It was placed about as far from the east end of the city commercial and shopping centres as the Great Western Millbay station was from the west end. Few passengers travelled to Friary from the Exeter direction, the majority preferring to leave the train at North Road. Patronage in the up direction was better because passengers made the extra effort to get to Friary in order to obtain a good chance of a corner seat of their choice. All Southern trains called at Mutley Station, but in the eyes of the Great Western Mutley's status was such that only their branch line services called together with the main line stopping trains.

The Southern did not count for much with Plymouthians in general and they still called it the "South Western". People always travelled to London by the prestigious Great Western with a shining King or Castle at the head of the train and not to Waterloo in a three coach train headed by an ancient looking Greyhound Class T9 4-4-0 of 1899 vintage. (To be fair, the two morning up and two afternoon down express trains also had three extra coaches to or from Portsmouth and Brighton). The Portsmouth service was important as it linked two important naval and dockyard establishments, the train being the only practical mode of travel for most occasions. Well remembered and regularly trotted out was the football excursion to Bournemouth which was said to have reached its destination just as the final whistle was blown. That incident just about summed up the South Western in the eyes of the local populace. Incidentally, the train would have travelled via Templecombe and the Somerset and Dorset Joint line.

In practical terms the Great Western service to Paddington was much quicker than the Southern service to Waterloo. The Cornish Riviera Limited did the journey in four hours in the summer, seven minutes longer in the winter. The down Atlantic Coast Express needed five and a half hours to reach Plymouth: the up train nineteen minutes longer.

General view of Friary Station with an Adams 0-4-4T in the right hand bay, probably on a Turnchapel train. Circa 1930's.

M J Dart collection

723 a Greyhound of class T9 an everyday sight in April 1937 emerging from Mutley Tunnel and coasting to a stand at Mutley Station. *P D Orton*

717 & 713 of class T9 (Greyhounds) on an up express soon after leaving the Friary terminus. Circa early 1930's. *M J Dart collection*

The basic timetable according to Bradshaw for May 1934 was:

			ACE*				Sundays	
Waterloo	dpt	8.40am	11am	12.40pm	3pm	6pm	11am	3pm
Brighton				11am				
Portsmouth & Southsea				12.40pm		5.34		
Friary	arr	3.10pm	4.31pm	6.55pm	8.41pm	12.9am	4.52pm	9.55pm
		6hrs 50	5hrs 31	6hrs 15	5hrs 41	6hrs 35	5hrs 52	6hrs 55

			ACE					
Friary	dpt	8.25am	10.10am	11am	2.10pm	3.50pm	9.50am	3pm
Portsmouth & Southsea	arr	2.15pm		4.39pm				
Brighton				6.34pm				
Waterloo		2.9pm	4pm	5.21pm	8.38pm	10.9pm	4.1pm	9.11pm
		5hrs 44	5hrs 50	6hrs 21	6hrs 28	6hrs 19	6hrs 11	6hrs 11

*Atlantic Coast Express

At the other end of the spectrum there was the 7.58am from Salisbury which took 6hrs 25mins to do the 150¾ miles to Plymouth, calling at all 41 intermediate stations, at an average speed of 24mph.

The express trains took almost two hours to cover the 62 miles from Friary to Exeter (Queen Street), now Exeter (Central). Comparing like with like Southern trains had to travel an extra seven miles between North Road Station and Exeter (St. Davids) but needed an extra thirty minutes to do the journey. Southern trains to and from Waterloo faced the extraordinary situation of travelling in the opposite direction to Great Western trains to and from Paddington, first between Friary Junction and Devonport Junction, and then between Cowley Bridge Junction and Exeter (St. Davids).

The express trains were almost monopolised by the elderly Greyhounds. Slow trains provided a wider variety of motive power, still principally Greyhounds, but also N class Woolwich Moguls. Occasionally, a 4-4-0 of Class K10 or L11 would appear, known to the local enthusiast fraternity as *Tea Party Fronts* because of the unusually wide platform in front of the smokebox door. They could often be seen on the ten o'clock arrival from Exeter (Queen Street). A further class of 4-4-0 needs a mention, that is the S11. They were Exmouth Junction engines, sub-shedded to Okehampton until they were transferred away in the mid thirties. They had a regular Sunday duty commencing with the first down stopper of the day from Okehampton, returning thence on the last of the day, with a return trip to Exeter and back on stopping services thrown in.

Unlike the Great Western, it was rare for anything surprising to arrive in Plymouth on the Southern. But there was a real surprise on 1st August 1931 when 643, an Adams Jubilee 0-4-2 of Class A12 arrived piloting a Greyhound on a strengthened summer Saturday service. It was the only 0-4-2 tender engine to have been seen by us in Plymouth and in all probability the last to visit Plymouth.

167 of class L11 with "Tea party front" at Bere Alston. Circa 1925.
F H C Casbourne/M J Dart collection

Lord Nelson class 859 *Lord Hood* at the west end of North Road Station en route to Devonport (Southern) for display during Navy Week. The only Lord Nelson to reach Plymouth before the end of steam on BR. August 1934.

H W Adams

17 of class T1 at Mutley station in April 1938 with gated stock on the 4.05pm from Friary, all stations and halts to Bere Alston and Tavistock.

P D Orton

A858 a Woolwich Mogul of class N passing through North Road Station on a freight for Friary. September 1932.
P D Orton

In the summer of 1936 Waterloo decided to upgrade the motive power, so that Exmouth Junction received over the ensuing two years eleven modern Class U1 Moguls numbered 1890 to 1900, although 1900 soon returned to London. With the outbreak of war the moguls left the area and the veteran Greyhounds resumed their former duties, soldering on until the arrival of the Bullied Pacifics in 1946. In fact, although in diminishing numbers, the Greyhounds could still be seen on class one duties towards the end of the 1950s. (The author has a photograph of 30710 in its 60th year on the three coach 2.25pm to Waterloo, taken in August 1958).

Now almost forgotten, a Southern 4-6-0 of the Lord Nelson class managed to reach Plymouth, but not over Southern metals west of Exeter. Because of weight restrictions it had to travel Great Western. It was 859 *Lord Hood*, sent down for display at Navy Days in 1934. Friary shed gave proud hospitality to that representative of their Railway's premier express engine class. It travelled in steam light engine from Friary each day to Devonport Southern Station where it was on display on the Tuesday, Wednesday and Thursday of that week. Also on display were:

A First Class dining car
A Kitchen and Pantry car
A Third Class corridor coach
A Third Class open coach
A general saloon

On the motive power front it has not proved possible to build up an allocation list for Friary shed to cover the whole period under review. However from various sources the standard allocation appears to be:

4-4-0 Greyhounds	4 or 5
0-4-4T Class T1	4
0-4-4T Class 02	5 to 7
0-4-0T Class B4	4
0-6-2T Ex PD&SWJR	2

Concerning the large T1 0-4-4Ts, three were used on the outer suburban trains to Bere Alson and Tavistock. Both Bere Alston and Bere Ferrers on the main line had very poor access into Plymouth with the railway having a virtual monopoly. Bere Alston was the junction for the Callington Branch, and whilst some of the Branch traffic went via Saltash, most of it went via Bere Alston. Hence, in the morning there was an arrival at North Road at 8.29 from Bere Alston and another at 8.44 from Tavistock, both worked by T1 tanks.

When individual engines were called in for Works they were replaced by another member of the class, so that in the decade of the 1930s no less than nineteen members of the class worked from Friary. Because of withdrawals, May 1939 saw the arrival of 0-4-4T, Class M7 number 35 as a replacement, the first member of the class to be seen in Plymouth following their prohibition after 252 left the road at speed back in 1898.

The small Class 02 0-4-4Ts had four areas of use:
The Plymouth inner suburban services
The Devonport pilot including the Dockyard transfer
The Turnchapel Branch (see Chapter 15)
The Callington Branch (see Chapter 15)

The inner suburban trains were made up of auto fitted gate stock and served ten stations and halts between Friary and St. Budeaux, although Weston Mill Halt closed in 1921. The total distance covered was $6^3/_4$ miles, all within the City boundary. Albert Road Halt was one of the more interesting of such places. It was a huge hole in the ground between two tunnels the platforms approached by long flights of steps which, in to-day's parlance would be deemed unsuitable for the elderly or those of impaired mobility.

There were four trains each day, except two afternoon turns which were Saturdays excepted, plus the 6.11am which worked forward to Tavistock as empty stock to form the 8.44 arrival from Tavistock mentioned above. During the decade 1930-9 thirty out of the 59 available members of the class visited Plymouth, but for some it was only a fleeting visit; four of them were subsequently transferred to the Isle of Wight.

The Devonport pilot passed through North Road light engine at 5.24am according to the 1932 Working Timetable and returned likewise back to Friary at

11.6pm. One of its duties was the Dockyard transfer which ran when required. Timings varied slightly from year to year, but in 1932 they were:

	arr.	dpt.
Devonport Southern	9.33am	
North Road	9.38	9.55 run around
Dockyard	10.00	10.45
North Road	10.50	11.02 run around
Devonport Southern	11.07	

Dockyard timings are only approximate.

Other traffic exchanges were in position between Devonport Southern and Millbay, worked by the Great Western, and also between Friary and Laira yard, that being the preserve of Southern 0-4-0Ts of Class B4 and would have included traffic to and from Cattewater branches. That sort of balanced reciprocal working between railways was quite common prior to nationalisation.

Reference has already been made to the N class Woolwich Moguls on passenger work. Exmouth Junction had a complete batch from 1826 to 1860, (with the exception of 1851 which was always at Salisbury) although some were for various periods sub-shedded to Barnstaple or Wadebridge. The class was responsible for all the main line freight traffic. In the Working Timetables the terminology was Freight trains on the Southern, but Goods trains on the Great Western.

An interesting train was the 8.07pm freight from Friary to Okehampton which was worked by a Class 700 0-6-0 tender engine, the last of that wheel arrangement to have a rostered regular duty in Plymouth. It probably arrived on the previous night's 8.55pm from Yeoford which stood at Devonport from 3.42am until 6.50am, arriving at Friary at 7.08am. The working was taken over by a Woolwich mogul early in the 1930s rumour being that the 0-6-0 had broken its connecting rod somewhere near Okehampton.

To conclude this chapter I have included two interesting footnotes which appear in the Working Timetable for the summer of 1932.

"The 11.37am from Exeter (Queen Street) calls at Meldon Quarry Platform on Fridays to set down a representative of the Engineers Department" and "On Saturdays, when required, the wives of the Company's employees returning from Okehampton". The wives had been picked up earlier in the morning by a special call by the 7.39am from Launceston.

"The 12.50am Newspaper train from Friary to Exmouth Junction to take newspapers for Bow and North Tawton on to Yeoford and returned by the 1.38am from Exmouth Junction Sidings".

700 class no E688 at Friary shed in April 1924. *F H C Casbourne/Stephenson Locomotive Society*

15. THE SOUTHERN RAILWAY BRANCHES

1. Turnchapel

From Friary station it was but 2½ miles to Turnchapel, a small village beside Hooe Lake, serving en route small communities at Plymstock and Oreston. The first train from Friary was at 5.35am, returning at 5.55am from Turnchapel. As it was only a ten minute journey there was a connection at 6.11am from Friary, all stations and halts to St. Budeaux – very much a workmens service, especially for the Yardees. Overall, there were 26 trains each way daily at irregular intervals, plus one Saturdays excepted and one additional on Wednesdays and Saturdays only, reflecting that Wednesday was an Early Closing Day, very much adhered to in the 1930s, even by the big departmental stores.

The Saturdays excepted service was at 5.39 from Friary which followed the 5.25 and was the only occasion when there were two timetabled passenger trains on the single line branch at the same time. The returning 5.25 crossed the outward 5.39 at Plymstock at 5.44 and 5.43 respectively according to the published timetable. The problem was that there was only one platform on the Turnchapel branch at Plymstock, so presumably the inward bound train passed through the platform and reversed to stand at the Yealmpton branch platform to allow the other train to pass. Sometime between 1934 and 1938 that unsatisfactory situation had been corrected by retaining the 5.25 at Turnchapel until 6.27 and returning the 5.39 back to Friary immediately after arrival at Turnchapel.

There were also 17 trains on Sundays commencing with the 9.15am from Friary. Both on week-days and Sundays the last train from Friary was at 11pm.

What is so extraordinary about the lavish service serving the three village communities is that there was competition. No! not only from the buses but from the sea! The Oreston and Turnchapel Steamboat Company (better known as the P & O Liners!) operated a 20 minute frequency ferry boat service from 8am until 10.30pm between the two villages and Plymouth Phoenix Wharf, adjacent to the Mayflower Stone in Sutton Harbour. For most purposes there was not much to choose between Friary Station and Phoenix Wharf for convenience except, perhaps, there was an adjacent tram service at Friary into the city centre, a mere five minute's walk.

The ferry company used vintage vessels of 1895 construction, namely Dart, Lively, Rapid and Swift. The Western National Omnibus Company provided a bus service with a 30 minute frequency to Hooe Lake, advertised as ¼ mile to Turnchapel station, but on the other hand, took their passengers to the Plymouth town centre.

The Turnchapel Branch had one thing in common with the Launceston Branch in as much as the area surrounding Turnchapel station was very popular with day trippers. There was the shingle Jennycliff beach, which by to-day's standards would be condemned out of hand. There was space for picnicking on Staddon Heights overlooking Plymouth Sound and it was very good walking country.

Little more than half a mile out from Friary there was Lucas Terrace Halt. On summer week-ends and Bank Holidays the platform would be lined with day trippers drawn from populace of high density Prince Rock and from the Beaumont Road area. At the end of the day the railway abandoned the timetable and ran a shuttle service to get the crowds home. The trains were exclusively worked by Adams 02 0-4-4Ts with two auto

B358 Stroudley class D1 at Friary Station whilst allocated to Plymouth for working the Turnchapel Branch. Circa 1930-31.

F H C Casbourn/Stephenson Locomotive Society

SOUTHERN–Western Section 360

PLYMOUTH and TURNCHAPEL (3rd class only).

Week Days.

Mls.		mrn	mrn	mrn	mrn	mrn	mrn	mrn	mrn	mrn	mrn	aft	aft	aft	aft	WSO	aft	aft	aft	aft	S X	aft	aft
	Plymouth (Friary)..dep.	5 35	6 18	6 48	7 18	7 50	8 16	8 48	9 40	1040	1127	1215	1248	1 22	2 6	2 40	3 17	4 22	4 57	5 25	5 39	6 6	6 40
¾	Lucas Terrace Halt.....	5 37	6 20	6 49	7 19	7 51	8 17	8 49	9 41	1041	1128	1216	1249	1 24	2 6	2 41	3 18	4 23	4 58	5 26	5 40	6 7	6 41
1½	Plymstock.............	5 42	6 23	6 53	7 23	7 55	8 21	8 53	9 45	1045	1132	1220	1253	1 27	2 10	2 45	3 22	4 27	5 2	5 30	5 44	6 11	6 45
2	Oreston...............	5 44	6 25	6 55	7 25	7 57	8 23	8 55	9 47	1047	1134	1222	1255	1 29	2 12	2 47	3 24	4 29	5 4	5 32	5 46	6 13	6 47
2¼	**Turnchapel**.........arr.	5 47	6 28	6 58	7 28	8 0	8 26	8 58	9 50	1050	1137	1225	1258	1 32	2 15	2 50	3 27	4 32	5 7	5 35	5 49	6 16	6 50

	Week Days—Contd.						Sundays.																
	aft	aft	aft	aft	aft	aft	mrn	mrn	mrn	mrn	aft	aft	aft	aft	aft	aft	aft	aft	aft	aft	aft	aft	aft
Plymouth (Friary)..dep.	7 30	8 25	9 9	9 55	1031	11 0	9 15	1010	1045	1125	1240	1 20	2 25	3 10	3 45	4 55	5 40	6 55	7 50	8 45	9 18	1020	11 0
Lucas Terrace Halt.....	7 31	8 26	9 10	9 56	1032	11 1	9 16	1011	1046	1126	1241	1 21	2 26	3 11	3 46	4 56	5 41	6 56	7 51	8 46	9 19	1021	11 1
Plymstock.............	7 35	8 30	9 14	10 0	1036	11 6	9 20	1015	1050	1130	1245	1 25	2 30	3 15	3 50	5 0	5 45	7 0	7 55	8 50	9 23	1025	11 7
Oreston...............	7 37	8 32	9 16	10 2	1038	11 9	9 22	1017	1052	1132	1247	1 27	2 32	3 17	3 52	5 2	5 47	7 2	7 57	8 52	9 25	1027	1110
Turnchapel.........arr.	7 40	8 35	9 19	10 5	1041	1113	9 25	1020	1055	1135	1250	1 30	2 35	3 20	3 55	5 5	5 50	7 5	8 0	8 55	9 28	1030	1113

Week Days.

Mls.		mrn	mrn	mrn	mrn	mrn	mrn	mrn	mrn	mrn	mrn	aft	aft	aft	aft	WSO	aft	aft	aft	aft	aft	S X	aft
—	**Turnchapel**........dep.	5 55	6 33	7 3	7 32	8 2	8 29	9 3	9 56	11 3	1142	1228	1 3	1 39	2 20	2 53	3 30	4 35	5 9	5 52	6 18	6 27	7 7
¼	Oreston...............	5 56	6 34	7 4	7 33	8 3	8 30	9 4	9 57	11 4	1143	1229	1 4	1 40	2 21	2 54	3 31	4 36	5 10	5 53	6 19	6 28	7 8
1	Plymstock.............	5 59	6 37	7 7	7 36	8 6	8 33	9 7	10 0	11 7	1146	1222	1 7	1 43	2 24	2 57	3 34	4 39	5 13	5 56	6 22	6 31	7 11
2	Lucas Terrace Halt.....	6 2	6 40	7 10	7 39	8 9	8 36	9 10	10 3	1110	1149	1235	1 10	1 46	2 27	3 0	3 37	4 42	5 16	5 59	6 25	6 34	7 14
2¼	**Plymouth**(Fr'ry) 348 arr.	6 5	6 43	7 13	7 42	8 12	8 39	9 13	10 6	1113	1152	1238	1 13	1 49	2 30	3 3	3 40	4 45	5 19	6 2	6 28	6 37	7 17

	Week Days—Contd						Sundays.																
	aft	aft	aft	aft	aft	aft	mrn	mrn	mrn	mrn	aft	aft	aft	aft	aft	aft	aft	aft	aft	aft	aft	aft	aft
Turnchapel.........dep.	8 5	8 40	9 22	1015	1043	1118	9 30	1025	11 5	1145	1255	1 40	2 40	3 25	4 0	5 10	6 0	7 20	8 5	9 0	9 40	1040	1118
Oreston...............	8 6	8 41	9 23	1016	1044	1119	9 31	1026	11 6	1146	1256	1 41	2 41	3 26	4 1	5 11	6 1	7 21	8 6	9 1	9 41	1041	1119
Plymstock.............	8 9	8 44	9 26	1019	1047	1122	9 33	1028	11 8	1148	1258	1 43	2 43	3 28	4 3	5 13	6 3	7 23	8 8	9 3	9 43	1043	1122
Lucas Terrace Halt.....	8 12	8 47	9 29	1022	1050	1126	9 37	1032	1112	1152	1 2	1 47	2 47	3 32	4 7	5 17	6 7	7 27	8 12	9 7	9 47	1047	1126
Plymouth(Fr'ry) 348 arr.	8 15	8 50	9 32	1025	1053	1130	9 40	1035	1115	1155	1 5	1 50	2 50	3 35	4 10	5 20	6 10	7 30	8 15	9 10	9 50	1050	1130

S X Saturdays excepted. WSO Weds. and Sats. only.

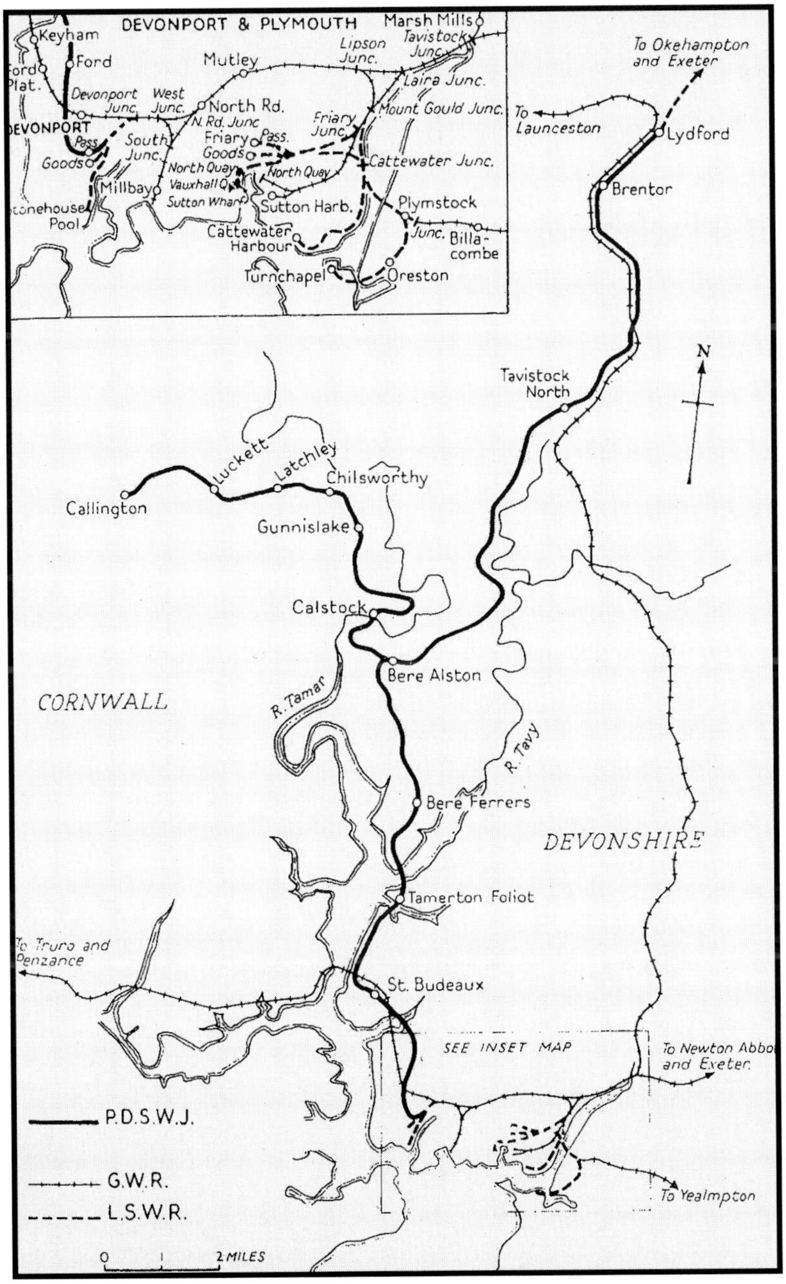

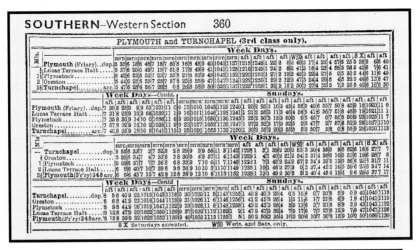

The Plymouth Devonport and South Western Railway Oakwood Press (1967)

Callington Station from the buffers end. *M J Dart collection*

fitted gate stock coaches well remembered by a small boy in short trousers sitting on horse hair seats. Gate stock was so called because entry/exit was effected by means of an off centre positioned metal gate open, to the elements, leading into the centre gangway seating accommodation. Perfectly safe in those days.

During the early 1930s the railway transferred in two former London Brighton and South Coast Railway (LB&SCR) Stroudley Class D1 0-4-2Ts B259 and B358 of 1882 vintage. (The Southern Railway in Plymouth survived largely on vintage motive power). The two Stroudleys worked the Turnchapel branch for about two years then returned from whence they came.

There was one afternoon freight train which ran on a "As Required" basis, worked by a Class B4 0-4-0T. There were three sources of traffic:

1. Bailey's siding. Baileys were timber merchants and the memory is very clear of timber floating on Hooe Lake whilst being thoroughly seasoned.
2. The branch was extended beyond Turnchapel Station by ten chains of heavily engineered track, through a short tunnel a deep cutting and a level crossing into an Admiralty establishment known officially as Turnchapel Wharf and situated on the opposite side of the Plym estuary to Victoria Wharf.
3. There was provision for coal and other freight at Plymstock and Oreston.

2. Callington

The first thing to be said is that the Branch from Bere Alston did not go to Callington but to Kelly Bray about a mile down the road.

In order to fully understand the economics of the Branch we will first look at the summer 1998 edition of the Great Britain Bus Timetable. Even to-day there is no bus service to Plymouth from Bere Ferrers, Bere Alston, Calstock or Gunnislake; the buses all go to Tavistock. Furthermore, there are only seven bus services between Callington and Plymouth. Turn to the road map, and except for Callington, it is still in 1998 a long detour to get into Plymouth. Turn that back to the 1930s when cars were still a luxury and the country roads undeveloped, then it can be understood that the Southern Railway had a virtual monopoly for both passenger and freight traffic on the branch. It also explains why the rail service still survives albeit only as far as Gunnislake. Additionally, it elaborates upon why it was necessary to run two morning commuter trains into Plymouth, the first, arriving at 8.29 starting from Bere Alston. (See Chapter 14).

The Southern inherited the branch at Grouping from the Plymouth Devonport and South Western Junction Railway together with its three engines, all constructed by Hawthorn Leslie in 1907.

0-6-0T	756	*A.S. Harris*
0-6-2T	757	*Earl of Mount Edgcumbe*
0-6-2T	758	*Lord St Levan*

758 *Lord St Levan* at Callington. Circa 1935. *M J Dart collection*

PSWJR 757 *Earl of Mount Edgcumbe* on the Callington Branch goods at Chilsworthy. *H W Adams*

Early on 756 departed for pastures new, never to return, whilst the other two were mainly employed on the freight traffic on the basis of one in steam and the other spare at Friary. Despite what has been said elsewhere, at least during the 1930s the spare engine was only seen through North Road station on extremely rare occasions.

The passenger trains became a natural for the small Adams Class 02 0-4-4Ts despite the fact that by the end of the 1930s they had all well passed their 40th birthdays.

During the season there was heavy traffic in Tamar Valley produce, flowers and, more particularly, strawberries. To give assistance even more elderly Adams engines were drafted in from Exmouth Junction in the shape of the 0395 Class 0-6-0s of 1881 vintage. They were serviced at Friary and could be seen running light engine to and from the Callington Branch.

Local enthusiasts rarely visited the Branch and therefore there are few memories to recall.

Finally, there was a short freight branch from Devonport Southern Station to Stonehouse Pool, from whence the LSWR had grand plans to capture some of the lucrative trans Atlantic traffic from the Great Western. That came to an unhappy end after the tragic Boat Train derailed at speed at Salisbury in 1906. There were 28 fatalities. By 1932 the remaining traffic on the Stonehouse Pool branch was probably very sparse. Although there were three paths available on the branch they were annotated to run as required. For us, railway enthusiasts as we were, we knew nothing of the Stonehouse Pool line, for even to us the Southern was the poor relation.

029 an Adams 0-6-0 constructed in 1885, and on the LSWR duplicate list since 1904. Seen here at Bere Alston, no doubt, on loan from Exmouth Jct to assist with the strawberry traffic on the Callington Branch. Circa 1930.

M.J Dart collection

16. EXCURSIONS

Many of the Restored Railways either have the original style booking offices which they inherited from British Rail, or they have realistic replicas. Original, or replica, they have a polished wood exterior, floor to ceiling, with one or more pigeon hole windows forming a barrier between the booking clerk and the passenger. One thing every booking office lacks on a Restored Railway is the row of leaflets strung up slightly above eye level advertising the various excursions currently on offer. The leaflets were printed on poor quality paper, sometimes tinted in pastel shades. The interested excursionist selected and plucked from the appropriate bundle suspended in front of him. Late offers, or those one off special offers were usually cyclostyled on to white foolscap duplicating paper and were often decidedly unprofessional in appearance.

Excursions fell broadly into three categories, day excursions, half day excursions and evening excursions. By inter railway agreement, half day excursions could not run before 9.30am and evening excursions before 4.30pm. The day excursions to Paddington, valid on the up midnight on Friday night and valid to return on any train up to the down midnight from Paddington on Saturday night were 17/6 (87½p) whereas the half day Sunday excursions by special train were only 12/6 (62½p). Apart from the Woolworths, probably the most popular of the evening excursion was to Newquay for half a crown (12½p).

According to an article in the Great Western Railway Magazine for April 1933, justification for Sunday excursions included provision for the self employed to get away for the day "having to attend to their business affairs for six days each week". Sunday excursions also afforded an opportunity for those who were not able to have a holiday at all. In effect, that meant those in employment without any entitlement to any holiday at all. It was not until the Holidays with Pay Act of 1938 that all employees were entitled to one week's annual holiday with pay. It was estimated at the time that several million became entitled to a holiday with pay for the first time.

According to the 1932 WTT, the Southern ran half day excursions each Sunday during the currency of the summer timetable, leaving Friary Station at 10am. There were four destinations, each in rotations, to Ilfracombe, Bude, Exeter and Bournemouth. The Exeter train provided a connection for Exmouth. Ordinary ticket holders were permitted to use those trains for stations between Friary and Okehampton. It was a good day out with mid evening departures from the resorts and a late arrival home. There was also a monthly day trip to Portsmouth and a half day to Waterloo annotated to run as required. An outstanding feature of the Waterloo train was that it was timetabled to run non-stop from Devonport to Exeter St. Davids. The excursions are summarised below with the arrival times at the resorts shown where known.

The Bournemouth train travelled via Templecombe and the Somerset and Dorset Joint Line.

Excursionists were hardy folk in those days, especially if it was an outing for the children to the seaside. What would one do in, say, Bude until 8.10pm if the weather turned wet after lunch, bearing in mind that weather forecasts (if any) were very much hit and miss affairs before the War. Even worse if it was a Sunday.

Friary	7.40am	Portsmouth	arr		dpt	7.53pm	Friary arr	1.11am
	9.50am	Waterloo				11.20pm		4.22am
	10.00am	Ilfracombe		1.36pm		7.20pm		10.51pm
	10.00am	Bude		12.21pm		8.10pm		10.33pm
	10.00am	Exeter		12.04pm		8.47pm		10.51pm

A perusal of the Great Western half day excursions for August 1939 reveals that such marathons were regular occurrences. Examples are:

Millbay	11.25am				
	Paignton	arr	12.56pm	dpt	8.35pm
	Millbay	arr	10.20pm	Fare	3/2 (16p)
Millbay	11.5am				
	Newquay	arr	1.25pm	dpt	8.10pm
	Millbay	arr	10.35pm	Fare	4/2 (21p)
Millbay	9.50am				
	Weymouth	arr	2.20pm	dpt	9.30pm
	Millbay	arr	2am	Fare	7/9 (38p)

The Weymouth train travelled via Durston and Yeovil (Pen Mill) and the return train was extended to Saltash, that is after a reversal at Millbay with a new engine on the other end.

For real marathons we have to turn to one off excursions all the way from Plymouth to Scotland using timetabled trains. The occasion was the British Empire Exhibition held at the Bellahouston Park, Glasgow. The Exhibition ran from Spring through to the Autumn in 1938. Mid-week tickets were available for 32/- (£1.60) by through coach on Wednesdays August 31st and September 14th with the following timings:

depart North Road	3.55pm Wednesday
arrive Glasgow Central	6.25am Thursday
	Through coach
depart Glasgow Central	5.40pm
arrive North Road	10.5am Friday
	Through coach

If the return train at 5.40pm was, perhaps, a little early, travel was permitted on the 11.25pm from Glasgow which finally brought the weary excursionist into North Road at 5.55pm, a journey of no less than 18½ hours. To be fair, the pamphlet warned that there would be a wait of one hour, two minutes at Preston in the early hours between 4.33am and 5.35am and almost three more hours at Crewe from 7.36am until 10.32am.

Excursions were also advertised on two dates on Fridays, up on the 3.55pm and returning on the Saturday night/Sunday mornings when the journey time was even worse. The 5.40pm through coach from Glasgow did not reach Plymouth until 11.56am, Sunday mid-day, an almost unbelievable time of 18¼ hours. The 11.25pm departure was even worse still than that not getting the traveller into North Road until 8.15pm on Sunday night after just 10 minutes short of 21 hours, or two days four hours and twenty minutes after setting out on Friday afternoon. In that case, the pamphlet failed to warn that there was a four hour wait at Preston in the small hours. The returning excursionist eventually joined the 11.55am through train at Crewe which took no less than 8 hours 22 minutes to reach North Road via Wem and the Severn Tunnel. Wem, an insignificant station between Crewe and Shrewsbury, which together with the Severn Tunnel, formed a restrictive route for ticket validity.

On 17th March 1939 there was a through excursion train to Edinburgh for the Scotland v England Rugby match at Murrayfield. Timings were as follows:

Friday	Plymouth North Road	dpt	8.10pm
Saturday	Edinburgh Princes St	arr	10.05am
Sunday	Edinburgh Princes St	dep	12.45pm
	Plymouth North Road	arr	2.45pm

14 hours each way for 30/3 (£1.51). Children age 3 and under 14 half price Children under three years of age Free.

Getting our feet back on to terra firma, always popular was the annual trip to Fry's chocolate factory at Keynsham and Somerdale for 9/3 (46p). The trip included a tour of the factory, followed by a dainty tea in the factory dining room, a box of chocolates and a short coach tour into the Somerset and Gloucestershire countryside. All for 9/3. (See "The Railways of Keynsham" RCTS 1997). The return train did not leave Bristol until 9.5pm and got back into Millbay at 1am where Corporation buses met the train. In pre-war days that would not be an unusual arrangement. The bus conductor would establish the various destinations for his passengers and, together with the driver, arrange a route of travel with complete disregard for conventional day time bus routes. The fare charged would be double, if not treble the normal day time fare for the distance travelled.

What was probably the greatest innovation for the decade was a joint effort between the Southern and Great Western Railways when, on Sunday 10th September 1933, they organised a sightseeing excursion from Exeter to Plymouth, out on the Southern via Okehampton, and back on the Great Western via Teignmouth and Dawlish. The fare was 4/- (20p). A restaurant car was provided catering for lunch, tea and light refreshments. It as certainly a sight for local enthusiasts to see Southern Greyhounds 732 and 733 climbing Hemerdon Bank on the way home.

As we have already noted, the word "Excursion" had quite an elastic interpretation. The GWR produced each summer a booklet varying in size from 24 to 28 pages entitled "Road and Rail Excursions and Timetables", of which there were several editions covering various geographical areas. The Totnes and Plymouth edition included:

1. A fare chart, 1st and 3rd class, for day return tickets from Totnes and Plymouth stations to all stations and halts in GWR Devon and Cornwall, Exeter and West thereof. Cheap Day Return tickets were issued at the single fare for the double journey, but they were not valid on the Cornish Riviera Express.
2. A complete main line timetable between Exeter and Truro, including arrival/departures times at Torquay/Paignton and Cornish branch line termini.
3. GWR operated bus timetables, which were continued after 1934 when the railway handed over the routes to other operators. (See also Chapter 6).

A comparison of day return fares between those of 1929 and those of 1939, eleven years later, show quite small increases. Examples:

		1929	1939	Inc
Millbay	to Penzance	10/- (50p)	10/6 (52½p)	5%
	to Princetown	2/9 (13p)	2/11 (14½p)	6%
	to Torquay	5/- (25p)	5/3 (26½p)	6%
	to Saltash	6d (2½p)	6½d (3p)	7½%

It was often cheaper to travel from North Road rather than Millbay. In 1939 the fare to Torquay was 3d cheaper from North Road, but passengers could avoid the extra at Millbay by taking a ticket to the less convenient station at Torre which was 3d cheaper than Torquay. From North Road, the fare to both stations was the same at 5/- Although three old pence seems an insignificant sum of money to those who have lived through the years of inflation, remember that an old penny would buy a cup of tea or even a Cornish pasty.

During the August Bank Holiday week the Dockyard shut down and the Yardees enjoyed their seven day annual holiday. Whilst they were on holiday the Dockyard was open to the public (in selected areas) for Navy Days, always a popular event. That brought an influx of excursion traffic into Plymouth from far and wide, some trains running through to Keyham where the station was situated right opposite the Dockyard gates. Otherwise, incoming excursions were generally run of the mill, but of significance were the annual day excursions from Swansea and Cardiff, both of which usually produced rare Saint 4-6-0s from Landore and Canton respectively.

Of even more significance were the Swindon Trip

WEDNESDAY, AUGUST 2nd

To FOWEY, PAR, NEWQUAY, ST. AUSTELL TRURO, PENRYN and FALMOUTH

Leaving at	From	Return Fares—Third Class: Fowey, Par or St. Austell	Return Fares—Third Class: Newquay or Truro	Return Fares—Third Class: Penryn or Falmouth	Return Train due back
a.m.		s. d.	s. d.	s. d.	p.m.
11 0	**PLYMOUTH (Millbay)**	3 2	4 2	4 9	9 55
11 5	DEVONPORT	3 2	4 2	4 9	9 50
11 10	KEYHAM	3 2	4 2	4 9	9 45
11 15	ST. BUDEAUX	3 2	4 2	4 9	9 40
11 20	SALTASH	3 2	4 2	4 9	9 35

ARRIVE—FOWEY 12-53 p.m., PAR 12-15 p.m., NEWQUAY 1-30 p.m., ST. AUSTELL 12-25 p.m., TRURO 12-55 p.m., PENRYN 1-25 p.m., and FALMOUTH 1-35 p.m.

RETURN—FALMOUTH 7-25 p.m., PENRYN 7-35 p.m., TRURO 8-0 p.m., ST. AUSTELL 8-25 p.m., NEWQUAY 7-15 p.m., PAR 8-40 p.m., and FOWEY 8†42 p.m.

*†—Passengers returning from Fowey arrive Saltash 9-56 p.m., St. Budeaux 10***A***9 p.m., Keyham 10***A***12 p.m., Devonport 10-4 p.m., and Millbay 10***B***27 p.m.*

A—*Change at Saltash.* **B**—*Change at Devonport.*

THURSDAY, AUGUST 3rd

To NEWTON ABBOT, TORQUAY, PAIGNTON and GOODRINGTON SANDS

Leaving at	From	Return Fares—Third Class: Newton Abbot	Return Fares—Third Class: Torquay, Paignton or Goodrington Sands	Return Train due back
a.m.		s. d.	s. d.	p.m.
11 0	SALTASH	3 2	3 2	10† 43
11 4	ST. BUDEAUX	3 2	3 2	10† 39
11 7	KEYHAM	3 2	3 2	10† 36
11 13	DEVONPORT	3 2	3 2	10† 30
11 25	**PLYMOUTH (Millbay)**	3 2	3 2	10 20
11 30	**PLYMOUTH (North Road)**	3 2	3 2	10 10
11 35	PLYMPTON	2 8	3 2	10 0

ARRIVE—NEWTON ABBOT 12-30 p.m., TORQUAY 12-50 p.m., PAIGNTON 12-56 p.m., and GOODRINGTON SANDS 1-0 p.m.

RETURN—GOODRINGTON SANDS 8-30 p.m., PAIGNTON 8-35 p.m., TORQUAY 8-45 p.m., and NEWTON ABBOT 9-10 p.m.

†—Change at Millbay.

EVERY SUNDAY

HALF-DAY EXCURSIONS, PLYMOUTH TO

LOOE 2s. 8d., FOWEY 3s. 2d., PAR 3s. 2d. and NEWQUAY 4s. 2d.

For full details see separate announcement

GWR

Attractive

HALF-DAY
EXCURSIONS

from

PLYMOUTH
DISTRICT
PLYMPTON
IVYBRIDGE
BRENT and
TOTNES

During AUGUST

Paddington Station,
July, 1939

JAMES MILNE,
General Manager.

EMPIRE EXHIBITION

AT BELLAHOUSTON PARK

GLASGOW

WEDNESDAYS, AUG. 31ST & SEPT. 14TH

LIMITED EXCURSION

TO

GLASGOW

Via SEVERN TUNNEL, CREWE & L.M.S.RAILWAY

Return Fare **32/-** Including ADMISSION to the EXHIBITION

Forward	A	
PLYMOUTH (North Road)	dep. 3.55pm	
GLASGOW (Central)	arr. 6.25am (Thurs)	
Return (Thursday)	**A**	**B**
GLASGOW (Central)	dep. 5.40pm	11.25pm
PLYMOUTH (North Rd)	arr. 10* 5am	5*55pm

NOTES - A. Through Coach. B - Change at Preston and Crewe. A wait is involved at the former station from 4.33am until 5.35am (Friday) and at the latter station from 7.36am until 10.32am. * - Friday

To reach the EXHIBITION, passengers travel by any train between GLASGOW (Central) or (St.Enoch) to Ibrox and from St.Enoch to BELLAHOUSTON PARK without additional charge.

Paddington Station.
August, 1938.

James Milne,
General Manager.

trains, a major feat of organisation to get the Swindon Works employees and their families off on to their annual holidays for the period of the annual Works shut down. As may be expected West of England resorts were among the popular destinations, so that there were usually three trains for Plymouth and Cornwall. The engines which had set out at dawn with their happy throng could be seen at the coaling stage at Laira by breakfast time. An obligatory visit to Laira was required because at least one, sometimes two, were in pristine ex works condition and, occasionally, from some far distant shed and therefore real cops.

From a report in the Great Western Railway Magazine in 1932 no less than 45% of the population of Swindon went on the Trip that year, a total of 18,544 men, women and children. Popular resorts included Weymouth which attracted 5050 trippers, and Weston Super Mare 4320. A total for Devon and Cornwall was not shown, but 480 made it to Penzance.

No record of the history of the railways in Plymouth during the 1930s would be complete without mention of the Seven Day Holiday Season Ticket. It brought a new dimension to holidays in a period when money was scarce and seven days was the extent of the annual holiday granted by employers to so many, the Dockyard included. In fact, it was a social revolution.

The Great Western put its toe in the water during the late 1920s, but it made little impact in Plymouth. Area No. 4 only covered the main line between Devonport and Totnes, together with the branches to Kingsbridge and Ashburton. The cost was 10/- (50p) for seven days unlimited travel. It was in 1933 for the same price (subsequently increased to 10/6 (52½p) that the area was extended west to include St. Budeaux, and east to the holiday resorts of Torquay, Paignton, Teignmouth and Dawlish that the idea finally took off. Such was the demand, that two special trains had to be provided from late July until the end of August. That had to be increased to a third train during August Bank Holiday Week, which as already mentioned, included the Dockyard holiday week.

Although the special trains set out from Saltash, that station was outside the ticket area. The trains called to pick up in the morning, and set down at the end of the day at St. Budeaux Platform, Keyham and Devonport as well as at North Road. No doubt, some Saltash residents purchased Cheap Day Returns to St. Budeaux – they would not have got past the Saltash barrier without. As we have already noted, excursionists were amenable to long days, so that the second return train did not get back into Millbay until nearly ten o'clock, where those for stations to Saltash needed to change into the 10pm Rail Motor. Late to bed and early to rise next morning for the 8.35 or 9.55.

Motive power was either a Castle or a Hall, or a Grange when they became available.

The special trains ran as under in 1938 on WEEK-DAYS ONLY. No special arrangements were made for the comparatively few who travelled on Sundays.

		SX	W SX	SO
Saltash	8.35	9.45	9.55	10.18
North Road	9.0	10.5	10.15	10.40
Newton Abbot	9.56	10.55	11.3	11.35
Torre	10.12	11.13	11.20*	11.54
Torquay	10.15	11.15	11.22*	11.58
Paignton	10.23	11.24	11.30*	12.5
Teignmouth			11.17	
Dawlish			11.27	
Exeter			11.49	
Duration	1st-27th August	1st-5th August	25th July 26th August	30th July to 27th August

*Excluding 1st-5th August

Exeter	6.10SX	
Dawlish	6.36SX	
Teignmouth	6.44SX	
Paignton	6.30	8.10
Torquay	6.37	8.17
Torre	6.41	8.23
Newton Abbot	7.0	8.45
North Road	7.50	9.40
Millbay		9.46
Saltash	8.15	
	W	
Duration 25th July 27th August		1st - 27th August

W = The train stabled overnight at Wearde Sidings. The two portions, Exeter and Paignton divided at Newton Abbot and combined there on the return journey.

Both Saltash and Exeter were outside the ticket's validity Paignton trains terminated there and commenced their return journeys from there.

28

HOLIDAY SEASON TICKETS

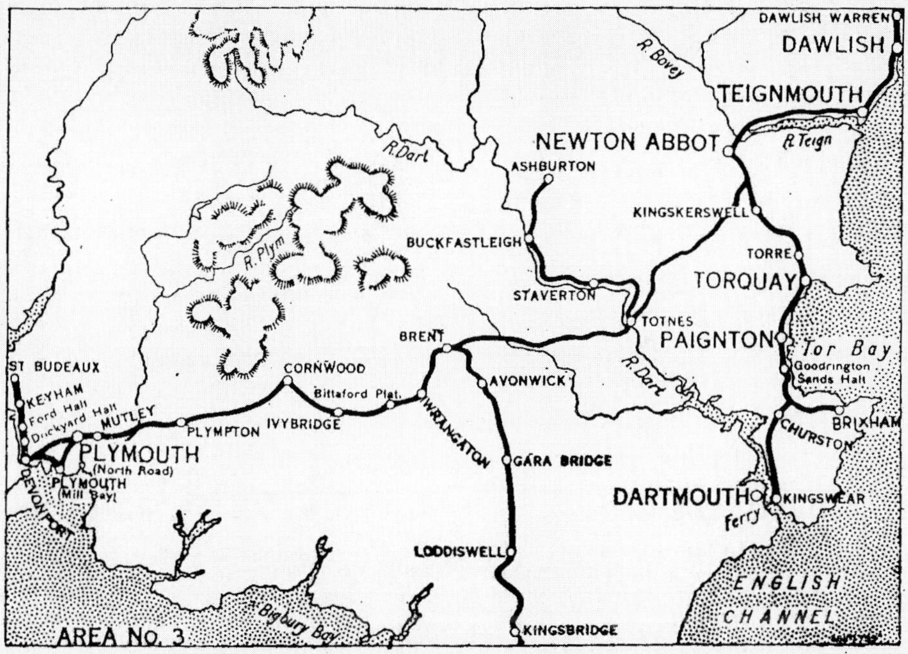

FIRST 15/9 CLASS

THIRD 10/6 CLASS

HOLIDAY SEASON TICKETS enable Tourists to make any number of Trips between the Stations in the area covered by the Ticket.

No. of Ticket.	AREA COVERED BY TICKET.	FARES FOR 7 DAYS. 1st. s. d.	3rd. s. d.
1	Penzance, St. Ives, Helston, Newquay, Truro, Falmouth	15 9	10 6
2	Truro, Fowey, Bodmin Road, Bodmin, Newquay, Chacewater, Falmouth	15 9	10 6
3	St. Budeaux Platform, Devonport, Plymouth, Kingsbridge, Ashburton, Dartmouth, Kingswear, Brixham, Torquay, Dawlish, Dawlish Warren	15 9	10 6
3a	As for No. 3 and including the River Dart—Totnes to Dartmouth	18 3	13 0
4	Ashburton, Totnes, Dartmouth, Kingswear, Brixham, Moretonhampstead, Teign Valley Line, Teignmouth, Exeter	15 9	10 6
4a	As for No. 4 and including the River Dart—Totnes to Dartmouth	18 3	13 0
20	Dartmouth, Kingswear, Brixham, Totnes, Teignmouth, Exeter, Sidmouth Junction, Sidmouth, Honiton, Exmouth	18 6	13 3
20a	As for No. 20 and including the River Dart—Totnes to Dartmouth	21 0	15 9
25	Fowey, Bodmin, Looe, Plymouth, Turnchapel, Bere Alston, Callington, Okehampton, Princetown, Tavistock	18 6	13 3

THE TICKET FOR YOUR HOLIDAY !

THE CHEAPEST MODE OF TRAVEL

SEVEN DAYS UNLIMITED TRAVEL

The back cover of the GWR Rail and Road Excursions and Time Tables booklet. Plymouth and Totnes edition. Summer 1939

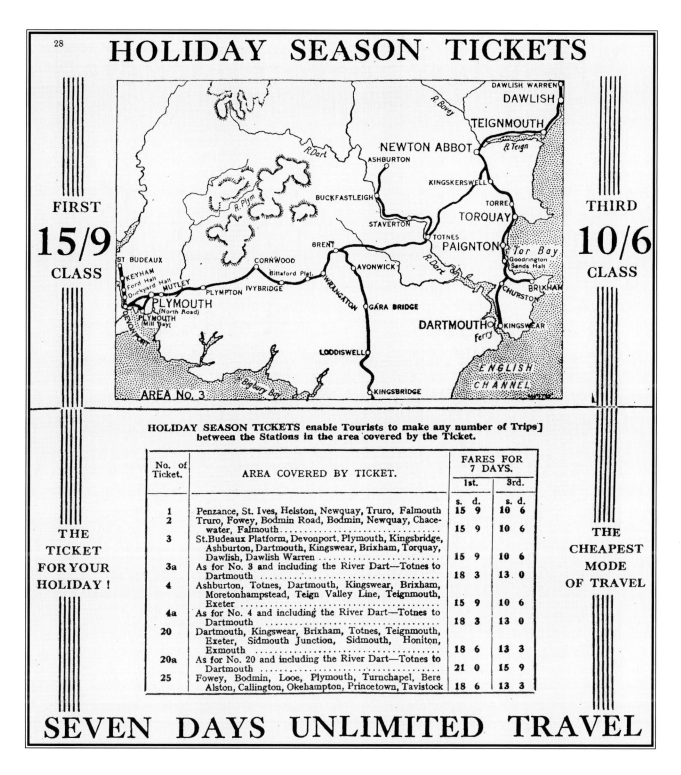

16

Holiday Season Tickets

7 DAYS UNLIMITED TRAVEL

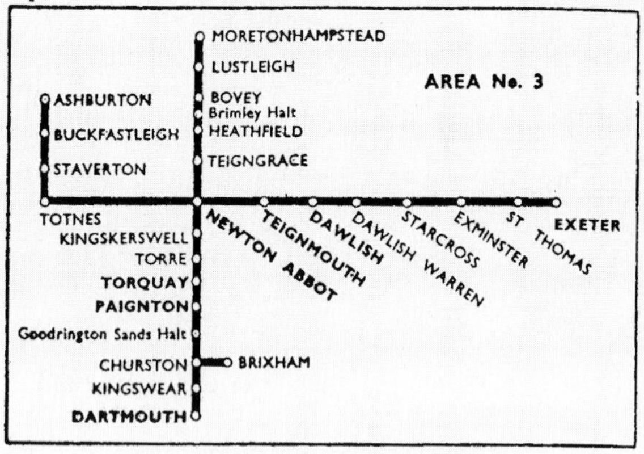

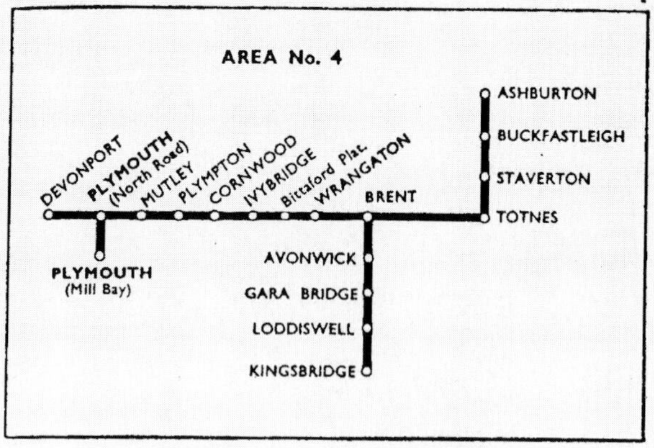

17/6 1st Class. 12/6 3rd Class. 15/- 1st Class. 10/- 3rd Class.

AREAS Nos. 3A and 4A available between the same Stations as Nos. 3 and 4 and including RIVER DART 2/6 extra.

WEEKLY SEASON TICKETS

ARE ISSUED BETWEEN ANY PAIR OF STATIONS IN THE AREA,

DARTMOUTH, MORETONHAMPSTEAD AND EXETER

For full particulars, see handbills obtainable at the Stations or Receiving Offices,

CONDITIONS OF ISSUE OF EXCURSION TICKETS AND OTHER TICKETS AT FARES LESS THAN ORDINARY FARES.

These Tickets are issued subject to the Conditions of Issue of Ordinary Passenger Tickets, where applicable, and also on the following conditions :—

Neither the holder nor any other person shall have any right of action against the Company or any other Railway Company or person, owning, working, or using any railway, vehicles, vessels or premises (whether jointly with the Company or otherwise) upon which such tickets may be available in respect of (*a*) injury (fatal or otherwise), loss, damage or delay however caused, or (*b*) loss of or damage or delay to property however caused.

The tickets are available only by the trains and on the days specified in the Company's Notices.

A ticket which covers the outward and return journey shall not be used for the return journey unless and until the outward journey has been completed. The tickets are not transferable.

If a ticket is used in contravention of these conditions, the holder will be required to pay the difference between the sum actually paid for the ticket and the full ordinary fare between the stations named on such ticket.

TICKETS ARE NOT TRANSFERABLE.

LUGGAGE ARRANGEMENTS.—Passengers holding Cheap Day Tickets may carry with them 60 lbs. of marketing goods at Owner's Risk, free of charge, all excess over that weight to be charged for.

Passengers returning from Shopping Centres may take with them, free of charge, at Owner's Risk, articles not exceeding in the aggregate 120 lbs. (1st class) or 60 lbs. (3rd class) which they have purchased for their own domestic use.

NO LUGGAGE OTHERWISE ALLOWED.

DOGS.—Dogs accompanying passengers are charged for at the Single Rate for the Double Journey, tickets available on day of issue or from Saturday to Monday (when tickets held by passenger are also so available).

The charge for a Dog accompanying the holder of a Walking Tour ticket is based on the greater (outward or return) distance.

NOTE.—Several of the Trains shown in this Folder will not run on August Bank Holiday, and others will run at altered times. Passengers desiring to avail themselves of Cheap Tickets on this day should see Special Pamphlets and Handbills.

Cheltenham Press, Ltd., Cheltenham and London.

GWR Timetables and Excursions booklet
Newton Abbot and Totnes edition. Summer 1931

Excursion and Cheap Tickets are issued

TO	FROM: Plymouth (Millbay) — FARES 1st	Plymouth (Millbay) 3rd	Plymouth (North Rd.) 1st	Plymouth (North Rd.) 3rd	Mutley 1st	Mutley 3rd
	s. d.	s. d.	s. d.	s. d.	s. d.	s. d.
Ashburton (* C)	7 0	4 3	7 0	4 3	7 0	4 3
Ashton (Devon)	9 0	5 6	8 9	5 3	8 9	5 3
Avonwick	4 3	2 6	4 0	2 6	4 0	2 6
Bickleigh	1 9	1 0	1 6	0 11	1 6	0 11
Billacombe	—	0 4	—	0 4	—	0 4
Bittaford Platform	3 0	1 9	3 0	1 9	2 9	1 9
Bodmin	6 6	4 0	6 6	4 0	6 9	4 0
Bodmin Road	5 9	3 6	5 9	3 6	5 9	3 6
Bovey	8 3	5 0	8 0	4 9	8 0	4 9
Brent	3 9	2 3	3 6	2 3	3 6	2 0
Brixham	9 9	5 9	9 6	5 9	9 6	5 9
Brixton Road	—	0 6	—	0 6	—	0 6
Buckfastleigh (* D)	6 6	4 0	6 6	4 0	6 3	3 9
Bugle	8 9	5 3	8 9	5 3	8 9	5 3
Burngullow	8 9	5 3	8 9	5 3	8 9	5 3
Burrator Platform	3 0	1 9	2 9	1 9	2 9	1 9
Camborne	14 0	8 6	14 0	8 6	14 0	8 6
Carbis Bay	16 3	9 9	16 3	9 9	16 3	9 9
Carn Brea	13 9	8 3	13 9	8 3	13 9	8 3
Chacewater	12 6	7 6	12 6	7 6	12 6	7 6
Christow	9 6	5 9	9 3	5 6	9 3	5 6
Chudleigh	8 3	5 0	8 3	5 0	8 0	4 9
Churston	9 3	5 6	9 0	5 6	9 0	5 6
Clearbrook Halt	2 3	1 3	2 0	1 3	2 0	1 3
Cornwood (E)	2 0	1 3	2 0	1 3	2 0	1 3
Coryton	6 0	3 6	5 9	3 6	5 9	3 6
Dartmouth	10 3	6 3	10 3	6 3	10 0	6 0
Dawlish	8 9	5 3	8 6	5 0	8 6	5 0
Dawlish Warren	9 0	5 6	8 9	5 3	8 9	5 3
Defiance	0 10	0 6	0 10	0 6	0 10	0 6
Devonport	0 4	0 3	0 4	0 3	0 4	0 3
Dockyard Halt	—	0 3	—	0 3	—	0 3
Doublebois	4 6	2 9	4 6	2 9	4 6	2 9
Dousland	2 9	1 9	2 6	1 6	2 6	1 6
Elburton Cross	—	0 6	—	0 6	—	0 6
Exeter	11 1	6 8	11 0	6 7	10 10	6 6
Exminster	10 3	6 3	10 0	6 0	10 0	6 0
Exmouth (H)	10 9	7 0	10 6	6 9	10 6	6 9
Falmouth	13 9	8 3	13 9	8 3	13 9	8 3
Ford	—	0 3	—	0 3	—	0 3
Fowey	7 6	4 6	7 6	4 6	8 6	5 0
Gara Bridge	5 0	3 0	4 9	2 9	4 6	2 9
Grampound Road	9 9	6 0	9 9	6 0	9 9	6 0
Gwinear Road	14 6	8 9	14 6	8 9	14 6	8 9
Hayle	15 3	9 3	15 3	9 3	15 3	9 3
Heathfield	7 9	4 9	7 6	4 6	7 6	4 6
Helston	16 3	9 9	16 3	9 9	16 3	9 9
Horrabridge	2 9	1 9	2 6	1 6	2 6	1 6
Ivybridge (B)	2 6	1 6	2 6	1 6	2 3	1 6
Keyham	0 4	0 3	0 5	0 3	0 5	0 3
Kingsbridge	6 3	3 9	6 3	3 9	6 0	3 9
Kingkerswell	7 6	4 6	7 3	4 6	7 3	4 3
Kingswear	10 0	6 0	10 0	6 0	9 9	6 0
King Tor Halt	4 6	2 9	4 3	2 6	4 0	2 6
Launceston	7 5	4 6	7 4	4 5	7 3	4 4
Lelant	15 9	9 6	15 9	9 6	15 9	9 6
Lifton	6 6	4 0	6 3	3 9	6 3	3 9
Liskeard	3 9	2 3	3 9	2 3	4 0	2 6

TO	FROM: Plymouth (Millbay) — FARES 1st	Plymouth (Millbay) 3rd	Plymouth (North Rd.) 1st	Plymouth (North Rd.) 3rd	Mutley 1st	Mutley 3rd
	s. d.	s. d.	s. d.	s. d.	s. d.	s. d.
Loddiswell	5 6	3 3	5 6	3 3	5 3	3 3
Longdown	10 0	6 0	10 0	6 0	9 9	6 0
Looé	5 9	3 6	5 9	3 6	5 9	3 6
Lostwithiel	6 6	4 0	6 6	4 0	6 6	4 0
Lustleigh	8 9	5 3	8 9	5 3	8 6	5 3
Luxulyan	8 3	5 0	8 3	5 0	8 3	5 0
Lydford	4X 9	2X10	4X 9	2X10	4X 9	2X10
Marazion	16 3	9 9	16 3	9 9	16 3	9 9
Marsh Mills (A)	0 10	0 5	0 8	0 5	0 8	0 5
Mary Tavy and Blackdown	4 3	2 6	4 3	2 6	4 0	2 6
Menheniot	3 3	2 0	3 3	2 0	3 6	2 0
Moretonhampstead	9 6	5 9	9 6	5 9	9 3	5 6
Nancegollan	15 6	9 3	15 6	9 3	15 9	9 6
Newquay	11 9	7 0	11 9	7 0	11 9	7 0
Newton Abbot	7 0	4 3	6 9	4 0	6 9	4 0
Padstow (Southern)	9 1	5 6	9 0	5 5	8 1	5 4
Paignton	8 9	5 3	8 6	5 0	8 3	5 0
Par	7 6	4 6	7 6	4 6	7 6	4 6
Penmere Platform	13 6	8 3	13 6	8 3	13 6	8 3
Penryn	13 3	8 0	13 3	8 0	13 3	8 0
Penzance	16 9	10 0	16 9	10 0	16 9	10 0
Perranporth (‡)	14 3	8 6	14 0	8 6	14 6	8 9
Perranwell	12 3	7 3	12 3	7 3	12 3	7 6
Plymbridge (K)	1 3	0 9	1 3	0 8	1 0	0 7
Plympton (F)	0 8	0 5	0 8	0 5	0 8	0 5
Praze	15 0	9 0	15 0	9 0	15 0	9 0
Princetown (G)	4 9	2 9	4 6	2 9	4 6	2 9
Probus and Ladock	10 3	6 3	10 3	6 3	10 3	6 3
Redruth	13 3	8 0	13 3	8 0	13 6	8 0
Roche	9 3	5 6	9 3	5 6	9 3	5 6
St. Agnes (‡)	13 3	8 0	13 3	8 0	13 3	8 0
St. Austell	8 6	5 0	8 3	5 0	8 6	5 3
St. Budeaux	0 5	0 3	0 8	0 5	0 8	0 5
St. Columb Road	10 6	6 3	10 3	6 3	10 6	6 3
St. Erth	15 6	9 3	15 6	9 3	15 9	9 6
St. Germans	2 3	1 3	2 0	1 3	2 3	1 6
St. Ives	16 6	10 0	16 6	10 0	16 6	10 0
Saltash	0 8	0 6	0 8	0 6	0 8	0 6
Scorrier	12 9	7 9	12 9	7 9	12 9	7 9
Shaugh Bridge (K)	2 0	1 3	1 9	1 0	1 9	1 0
Shepherds (‡)	15 0	9 0	15 0	9 0	15 0	9 0
Starcross	9 6	5 9	9 3	5 6	9 3	5 6
Staverton (*)	5 9	3 6	5 9	3 6	5 9	3 6
Steer Point	—	0 9	—	0 9	—	0 9
Tavistock	3X 4	2X 0	3X 4	2X 0	3X 3	2X 0
Teigngrace	7 6	4 6	7 3	4 6	7 3	4 3
Teignmouth	8 0	4 9	8 0	4 9	7 9	4 9
Torquay	8 3	5 0	8 0	4 9	8 0	4 9
Torre	8 0	4 9	7 9	4 9	7 9	4 9
Totnes	5 0	3 0	5 0	3 0	5 0	3 0
Truro	11 3	6 9	11 3	6 9	11 3	6 9
Trusham	8 9	5 2	8 6	5 0	8 6	5 0
Wadebridge	7 10	4 9	7 10	4 9	7 9	4 9
Wrangaton	3 3	2 0	3 3	2 0	3 0	1 9
Yealmpton	—	0 11	—	0 11	—	0 11
Yelverton	2 6	1 6	2 3	1 6	2 3	1 3

*—Rail Motor Car, one Class only over Ashburton Branch. ‡—Rail Motor Car, one Class only over Chacewater to Newquay Branch.
A—Passengers booking at Millbay, North Road, or Mutley may return from Plympton. B—Passengers may return from Yealmpton.
C—Passengers may return from Buckfastleigh or Princetown. D—Passengers may return from Brent or Princetown.
E—Passengers may return from Shaugh Bridge or Bickleigh. F—Passengers booking at Millbay, North Road, or Mutley, may return from Marsh Mills. G—Passengers may return from Tavistock. H—Passengers change at Starcross and proceed by Stacross-Exmouth Boat Service. K—Passengers may return from Plympton.
X—These tickets are available via G.W. or Southern Rly on the Return journey only.

Passengers holding Cheap Day Tickets are allowed to alight at a Station short of destination in either direction on surrender of ticket, and to return from any intermediate Station.

Fare chart from the GWR Time Tables and Excursion booklet.
Plymouth edition summer 1929

17. GOODS TRAINS AND TRANSFERS

Goods trains were unglamorous and were only of passing interest to those of us who gathered in "The Lane". Therefore, this chapter is thin upon reminiscences and is only produced with a larger proportion of help from research than some other chapters.

In its heyday goods traffic was a highly labour intensive operation for the railway, even if we only concentrate upon the train movement side. Long distance unfitted trains were unbelievably slow, the 3.50pm from Swindon not reaching Laira until 3.26 next morning. The classic, undoubtedly, was the 2.30pm from Laira yard which did not reach its destination at Birmingham Bordesley until 5.33pm the next day, still shown in the Working Timetable as the 2.30pm from Laira! Trains classed as unfitted were those where the only control over the train rested upon the engine's brakes and the guard in his brake van. Part of the slow progress of the unfitted goods trains was the necessity to stop at the top of an incline to pin down a proportion of individual wagon brakes and to stop again at the bottom to release those brakes. Goods trains were always side tracked into loops whilst braking operations were carried out to keep them out of the way of faster moving passenger traffic. In the period we are covering unfitted goods trains were the norm.

During the 1930s there were the much advertised express goods services radiating from Paddington (Goods) which were partially fitted, i.e. the first specified number of wagons behind the engine had to be fitted with continuous vacuum brakes. One such was the 9.32pm which was through North Road at 5.23 next morning and only conveyed through Cornish traffic. Plymouth traffic was on the following 10.10pm which worked right through to Millbay, arriving at 6.38am. That train was hauled by one of the 47XX large 2-8-0s, of which Laira always had one on its books, alternating each night with a London engine of the same class. By way of contrast, the 10.30pm from Reading (known as "The Biscuit" because of the town's association with the biscuit firm of Huntley and Palmer) did not arrive at Laira until 1.17pm the next day. The Reading engine which worked on alternate days was for many years the preserve of Mogul 9305. The Reading Bulldogs which appeared occasionally on the Laira coal stage were probably off that train. A notable example, seen on a number of occasions, was 3394 *Albany* fitted with the Westinghouse brake, the pump being prominent on the side of the boiler.

2818 of class 2800 on the 2.30pm from Laira to Birmingham Bordesley Sidings (due there 5.33pm next day) ascending Hemerdon Bank, with a bank engine at rear. April 1939. *P D Orton*

100 of class B4 approaching Friary Jct. with a transfer service from Laira Yard to Friary Yard. This represents traffic brought by the GWR into Laira Yard and consigned to various destinations on the Southern. Circa 1930.

F HC Casbourn/Stephenson Locomotive Society

Armstrong Standard Goods (1868 vintage) No 436 seen passing through North Road Station returning to Laira Yard with the Devonport (Valletort) transfer service a week after arrival at Laira after transfer from Exeter. 8 September 1928.

M J Dart collection

Main line goods trains running to and from Cornwall were serviced at Tavistock Junction where Plymouth traffic was detached and later tripped to Laira yard. There it would be sorted for the multifarious destinations within the Plymouth area. A glance at the shunter roster for the downside at Tavistock Junction reveals that it only covered the night shift, the period when most down goods trains arrived and/or departed. In the summer Working Timetable (WTT) for 1932 there were recorded no less than nine goods trains into Cornwall between midnight and 6am (Mondays excepted), two of which started from Millbay and all went through to Truro or Penzance, except for one which terminated at St. Blazey.

As far as the Great Western was concerned, the hub of the business was Laira yard where shunting went on day and night from 5am on Monday until 6am on the following Sunday morning. (A personal reminiscence may be permitted here concerning a somewhat stressed young married unable to sleep at three in the morning, his wife having just departed to hospital to deliver our first born. Insomnia was accompanied by the continuous shunting from the nearby Laira yard with the distinctive sharp staccato of a pannier, followed by the clashing of buffers).

Millbay Goods also had all night shunting as this was the principal commercial depot for Plymouth, both receiving and despatching merchandise. Millbay goods was also the base for traffic to and from Millbay Docks. Two Class 1361 0-6-0STs were allocated for work in the docks and they were stabled in their own shed in the docks at week-ends. There was also a subsidiary yard at Devonport (Valletort) and small reception sidings at Plympton, Keyham and Saltash.

Distribution of inward traffic and collection of outward was by means of transfer trains, often well loaded. Transfer trains were a common enough sight in most industrial and commercial centres. The WTT for the summer of 1932 shows that there were no less than 33 regular daily transfers between yards in the Plymouth area on Tuesdays to Fridays, with some variations on Mondays and Saturdays. That total includes transfers between the Great Western and Southern yards at Friary and Devonport.

With so much of the traffic physically transferred between wagons and ultimately from wagons to road delivery vehicles it is quite understandable that claims for damage poured into District Goods Managers' Offices. (DGMOs).

The Dockyard had its own internal railway system, connected by a trailing spur into the down Cornwall main line just beyond Keyham station. This meant that trains had to be propelled into the Dockyard and had to

1362 of class 1361 passing Mutley station in April 1937 returning to Laira Yard having shunted the small District Engineer's yard adjacent to North Road station. The yard was accessed by a gated level crossing over Glen Park Avenue. The site is now part of the station car park. The job was a Thursdays only working usually with a Dock Tank or small Pannier. *P D Orton*

ROD 3049 at Laira in May 1934, its home shed. *H W Adams*

1799 of class 1854 light engine on the down line between Plympton and Tavistock Jct. Still quite rural in April 1939 with no up and down goods loops. *P D Orton*

reverse direction when leaving the yard for Devonport. Entry into the Dockyard was through heavy solid doors (as might be expected for entry into Government property_ and they were only normally opened when traffic was transferred. The GW train was scheduled to leave Valletort yard at Devonport at 12.18(SX), returning to base at 1.30pm. There was a second Government establishment at Bull Point, just beyond Weston Mill Viaduct, where the short branch line was visited on an As Required basis.

When it was available, the regular Devonport Goods transfer engine was pannier 1755. That is except for a few months at the end of 1928 when it gave way to an ancient Armstrong Standard Goods 0-6-0 436 of 1868 vintage and, therefore, already 60 years of age. It was a source of great amusement to the local enthusiasts of the day having seen nothing remotely like it before. A distinctive feature of this venerable machine was a non standard number plate, dating back to 1876, when Wolverhampton built engines first received numberplates in lieu of painted numbers. (See Part 1, page 43, of Locomotive of the GWR – RCTS 1951). The regular driver of 1755 was somewhat portly and, no doubt, found the footplate of 436 more spacious than the cramped cab of 1755. Laira only had 436 between September and December 1928 when it returned to Exeter from whence it came. Why it came to Laira is a mystery.

GOODS TRAIN TIMINGS

2.30pm Plymouth Laira to Birmingham Bordesley.

	arr	dpt
Laira		2.30pm
Totnes	3.41pm	4.52
Newton Abbot (Hackney)	5.30	10.25
Exeter	11.15	12 ngt
Wellington	1.6am	1.25am
Taunton	1.44	2.0
Castle Cary	3.9	3.16
	Calls Frome RR	
Westbury	4.10	4.45
Chippenham	5.31	5.40
Swindon	6.23	10.10
Oxford	12.17pm	12.57pm
Aynho Junction	1.40	2.5
Banbury	2.21	
Leamington	4.0	4.15
Bordesley	5.33pm	

10.30pm Reading to Laira

	arr	dpt
Reading Low Level		10.30pm
Reading High Level	10.35pm	11.20
Newbury Racecourse	12.35am	2.38am
Westbury	4.2	4.17
Taunton	5.27	6.25
Exeter	7.35	8.10
Newton Abbot (Hackney)	8.55	10.35
Ashburton Junction	11.17	11.49
Tavistock Junction	12.58pm	1.12pm
Laira	1.17	

3.50pm Swindon to Laira

	arr	dpt
Swindon		3.50pm
Chippenham	4.21pm	4.40
Westbury	5.44	6.35
	Calls Melksham RR	
	Holt RR	
Castle Cary	7.15	7.35
	Calls Frome RR	
Taunton	8.26	8.55
Exeter	10.15	11.40
Dawlish Warren	12.1am	12.25am
Newton Abbot (Hackney)	12.50	1.45
Laira	3.26	

No. 6.

TRANSFER TRAINS BETWEEN SALTASH, PLYMOUTH AND LAIRA, AND LAIRA AND SUTTON HARBOUR.

No.	Time.	From	To	To be worked by	To Convey
1	2.10 a.m.	MX Laira	Saltash‡	Laira Transfer Engine	‡ Tuesdays to Sundays.
2	4. 0 a.m.	MX Saltash	Laira‡		
3	6.25 a.m.	Laira	Plymouth		
4	7.15 a.m.	Plymouth	Devonport		
5	8.50 a.m.	Plymouth	Laira	MO 47XX; off 10.10 Paddington	Traffic and Empties from the Plymouth Goods Yard and Millbay Docks.
6	8.55 a.m.	Laira	Plymouth		
7	10.48 a.m.	Laira	Plymouth		
8	12.15 p.m.	Plymouth Docks	Laira		
9	1. 8 p.m.	Laira	Plymouth	Class A Transfer Engine.	Traffic and Empties for Plymouth Upper Yard. S.T. 241.
10	5.30 p.m.	Plymouth	Laira		
11	6.35 p.m.	Laira	Plymouth	Engine of 8.0 p.m. Laira to Truro.	
12	7.55 p.m.	Plymouth	Laira	Engine of 5.16 p.m. ex Exeter.	Traffic for 3.30 Penzance and 7.48 p.m. ex Truro.
13	9. 5 p.m.	Laira	Plymouth	Engine off 10.10 p.m. Tavistock.	Traffic for the Lanson and Tavistock and Yealmpton trains.
14	11.30 p.m.	Plymouth	Laira		
16	6. 5 a.m.	MX Plymouth	Devonport		
17	7.18 a.m.‡	MX Laira	Devonport	Devonport Transfer Engine	‡ 6.55 a.m. Mons.
	12.18 p.m.	Devonport (SX)	Keyham		
18	1.30 p.m.	§Keyham (SX)	Devonport¶		§ On Saturdays leaves Keyham 11.10 a.m.
	2.18 p.m.	Devonport	Laira		¶ RR Devonport to Bull Point.
	3. 5 p.m.	Laira (SX)	Devonport		
19	6.40 p.m.	Devonport (SX)	Laira		
20	2. 0 a.m.	Laira	Plymouth	MX	
21	2.25 a.m.	Plymouth	Laira		
22	3.30 a.m.	Laira	Tavistock Junc.		
23	4.50 a.m.	Tavistock Jct.	Plymouth		
24	5.35 a.m.	Plymouth	Tavistock Junc.		
25	8.20 a.m.	Tavistock Jct.	Laira		
26	1.30 p.m.	Laira	Sutton Harbour		
27	5.30 p.m.	Sutton Harbour	Laira ‡		‡ Shunts Mt. Gould until 9.0 p.m.
28	8.25 a.m.	Laira	Tavistock Jct.	Shunting Engine	Shunts Plympton Yard and Tavistock Junction until 3.0 p.m.
29	9. 0 a.m.	Tavistock Jct.	Plympton		
30	10.25 a.m.	Plympton	Laira		
31	7.45 a.m.	Laira	Sutton Harbour	Sutton Harbour Shunting Engine	Traffic to and from Sutton Harbour.
32	1.30 p.m.	Sutton Harbour	Laira		
33	12. 0 night	Plymouth and	Devonport S.R. back.	SX	S.R. traffic.
34	6.10 p.m.	Plymouth and	Devonport S.R. back.	SO	
35	9.50 a.m.	Tavistock Jct.	Laira (Suns.)	"D" Class Engine	Plymouth District Branch Traffic and Traffic for 9.35 a.m. Laira and St. Austell.
	10.20 a.m.	Laira	Plymouth		Meat traffic off 10.10 p.m. Paddington.
36	1.35 p.m.	Tavistock Jct.	Laira (Suns).	Trainmen off 10.30 p.m. Reading	Plymouth District Traffic.

Extract from the Working Timetable for the summer 1932
For 'Plymouth' read "Plymouth Millbay".
Under duty 14 note "Lanson", but Yealmpton is spelt correctly.
(PRO RAIL 937/158)

18. THE CATTEWATER AND SUTTON HARBOUR BRANCHES

Cattewater was the industrial area of Plymouth with a thriving River Plym waterside. It was served by both the Great Western and Southern Railways, the Southern having the benefit of the waterfront. The Great Western branch reached into Sutton Harbour where it was joined by a short steeply graded Southern branch connected direct to their Friary goods yard. It reached Sutton Harbour via a short tunnel under Exeter Street. By the date of this history the lines around the harbour were largely moribund with very little traffic on offer.

In the Cattedown area there were situated both the gas works and the electricity generating works. Each had their own private wharfs to receive their seaborne coal. The gas seaborne coal came from the North East and William Cory were the agents. From the gas works there were the residual products outgoing by rail, especially coke, and from the electricity works there was clinker. On the other hand, tar from the gas works went to the waterside tar distillery which also received the raw product by rail from other gas works in Devon and Cornwall. After treatment the final product was dispatched by road for local use, or by rail as tar, creosote or chemicals.

Victoria Wharf was where most of the seaborne merchandise was received. It was serviced almost daily by ships of Coast Lines Ltd who had their own Manning Wardle 0-4-0ST shunter, named *Alice*.

Coast Lines vessels discharged a range of cargo for onward distribution. There was only a limited amount of general cargo outward bound, for the Plymouth hinterland produced relatively little for export. From Crispin Gill's excellent book, *Plymouth River*, published in 1997, is extracted a list of cargoes landed at Victoria Wharf.

Soap from Unilever, Liverpool
Soap from Proctor & Gamble
Guiness stout from Liverpool
Coal from the East Coast
Flour from the CWS Bristol
Sugar from Tate & Lyle on the Thames
Oil cake for animal feed
Fertiliser
New potatoes from Brittany in season
Strawberries in season
General merchandise transhipped from London and Liverpool.

Most of that, other than for local collection, or delivery, would have accrued to the Southern Railway for onward transit. In addition to the seaborne traffic, there were concerns such as Fison's for fertilisers and British Oxygen who both provided bulk traffic for the railways.

An important source of traffic was petroleum products which came in by sea for Shell Mex, BP, and Esso, received for bulk storage and then distributed by rail as required, or locally by road.

There was sufficient traffic to warrant two daily trips, Mondays to Fridays, both Great Western and Southern. The Working Timetable also provided for two extra Southern trips to run on a "As Required" basis. The Southern traffic went to Friary and the Great Western to Laira where some of it would reappear in the consist of the transfer trains between the two yards. The two yards then sorted the wagons once again for onwards dispatch towards destination by the appropriate main line goods train.

For trains serving the Cattewater the Great Western used small pannier tanks of Class 1901 or 2021, and the Southern Class B4 0-4-0Ts.

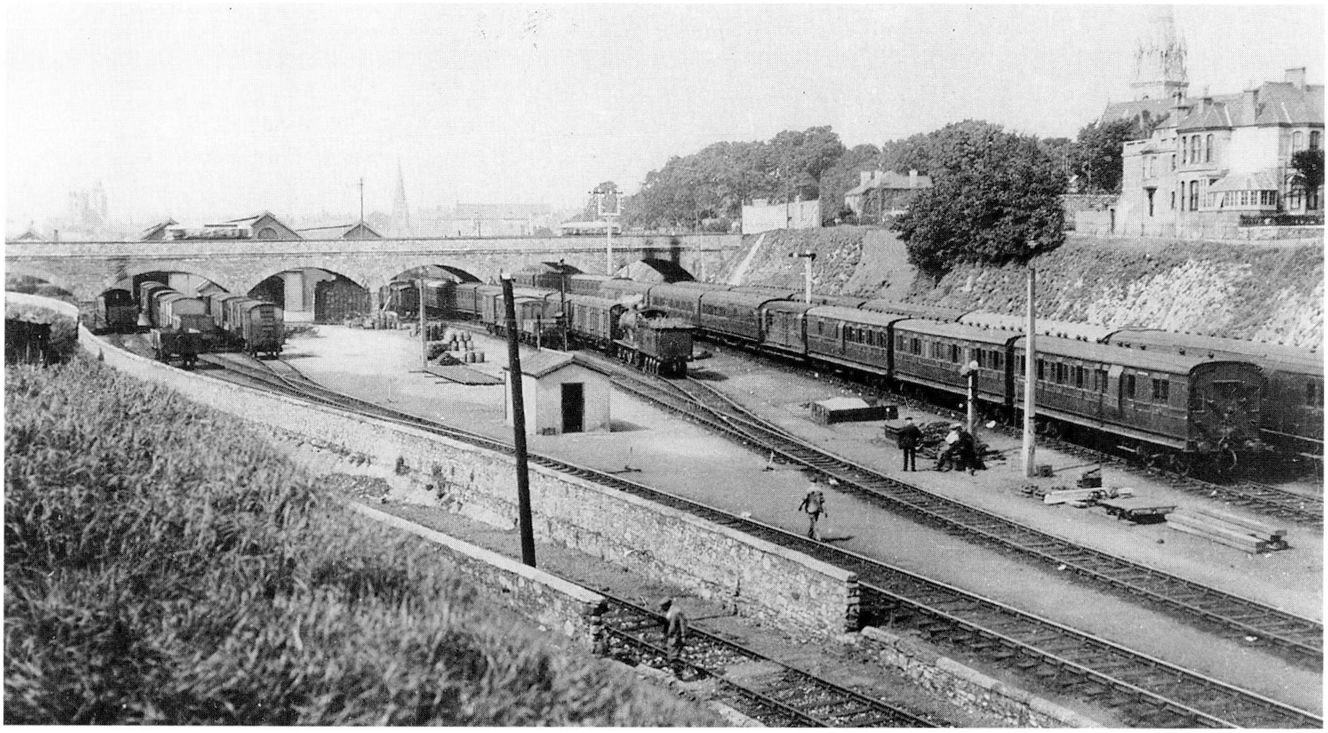

Plymouth Friary Yard with a class T9 shunting. SR Sutton Harbour Branch is descending between walls in foreground. Circa mid 1930's. *M J Dart collection*

1930 of 850 class on Laira to Sutton Harbour GWR transfer goods at Friary Jct. This vividly illustrates the volume of traffic generated on the Sutton Harbour Branch. March 1925. *M J Dart collection*

Class B4 0-4-0T 94 seen by the Cattewater waterside in the 1930's. The only class to work on the harbourside. *H W Adams*

Approaching Lucas Terrace Halt is 30094 with a transfer freight from Cattewater to Friary in November 1955. Although an out of period photograph, if viewed with that of 1930 (page 103), they graphically illustrate the volume of traffic generated by the two industrial branches at Cattedown. *Authors collection*

Frontage of North Road Station in mid 1930s. *Authors collection*

19. RECONSTRUCTION OF NORTH ROAD STATION

In keeping with the spirit of the age, the GWR had grand plans for the reconstruction of North Road Station, and not before time too! The platform accommodation had become inadequate to cater for an ever expanding summer week-end holiday traffic. Both the up and down side buildings of ramshackle appearance were life expired edifices of wooden construction and decidedly shabby. Work commenced early in 1938 with the closure of the up side approach road from Pennycomequick together with the Birdcage Walk from the Mutley direction. That permitted the demolition of the upside booking office and other administrative buildings, leaving the main up platform with a roof, but otherwise exposed to the mercy of the weather. Memory is defective, but from a photograph it would appear that the island platform was devoid of buildings or shelter.

A temporary footbridge was needed, the original one having been removed, it was open to the elements and was constructed from such assorted oddments which were available. The area once occupied by the approach road became the construction site for the new up side track work.

Concurrently, the Houndiscombe bridge at the Mutley end of the station was rebuilt to provide for additional tracks, and at the west end of the station was the bridge over the busy Pennycomequick Hill was also replaced. There was also a replacement for North Road East signal box.

Work stopped abruptly when war broke out, but not before Mutley Station was closed on 3rd July 1939, the final Saturday of the then winter service. Mutley Station was expendable because it was only 24 chains to North Road Station. At least to the onlookers, there was an amusing incident when a train from Mutley went off without the guard and he was watched walking from Mutley to North Road to rejoin his train.

The grand plans of the Great Western were brought to fruition in 1962, including the conspicuous tower block. Dr. Beeching came to open the new station which he described as "A white elephant". For once he was right. However, some good did eventually come out of the reconstruction when the excess platform accommodation was taken over by Royal Mail and it now forms an integral part of the Railnet network.

North Road Station (east end) prior to redevelopment. Birdcage Walk still in situ, but now underneath the upside sidings adjacent to platform 8. October 1937. *H W Adams*

North Road Station (west end) prior to redevelopment. Upside buildings on left and Parcels Office on far right. October 1937. *H W Adams*

North Road Station. The temporary footbridge under construction in 1938 made up of oddments – three styles of cross girders and three styles of stairways. *H W Adams*

Mutley Station a few weeks before closure with a new crossover and upside siding already in place. May 1939.
H W Adams

New signal gantry, looking west from the remains of Mutley Station up platform, down platform demolished. Sixteen signal arms but only four in use. Late 1939/early 1940.
H W Adams

20. POSTSCRIPT

Three of the four principal stations in Plymouth have disappeared without trace. The Great Western's line from Millbay to North Road has been obliterated. On the site of Millbay station there has arisen a complex with a conference centre, an ice rink and a leisure pool which is billed as "The Premier concert and Leisure venue in the South West". Never again will there by any Boat Trains from Millbay Docks. The Southern Railway has fared no better for both their principal stations have vanished: Friary Station has been replaced by housing and Devonport Station by the Plymouth College of Further Education (PCFE). Their main line between Devonport Junction and St Budeaux has vanished, only the tunnels remain as a reminder.

The disappearance of those three stations has been no great loss to the City of Plymouth. Of far greater importance is the vast improvement in the timetable, evidenced by range of destinations now available, together with the frequency and speed of travel, and as illustrated in the accompanying Table. For example, there are now First Great Western trains to and from London via Bristol serving Bath, Chippenham and Swindon at the time most people wish to travel. London has sixteen trains a day instead of seven, and amongst those there is one significant event to be recorded. Turning the clock back to the 1930s there was great excitement when the Great Western Railway achieved a timetabled four hour non-stop run from Paddington to Plymouth on the down Cornish Riviera Express during the summer service. With the introduction of the winter timetable on 24th September 2000 another landmark was reached, when one minute was shaved off the arrival time at Paddington of the up Golden Hind (05.15 from Penzance, 07.00 from Plymouth) to complete the journey in 2hrs 59 minutes. An intriguing point about the Golden Hind is that it is six minutes faster than the up Cornish Riviera, yet calls at two additional stations, namely, Newton Abbot and Taunton.

If there were a league table surely pride of place go to Birmingham where the journey time has been reduced by almost 30% and the number of through trains increased from two to eleven. Conversely, although the pre war timetable showed through trains to a number of destinations, one needs to question how many passengers were prepared to use those trains and put up with the inconvenience of arrival in the small hours of the morning. That is now a thing of the past.

Finally, it is worthy of note that Plymouth and Penzance now have the only sleeping car service with an English destination. All the other remaining sleeping car destinations are in Scotland.

Plymouth Millbay from the air. Millbay passenger station is centre right, the goods shed the ribbed roof bottom right, Union Street runs top right to bottom left with the Octagon the large open space just left of centre. Circa 1930. *Authors collection*

Site of railway at Millbay in 2000. Passenger station was to centre left and the railway bridge over Union Street was to left of the Toys r Us circular building. The line to North Road passed to left of the dual carriage way straight ahead on right of picture through the modern white houses where road curves right. *Authors collection*

COMPARISON OF THROUGH TRAIN SERVICES
WINTER 1933/4 AND WINTER 2000/01
MONDAYS TO FRIDAYS

TO	WINTER 1933/34				WINTER 2000/01						
	Number	Fastest Train		Note	Number	Fastest Train		Operator(s)	Acceleration		Note
Paddington	7	4hrs	15 mins	1	16	2hrs	59 mins	FGW	1hr	16 mins	
Waterloo	5	5	35		0						
Bristol	8	2	52	2	19	1	54	FGW 4 VII WW5	58	2	
Cardiff	0				2	3	12	WW			
Birmingham	2	5	20	3	13	3	25	VII WW2	1	55	
Liverpool	4	8	29	4	1	5	45	V	2	44	
Birkenhead	3	8	44	5	0						
Manchester	3	7	53	6	3	5	31	V2 WW1	2	22	14
Leeds	0				4	5	32	V			
Newcastle	1	11	19	7	4	6	48	V	4	31	
Edinburgh	1	14	00	8	3	8	41	V	5	19	15
Glasgow	2	12	50	9	1	8	17	V	4	33	
Aberdeen	1	17	30	10	1	11	50	V	5	40	
Penzance	10	2	20		22	1	49	FGW16 V11 WW9		31	16
Exeter GWR	20	1	09	11	36		51	FGW 8 V4 WW10		18	17
Exeter SR	10	1	39	12	0						
Portsmouth HBR	2	5	41	13	1	3	59	WW	1	40	18
Brighton	1	7	14		0						

All times calculated from North Road
FGW = First Great Western, V = Virgin, WW = Wales and West

NOTES

1. Includes the Sleeper and one arrival at 2.40am
2. Includes the Sleeper both in 1933/34 and in 2000/01
3. Birmingham Snow Hill
4. One arrived at 1.05am and another at 5.55am
4 Birkenhead Woodside via Severn Tunnel, Hereford and Chester
6. Two of the trains arrived at 3.22am and 6.03am
7. Arrival time 1.19am
   In 1933/34 there was only one practical day time service to Newcastle 10.30am from Plymouth, arrival at Newcastle 101.10pm. Journey time 11hrs 40 min. with one change at Bristol.
8. Arrival time 4am.
9. One journey was overnight on the 8pm departure.
10. Journey time 21hrs 3 min for a Sunday arrival.
11. The seven all stations trains from North Road to Exeter St. Davids averaged about two hours to complete the journey.
12. Southern Railway timings are also between North Road and Exeter St. Davids.
13. Via Templecombe and Salisbury to Portsmouth and Southsea.
14. The Wales and West train routed via Severn Tunnel and Hereford. The Virgin trains via Birmingham and The Potteries.
15. The fastest train was the 9.22am from Penzance, 11.15am from North Road via the East Coast. The Aberdeen train via the West Coast was 24 minutes slower.
16. The fastest train to Penzance was the *Golden Hind*, 18.03 from Paddington, 21.12 from Plymouth, arriving Penzance at 23.01.
17. The fastest train was the 11.15am to Edinburgh.
18. Via Westbury and Salisbury.

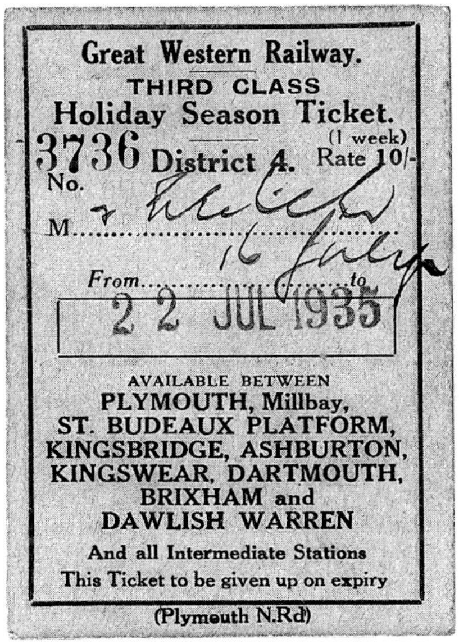

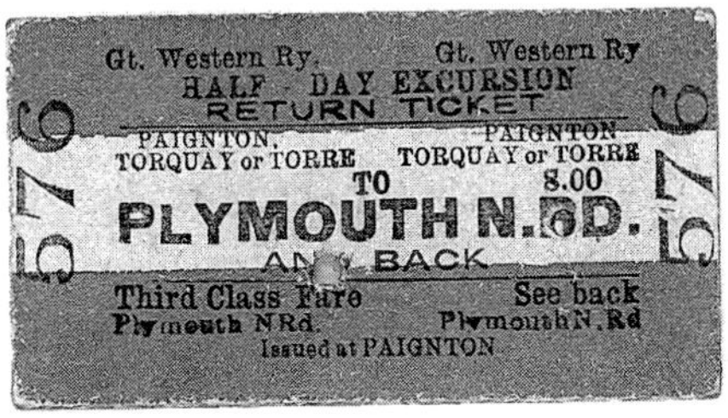

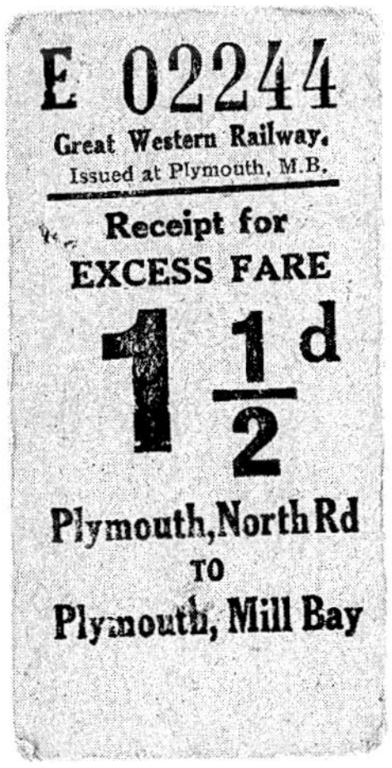

Appendix A

Laira Allocation		31st December												
		1927	1928	1929	1930	1931	1932	1933	1934	1935	1936	1937	1938	1939
4-6-0	King	2	8	8	8	8	8	8	7	8	8	8	8	8
	Castle	12	7	7	7	6	8	10	12	13	10	11	10	13
	Star	2												1
	Hall			8	7	8	5	7	7	7	9	9	8	6
	Grange										1	1	2	1
2-8-0	47XX	1	1	2	1	1	1	1	1	1	1	-	2	2
	30XX ROD	3	2	2	1	1	1	1						
	28XX	3	3	3	3	2	3	4	3	4	3	3	3	3
2-6-0	43XX 53XX 63XX 73XX	12												
	83XX		13	7	6	6	5	6	10	8	7	6	5	7
	26XX Aberdare	3	4	3	4	3	4	3	1	1	1			
4-4-0	Bulldog	4	3	3	3	3	4	6	8	9	8	6	6	6
	Duke			2	3	2								
2-8-0T	42XX								1	1	1			
2-6-2T	31XX	2	4	3	4	3	3	3	2	2	2	2	2	3
	45XX	7	10	11	8	8	8	8	9	10	13	12	7	9
	44XX	4	3	3	1	6	4	4	3	1	2	2	2	2
0-6-0T	Large 1076 auto	8	6	8	8	8	2	2	2	2				
	1076 non auto	1	1	1		1	1	1	1	1				
	64XX auto						4	4	5	7	7	7	7	7
	1813									1	2			
	1854	3	5	5	7	5	3	2	3	2				1
	2721									1	1	3	2	2
	57XX				1	1	1	1	3	4	4	4	5	9
	74XX											1	1	1
Small	1361 Dock Tank	5	5	4	4	4	4	5	5	5	4	5	4	4
	850 and 1901-2020	9	6	6	4	3	6	6	5	6	3	2	1	
	2021		1		1			1			1	2	2	3
	TOTAL	81	82	86	81	79	75	83	88	94	88	84	77	88
TOTAL Shunting Tanks	included above	18	18	16	17	14	15	16	17	20	15	17	15	20

The following classes do not appear on the allocation schedule because they were not present at a 31st December year end:

Armstrong Standard Goods 0-6-0	436	for year 1928
Pannier 0-6-0T, auto fitted the 1st	5400	1931
Auto fitted 0-4-2Ts	4827/9	1937
Dukedog	3226	1939

Additionally, 3270 *Earl of Devon* failed to be included within the *Duke* Class for 1928.

A study of the schedule will illustrate how the older classes gradually faded away as new construction took their places. The one exception were the Bulldogs, where growth in holiday trains brought about the need for extra engines for piloting duties.

It was the practice to paint the engine's home shed in white letters on the cab roof just above the Driver's head. That can be seen to-day on 6000 *King George V* in the Great Western Steam Museum at Swindon, where the letters PDN are placed in the correct position on the interior of the cab roof. Standard abbreviations were used, thus LA for Laira and PDN for Old Oak Common, hence London based engine were always referred to as Paddington engines. In non standard form was NA or NA for Newton Abbot.

Appendix B
SUNDAY AFTERNOON VISITS TO LAIRA SHED

Date	3rd August 1930	21st August 1932	6th January 1935	3rd April 1938
4-6-0				
KING	6002 6004 6010 6012 6016 6023 6024	6002 6004 6010 6016 6020 6022 6024 6028	6000 6004 6016 6022 6028	6004 60016 6020 6021 6022
CASTLE	4032 4094 4096 5007 5008	4081 5002 5007 5009	4077 4088 4092 4094 5009 5028	4032 4092 4097 5013 5043
HAll	4905 4910 4954 4978	4926 4938 4960 4976	4946 4951 5957 5916	4951 4982
STAR	4013 4029			
SAINT				2913
4-4-0				
DUKE	3272 3282 3284 3289			
BULLDOG	3368 3424	3393 3401 3416 3424	3342 3393 3419 3424	3393 3431
2-8-0				
47XX	4708	4705	4704	4703
28XX	2846 2849	2812 2846 2858 2860	2812 2819	2819 2839
ROD	3039	3049		
2-6-0				
ABERDARE	2620 2648 2660 2675	2648 2675 2676		
MOGUL	8309 8361 8387	8363	8325 8342 8374 8376 8388	8337 8357 8381
2-8-0T			4298	
2-6-2T				
31XX	3181 3187	3180 3181 3186	3180 3186	3186
44XX	4401 4404		4409	4402
45XX	4523 4526 4542 4544 4598	4545 4591 5502 5526	4523 4598	4534 4545 4598 5531 5573
0-6-0T				
1076			1562	
1076 Auto	738 1167 1235 1252 1570	1167 1252 1570	1167 1271	
1854	1703 1717 1755 1897	1703 1717 1755 1895 1900	1755 1761	
1361	1363 1365	1361 1364	1362	1362 1364
1901	1922	1905 1922 1973 1985	1905 1993 1999	1909
2021			2050	2116
2721				2725 2780
57XX		7760	9711	7715 9770
64XX		6407 6409	6406 6407 6408 6414	6419
TOTAL	56	54	48	35

The 1938 figure may have been distorted as a result of broccoli traffic.

APPENDIX C

No. 6. 123

BANKING AND SHUNTING ENGINES.

Station.	Engine Number.	Starting Time.	Authorised Hours. Monday.	Tuesday.	Wednesday.	Thursday.	Friday.	Saturday.	Sunday.	Total hours per week.	Particulars of Work.
											12.30 p.m.)
Tavistock Junction ..	1	1.50 a.m.	3	—	—	—	—	—	—	3	Banks 1.15 a.m. Plymouth, 3.30 a.m. Tavistock Jc., 4.5 a.m. and 4.30 a.m. ex Laira.
	2	3. 0 p.m.	5¾	5¾	5¾	5¾	5¾	5¾	—	84½	
	3	9.30 p.m.	7½	7½	7½	7½	7½	6	—	43½	Banks 9.43 p.m. ex Laira and all trains up to and including 4.30 a.m.
	4	12.45 p.m.	1¼	1¼	1¼	1¼	1¼	1¼	—	7½	Shunts Up Sidings.
	5	10. 0 p.m.	8	8	8	8	8	8	—	48	Night Shunting.
	6	9. 0 a.m.	—	—	—	—	—	—	8	8	
Laira ..	1	6. 0 a.m.	18	24	24	24	24	24	6	144	Shunts Up Sidings and Mount Gould as required.
	2	5. 0 a.m.	19	24	24	24	24	24	6	145	Shunts Mount Gould and form 7.45 a.m. Laira Sutton Harbour, 10.0 a.m. Laira Yamton, 11.20 a.m. S.R., 10.48 a.m. and 1.8 p.m. Laira to Plymouth and shunt Down Side as required.
	3	5. 0 a.m.	3½	3½	3½	3½	3½	3½	—	21	Shunting by Sutton Harbour transfer engines off 2.40 p.m. and 5.30 p.m. ex Sutton Harbour.
North Road (Passenger).	1	3. 0 a.m.	20	20	20	20	20	20	4	124	
Millbay (Passenger)	1	4.30 a.m.	22½	22½	22½	22½	22½	22½	—	135	Shunting at Passenger Station and Harwell Sidings.
	2	*	7½	7½	7½	7½	7½	7½	1	46	* Shunting performed by various Train Engines.
	3	6. 0 a.m.	—	—	—	—	—	—	20½	20½	
Millbay (Goods)	1	6. 0 a.m.	18	22	22	22	22	22	4	132	Shunts Yard. To be released on completion of work.

Extract from the Working Timetable for the summer 1932 Under duty Laira 2 note the spelling "Yamton", but spelt correctly on page 115 of the same edition of the timetable.
(PRO RAIL 937/158)

APPENDIX D
PRE WAR PURCHASING POWER

Undoubtedly, one of the problems the modern reader will face is coming to terms with what appear to be ridiculous money values. To help with that there appears on page 117 a selection of advertisements for the period which have been taken from Brendon's local Plymouth Timetable, the Great Western Railway Magazine and the period tariff kindly supplied by the Duke of Cornwall Hotel. That noble pile was constructed in 1863, and is immediately opposite the one time Millbay Station and, therefore, ready to greet guests arriving at Plymouth's principal railway station of the day. (North Road Station was not opened until 1876). In the 1930s the Duke of Cornwall Hotel was up market (and indeed still is) with bed and breakfast at 9/- (45p). Rather expensive. Just down the road in Union Street was the Farley Hotel, where it was at the lower end of the market at 6/6 (32½p). For B&B, as we know it to-day, Paddington prices were only 3/6 (17½p) to 4/- (20p). Prices were finely graded and 6d or 2½ p was a significant sum of money. The Duke of Cornwall was more than double what could be had at Paddington, but like to-day, you got what you paid for.

It is difficult to conceive how a three course lunch could be provided for 1/9 (9p) in Plymouth's principal departmental store, or high tea even cheaper for 7½p. Equally difficult to believe was an ounce of tobacco for 10d (4p).

Before the War, Swindon sold off engine name plates, together with numberplates and the price I seem to remember was 17/6 (87½ p) delivered to your local station.

The bureau bookcase at which I have sat to write this book was purchased new for my 21st birthday (not eighteenth) and the price was £6.15s 0d (£6.75p), so expensive it had to be paid in two instalments. A recent valuation put the value of that piece of furniture at £400; quite modest compared with the escalating value of nameplates. All that has to be related back to earnings. A man earning £4 was among the elite; many were earning less than £3 for a 48 hours week. Remember too, a married woman was a housewife, not the provider of a second income.

The Duke of Cornwall Hotel, Plymouth.

TARIFF.

—o—

			s.	d.
APARTMENTS.	Bedrooms (Single) inclusive of attendance ...	from	5	6
	ditto (Double) „ „ ...		12	6
	Dressing Room		2	6
	Sitting Room	from	7	6
	Board	per day	10	0
	Bedroom	„	2	6
	Sitting Room or Bedroom Fire, per day ...		4	0
	Bedroom Fire, Evening only		2	0
	Hip or Sponge, in Bedroom		1	0
	Hot or Cold, in Bath Room		1	0
BREAKFASTS.	Table d'Hote, as per daily Menu		3	6
LUNCHEONS.	Table d'Hote, as per daily Menu		3	0
AFTERNOON TEAS	... ...		1	0
DINNERS.	Dinners à la Carte, charged according to order.			
	Table d'Hote Dinner, 7-0 p.m.		6	0

NO CHARGE FOR ATTENDANCE.

Passenger Lift to each Floor.

APARTMENTS.

(Rate for insertion, 5d. per word).

LONDON.—Mrs. Davies, 11, Delamere Street (adjoining Upper Westbourne Terrace), W.2. Bed/Breakfast, 3/6. Special terms permanency.

LONDON.—Mrs. Phillips, 6, Westbourne Square, W.2. Bed/Breakfast, 3/6. 4 mins. Paddington station.

LONDON.—Bed/Breakfast, 3/6. Mrs. Hackett, 16, Delamere Street, Paddington, W.2. Five minutes from station.

LONDON.—Bed and Breakfast, 21/- weekly.—Mrs. Maulkin, 17, Errington Road, Fernhead Road, W.9.

LONDON.—Stay at a Western home. Bed/Breakfast, 4/-; weekly, 24/-. Liberal table, bath, 'phone, electric light, gas fires. Homely. 21 rooms. Quiet district, close Paddington.—Mrs. Collins, 20, Upper Westbourne Terrace, Paddington, W.2, adjoining Westbourne Square.

LONDON.—Watts, 29, Great Western Road, Westbourne Park, Paddington. Bed and Breakfast, 6/6 double.

LONDON.—Superior accommodation. Bed/Breakfast, 4/-. Double, 25/- weekly. Modern furnishing; artistically decorated. Clergyman writes: "Beautifully clean; splendid food and service."—Robinson, 14, Westbourne Square, W.2. 'Phone Abercorn 3547.

MEET YOUR FRIENDS AT SPOONERS RESTAURANT

TABLE D'HOTE LUNCHEONS 1/9

HIGH TEAS 1/6

with Brown or White Bread and Butter

SPOONERS

THE DEPARTMENTAL STORE

PLYMOUTH · PHONE 494

OGDEN'S

St. JULIEN

TOBACCO

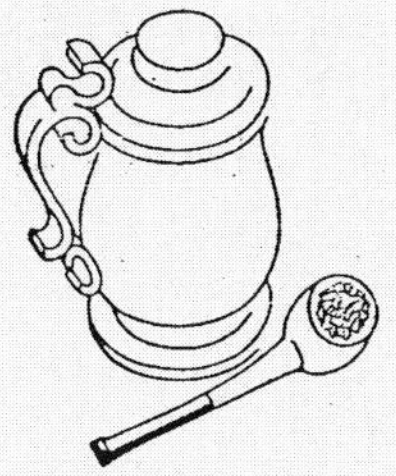

The Empire blend (at 10d an ounce) is now obtainable in a 2-ounce Pocket Vacuum Tin—at 1/8d

FARLEY HOTEL, PLYMOUTH

FAMILY AND COMMERCIAL

MODERATE TARIFF. BED AND BREAKFAST FROM 6/6. HOME COMFORTS.

LONDON. YORK HOTEL, Waterloo Station.

BED, BREAKFAST AND ATTENDANCE FROM 8/-.

Telephone No.:—HOP 948. *ELECTRIC LIGHT.*

SOME OTHER RCTS BOOKS

THE RAILWAYS OF KEYNSHAM

Featuring Fry's Chocolate Passenger and Freight Operations

Readers of this budget priced book will not merely find the facts and figures of Keynsham's railways, they will feel the atmosphere of the place through local personalities and staff. Imagine the heavy smells of smoke and fog mixing with chocolate. All the necessary detail is here, from the first coming of the railway, the arrival of Fry's, the creation of Fry's own railway infrastructure, the freight and passenger services provided for the factory, the growth years, decline, threat of closure and above all a happy ending with a buoyant present day scene (a new service to Filton Abbey Wood added recently). The Bristol-Bath route and Keynsham's four other industrial sidings are also comprehensively covered. Author Russell Leitch can claim fifty years of interest in Bristol area railways. Who better to take us on this fascinating trip to the past?

Laminated cover, 160 pages 80 illustrations including 7 maps and drawings

BRITISH RAILWAYS STANDARD STEAM LOCOMOTIVES

Volume 1 Background to Standardisation and the Pacific Classes

Immediately British Railways was formed in January 1948, the railway Executive instructed Robert Riddles to design a series of standard locomotive designs. The intention was to gain material savings in running and maintenance costs by adopting as standard the best practices of the four independent companies. In this major new series, the Society presents for the first time the complete story of British locomotive standardisation from the days of the Robinson ROD 2-8-0s to the twelve BR Standard designs totalling 999 locomotives. This book, by Paul Chancellor and Peter Gilbert, presents the Standards design history and for each of the 66 locomotives in the popular Britannia, Duke and Clan classes its complete construction, modification, allocation and operating history.

Casebound, page size 212 x 272mm, 184 pages, 151 illustrations including 17 in colour

BRITISH RAILWAYS STANDARD STEAM LOCOMOTIVES

Volume 3 The Tank Engine Classes

From Penzance to Wick, the Standard tank classes were designed to modernise secondary route power. Railway enthusiasts throughout the land became familiar with their high running plates which gave the 230 engines of three types their "family" appearance. Author Paul Chancellor presents their full story, from their design origins, construction, modifications, allocation, use and liveries. Whether these engines hauled you reluctantly to school – your reviewer's experience – or you only came across them in preservation, the Class 4's handsome curved tank sides will evoke many a nostalgic memory. With their construction at all six main workshops, local livery variations and national use, there is something for everyone to savour in this book, the second in the Society's BR Standard series. Diagrams of each design are included.

Casebound, page size 212 x 272mm, 189 photographs including 16 in colour.

WESTERN CHANGE

Summer Saturdays in the West 1957-1995

Author Paul Chancellor brings four generations of change alive. From Halls and Granges struggling with fourteen bogies through the hydraulic and diesel electric locomotive eras to today's HSTs, traffic surveys taken by RCTS members present the changing canvas of summer Saturday railway operation. The steam to diesel transitional period is particularly featured including the temporary resurgence of steam in 1962 when diesels were transferred north. Diesel availability shortfalls and steam substitution records continue the Society's reputation for using operational detail to eloquently balance the nostalgia with realism.

Laminated cover, 169 pages, 69 photographs and maps.

ORDER THIS BOOK WITH ANOTHER RCTS BOOK FOR JUST £5.00

RAISING STEAM ON THE LMS

The Evolution of LMS Locomotive Boilers

This absorbing read opens at Grouping with an LMS locomotive fleet of poor steaming designs unsuited to the heavy and growing traffic levels. The Board's historic decision to hire Stanier from the rival Great Western and his revolutionary work to equip the LMS with a more suitable fleet revolved around more effective raising and use of steam. The complete story is presented here, from early LMS practice based on pre-Grouping designs, through Stanier's importation of GWR practices, early results and comprehensive details of his design improvements culminating in the largest British pacifics, the Coronation class. The necessary technical content is presented by author Arthur Cook concisely in useful tables and an Appendix, allowing the text to be presented in an infectious, readable style. Readers can almost imagine themselves in the mutual improvement classes at the running shed!
Casebound, page size 180 x 235mm, 233 pages, 138 photographs and drawings, including one in colour

LMS DIESELS

Locomotives and Railcars

Today's British motive power fleet is a tribute to the pioneering work of the LMS. Cl 56, 58, 60 and HST power cars use AC generators based on the 10800 *Hawk* development and Cl 77 electrics used LMS designed bogies. Cl 40, 50 and DP2 used LMS designed engines and Peak Cl 44-46 used cab design from the famous 10000 and 10001. Our first generation dmmus owe much to the 1938 80000-2 LMS railcars. And, of course, our Cl 08 and 11 bear testimony to the quality of their LMS design 60 years ago. Author Edgar Richards takes readers through the fascinating history of LMS diesel development. From the first steam conversion in 1932 to the rugged 0-6-0 shunters built in large numbers for war service at home and abroad, the revolutionary main line 10000, 10001 10100 and 10800, and the Michelin, Coventry and LMS railcars, in total 208 locomotives, 15 railcars and 5 trolleys were operated by the LMS. Full details of their design, construction, modification, liveries, allocation and use are included. The book includes much new material and is highly recommended.
Casebound, 219 pages, 125 illustrations.

LMS LOCOMOTIVE NAMES

The Named Locomotives of the LMS and its Constituent Companies

The LNWR had a vigorous naming policy and the Midland Railway an equally determined anti-naming stance. The 1923 grouping set the stage for an absorbing battle within the management teams over naming policy with Derby's early policy success followed by Crewe's ultimate victory. Author John Goodman's absorbing read presents the full story of the LMS and its constituent companies' naming policies and the history of each named engine owned by the LMS, a total of 812. The LNWR contributed 668 of these and a complete presentation of its complex re-naming system is an invaluable inclusion.
Casebound. 211 pages, 124 photographs, 25 drawings.

THE BIRKENHEAD RAILWAY

(LMS & GW Joint)

Today's successful electric railway between Chester and Birkenhead is in sharp contrast to the earlier story of the line. At first passengers were the major earner, but opening of other lines at Chester and the development of Ellesmere Port brought major freight operations. The main line was quadrupled, and the dock system eventually grew to 48 miles. Author Bruce Maund brings to life the detailed and fascinating tale of the complete system, the machinations of expanding railway companies to get control and, in the end, an object lesson in how two great rivals found a satisfactory *modus operandi* to run it with reasonable harmony for almost 90 years. Compulsory reading for all those involved in today's fragmented railways!
Page size 212 x 277mm, laminated cover, 102 pages, 140 illustrations

RCTS Publications List

*UK Post Free
Overseas add 40%
When ordering please quote PLY1

Title of Book	*ISBN No*	**Price*
Locomotives of the LMS		
Locomotives of the LNWR Southern Division		
LBR, LNWR and Wolverton Loco Works	0901115894	£27.95
Raising Steam on the LMS	**0901115851**	**£24.95**
LMS Diesels	**0901115762**	**£19.95**
LMS Locomotive Names	**0901115797**	**£18.95**
Highland Railway Locomotives 1855-1895	0901115649	£12.95
Highland Railway Locomotives 1895-1923	090111572X	£16.95
Special Offer set of Highland Railway		£23.50
BR Standard Steam Locomotives:		
Vol 1 Background and the Pacifics	**0901115819**	**£19.95**
Vol 3 The Tank Engine Classes	**0901115770**	**£18.95**
The Birkenhead Railway	**0901115878**	**£14.95**
The Great Northern Railway in the East Midlands		
The Erewash Valley lines, Pinxton Branch,		
Awsworth-Ilkeston, Heanor & Stanton Branches	0901115886	£15.95
Nottingham Vic, GC, Leen Valley Network	090111586X	£14.95
Colwick Yards, London Rd-Gedling-Basford	0901115843	£13.95
The High Level Bridge and Newcastle Central Station	1873513283	£ 9.95
The Railways of Keynsham	**0901115827**	**£ 9.95**

SPECIAL OFFER - BUY THIS BOOK WITH ANOTHER FOR JUST £5.00 (NETT PRICE)

Western Change-Summer Saturdays in the West	**0901115789**	**£15.95**

A Travellers Guide to Robin Hood line	0901115835	£2.95
Special Offer Set of Gt Northern Loco History		£40.95 (NETT)
Gt. Northern Locomotive History		
1: 1847-1866	0901115614	£12.95
2: 1867-1895	0901115746	£19.95
3A: 1896-1911	090111569X	£19.95
3B: 1911-1923	0901115703	£16.95
Locomotives of the LNER:		
Part 1 Preliminary Survey	0901115118	£12.95
Part 2A Tender Engines A1-A10	0901115258	£14.95
Part 2B Tender Engines Classes B1-B19	0901115738	£13.95
Part 9A Tank Engine Classes L1-L19	0901115401	£10.95
Part 9B Tank Engines Q1-Z5	090111541X	£10.95
Part 10A Departmental Stock, Engine Sheds, Boiler and Tendering Numbering	0901115657	£10.95

Available from:–
Hon Assistant Publications Officer
Hazelhurst
Tiverton Road
Bampton
Devon EX16 9LJ